Law in the United States

An Introduction

Andrew M. Thornley

Kendall Hunt
publishing company

Cover image © Shutterstock, Inc.

Kendall Hunt
publishing company

www.kendallhunt.com
Send all inquiries to:
4050 Westmark Drive
Dubuque, IA 52004-1840

ISBN 978-1-5249-2337-2

Published in the United States of America

contents

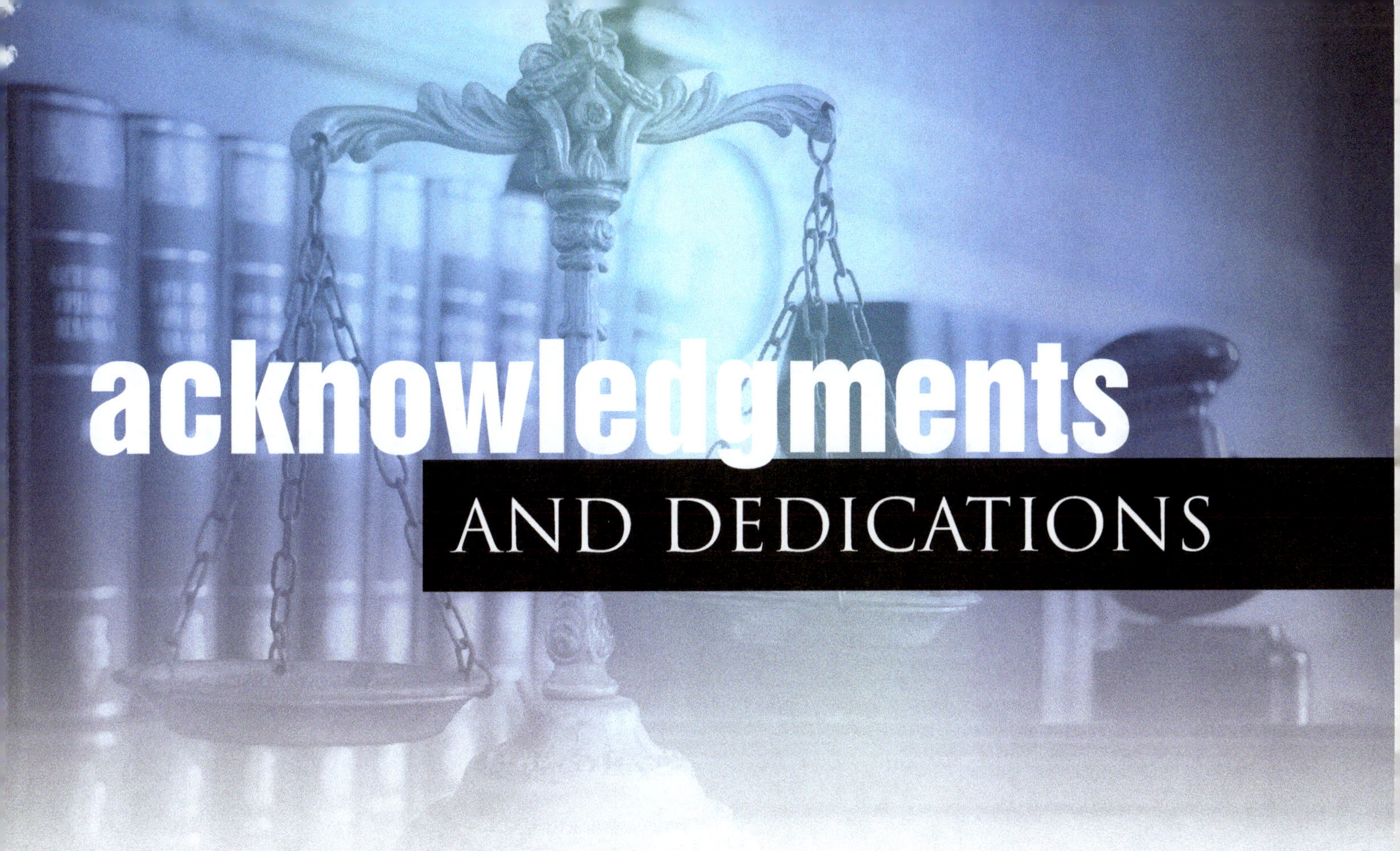

acknowledgments AND DEDICATIONS

For their excellent research assistance, sincere thanks to Lora Chowdhury, Alex Guevara, Micaela Pina, Travis Renna, Erin Schwartz, Kathryn Thiel, Johnathan Trimble, Taylor Yetter, Taylor Crisp, and Karen Johnston. It was my sincere pleasure to work with you, and I wish each of you nothing but the best.

For being such a supportive publisher, genuine thanks to Kendall-Hunt. Thank you for making the process of writing my first book a great experience.

Finally, I dedicate this book to my family, friends, and students, for whom I am daily thankful and by whom I am immeasurably blessed.

preface

This book's title, *Law in the United States: An Introduction*, expresses what I intend this book to be: an introduction. Not a comprehensive examination of law but a basic study of law. Law is a vast topic, made up of a multitude of far-reaching subtopics. Each chapter of this book covers a topic large enough for its own book. As such, each chapter is a basic overview. My goal is not to make readers experts on the law (not least because I have so much more to learn) but rather to give readers a basic understanding of the laws of the United States.

To that end, and just as I teach classes, I have tried to speak plainly throughout the book. In the classroom, if I understand concepts but fail to convey them in ways that resonate with students, I would fail as a teacher. The same is true for this book: If this book states concepts correctly but in ways that do not make sense to readers, I would fail as an author. I do not want to be correct but confusing. I want to be correct and clear. My hope is readers understand my words. I do not care about fancy language or advanced legal speak. I care about learning. I care about communicating content in ways readers easily comprehend. I truly hope this book accomplishes that goal.

Finally, I did not write this book for a specific audience, to the exclusion of all others. Rather, I wrote the book for anyone interested in learning some basics about law in the United States. My hope is the book is useful for any reader, from lawyers to laypersons, from law students to those who never intend to go to law school.

It has been my sincere pleasure to write this book. I hope it teaches you something; and, if I may be a bit greedy, I hope you enjoy it.

chapter 1 LAW

WHAT IS LAW?

© Kalmatsuy, 2014. Used under license from Shutterstock, Inc.

DEFINITION

For a legal book, it seems appropriate and necessary to begin with an understanding of the meaning of the word *law*. Before we walk, let's crawl, because a firm grasp of the basic idea of *the law* will inform everything we explore throughout this book.

In my classroom, whenever I want students to understand a basic concept, I ask them to imagine an alien lands on our planet. The alien has never been here and knows nothing at all about our land, our people, or our lives. How would you define *law* for our foreign visitor?

I don't claim to possess the best possible definition of law, but for our purposes, I feel confident in a simple one: the binding rules of a given society. There are certainly longer possible definitions (and, obviously, this book will go into so much more detail) but to convey the basic notion of *law*, this brief definition will suffice. Law is the set of rules governing a group of people. Law is the set of rules applicable binding upon a group of people. By *binding*, I mean there are consequences for not adhering to the rules. Laws are not suggestions. They aren't optional. They are rules that, if broken, yield repercussions.

RELEVANCE

If you're like many people, when you think of *the law*, you think of the concept of breaking the law. You think of crimes. You think of police and mugshots and criminal trials a la *Law & Order*. Perhaps you think you needn't worry about the law, because you never plan to commit a crime. Indeed, criminal law is a big piece of the legal pie, but the pie is so much bigger, and the slices — some big, some small — are more numerous than you probably think. Even for those who plan to commit nary a single crime in their lives, learning more about the law is a good idea.

The law is relevant to everyone. Law is all around us. You may not realize it, but it's there. It's always there. In fact, name any situation, and there is a possible scenario in which the law is involved. Buying a car? Sales law. Leasing an apartment? Landlord-tenant law. Mowing lawns for pay? Contract law. Starting a business or gifting money to loved ones? Tax law. Even if you're all alone, walking down a sidewalk in your neighborhood, the law is there, ready for duty, in case something triggers it. Keep reading!

CLASSIFICATIONS OF LAW

Before breaking down law by specific subject area, it is important to put the law into broader classifications. What follows is not an exhaustive breakdown, but it is sufficient for our purposes; and an understanding of these major breakdowns is crucial to our understanding of the subsequent material.

PRIMARY V. SECONDARY

Primary law is binding law. Before you say it, yes, this is redundant. We just learned law is the set of rules binding upon a certain group of people. Therefore, if a rule is binding, it's a law. The redundancy notwithstanding, primary law is any law that is binding. By contrast, secondary law is not binding. Unlike primary law, there are no legal consequences when one doesn't adhere to secondary law. As such, secondary law is not technically law, since law, by definition, is binding. Whereas primary law is controlling, secondary law is not. To avoid confusion, it might be helpful to refer to secondary law as *secondary authority* or *secondary legal authority*.

So, what are some examples of each? Let's start with primary law. What are some of the rules binding upon us? Stated differently, what sources produce binding rules for us? Where does the law come from?

SOURCES OF PRIMARY LAW (NON-EXHAUSTIVE LIST)

SOURCE	EXAMPLE
U.S. Constitution	Well, there's only one: the Constitution of the United States (1787)
State constitutions	Texas Constitution (1876)
Legislation passed by U.S. Congress	Endangered Species Act (1973)
Legislation passed by state legislatures	Wisconsin Criminal Code, Wisconsin Statute & Annotations, Chapters 939-951
Federal-court decisions/ rulings	*Roe v. Wade*, Supreme Court of the United States, 410 U.S. 113 (1973)
State-court decisions/ rulings	*Griffin v. The State*, Supreme Court of Georgia, 288 Ga. 833 (2011)
Federal-agency regulations	Code of Federal Regulations, Title 26: Internal Revenue, Section 1.1-1: Income tax on individuals. Subsection (b), in part: "*Citizens or residents of the United States liable to tax.* In general, all citizens of the United States, wherever resident, and all resident alien individuals are liable to the income taxes imposed by the Code whether the income is received from sources within or without the United States."
State-agency regulations	Kansas Administrative Regulations, Agency 40. Insurance Department, Article 12. Sale of Stock, Section 40-12-4. Stock insurance companies; sale of stock; permit; amount paid-in; requirements: "A domestic insurance company in the process of organization and offering its stock for sale under a permit issued by the commissioner of insurance shall not be issued a certificate of authority to transact the business of insurance, as required by K.S.A. 40-214, until the full amount of stock authorized under the permit has been paid-in."
City ordinances	Rules of the City of New York (New York), Title 1: Department of Buildings, Section 6-01: Erection and Dismantling of Climber/Tower Cranes, Subsection (j): "No Climber/Tower Crane shall be erected, operated, or disassembled in any roadway, sidewalk, or street unless a permit is first obtained from the Bureau of Highways of the NYCDOT."

Get the idea? Each of the sources of law listed in the table is binding upon certain people (we'll expound upon *certain people* in a bit). The sources of law listed above aren't suggestions. If not followed, there are consequences. This is the very nature of primary law: if it applies to you, it is legally binding upon you.

How about secondary law? Where do we get legal authority that is not technically law? From what sources do we derive the non-binding stuff?

SOURCES OF SECONDARY LAW (NON-EXHAUSTIVE LIST)

SOURCE	EXAMPLE
Legal textbook/coursebook	This book!
Legal-journal article	Ferrell, Allen. *A Proposal for Solving the 'Payment for Order Flow' Problem, 74 California Law Review* 1027 (2001)
Legal dictionary	*Black's Law Dictionary*
Legal encyclopedia (compilation of legal articles)	*American Jurisprudence, 2d* (Am.Jur.)
Legal brief (a document filed with a court in support of a certain side in a legal case)	*The Brandeis Brief* (as it has come to be known), a 113-page brief filed in 1908 by Louis Brandeis, on behalf of the State of Oregon in the U.S. Supreme Court case *Muller v. Oregon*, 208 U.S. 412 (1908)
Restatements of Law (a set of treatises on a range of legal subjects, published by the American Law Institute)	*Restatement Second, Contracts*

What these (and other) sources of secondary law have in common is they are meant to summarize and/or explain and/or comment on primary law. They are examinations of binding legal authority. And since these sources are not binding law, there are no legal consequences for not adhering to them. A simple contrast is instructive: if a state's penal code (i.e., its list of actions that constitute crime in that state) states murder is a crime, the law of that state is, in fact, murder constitutes a crime. Someone who commits murder faces the consequences (e.g., prison) for committing a crime — for violating primary law. Meanwhile, if a law professor writes a paper stating wearing red sweatshirts should be a crime, no one will face legal consequences for wearing a red sweatshirt. Why not? Because the professor's paper is secondary law. It is not controlling legal authority. It is simply a paper with comments about amending the penal code (primary law). Unless a state decides to add "*the wearing of a red sweatshirt*" to its list of crimes, feel free to wear your favorite red sweatshirt as much as your heart desires, because doing so won't get you fined or arrested.

FEDERAL V. STATE

If you are in the United States, at any given moment, you are bound by two sets of laws: the laws of The United States of America (i.e., federal law) and the laws of the state where are you present (i.e., state law). If I'm having a fish taco for lunch in San Diego, I'm bound by the laws of the U.S. and the laws of California. If I'm in Times Square on New Year's Eve, I'm bound by the laws of the U.S. and the laws of New York. And so forth and so on. Federal law has power over you in every state, but the state laws that govern you change as you move among the states.

By far, most of the laws that govern us are state laws. Why? The framers of the U.S. Constitution decided (via the Tenth Amendment) the U.S. Congress could make laws in specific (i.e., enumerated) areas, and all other areas were fair game for the various state legislatures: "*The powers not delegated to the United States by the Constitution, nor prohibited by it to the states, are reserved to the states respectively, or to the people*" (U.S.

Constitution, Amendment X). And since only a handful of areas were specifically listed in the Constitution as powers of the federal government, most areas of legislative power were reserved to the state governments. In other words, the framers cherry picked the areas of federal purview and left the rest to the states.

© Hong Vo, 2014. Used under license from Shutterstock, Inc.

If it helps you to remember most of the laws in the United States are state laws, imagine a whole pizza. One small slice of the pizza represents all of the country's federal laws. All of the other pieces represent the laws of the 50 states.

CRIMINAL V. CIVIL

Imagine we have a list of all of the things that could possibly land you in trouble with *the law* (meaning the things that could lead to legal repercussions, such as fines, probation, or incarceration). Let's call the items on this list *legal offenses*. Legal offenses are either criminal or civil, in nature.

Criminal law is the body of law dealing with, you guessed it, criminal offenses, or crimes. Civil law, meanwhile, deals with civil offenses. No surprise there, right? The government pursues criminals via criminal prosecutions, and private parties (and, sometimes, the government) pursue civil wrongdoers via lawsuits. (The government can also sue, but we will save that discussion for another time.)

Going a little deeper, let's break down criminal wrongs into two types and civil wrongs into two types.

Crimes are categorized according to severity. The less serious crimes are referred to as *misdemeanors*, while the more serious crimes are known as *felonies*. Some misdemeanors and felonies are further divided into classes/degrees, based on the nature of the criminal act. The more serious crimes yield the more serious punishments. Generally, misdemeanors are punishable by monetary penalty (fines) and/or incarceration of no more than one year. Meanwhile, felonies are punishable by incarceration of more than one year or even death. Moreover, unlike with misdemeanors, felony convictions can lead to the loss of certain rights and privileges (e.g., right to vote, right to purchase firearms) that may or may not ever be restored.

Unlike crimes, commission of a civil wrong won't land you in jail or prison or death row. Instead, civil wrongs are punishable by monetary and non-monetary penalties not involving incarceration.

Before moving on, note the same legal offense can invoke criminal law *and* civil law. Stated differently, an action can be a criminal wrong *and* a civil wrong. In such cases, the wrongdoer potentially faces criminal prosecution and a lawsuit.

STATUTORY V. REGULATORY V. COMMON

Another way to classify laws is based upon which branch of government (federal or state) creates the law at issue. For purposes of explanation, imagine Kansas has a law banning its residents from flying kites in any public park in Kansas. Which branch of the Kansas state government created the law? Was it the Kansas Legislature (legislative branch)? Was it a state regulatory agency (executive branch)? Was it a Kansas state court (judicial branch)? The answer will tell us whether Kansas' kite ban is statutory law, regulatory law, or common law.

Statutory law is law enacted/passed by the legislative branch. The U.S. Congress and the various state legislatures create law via legislation. Such statutes are, fittingly, statutory law. (Some refer to statutory law as *written law*.) Statutory law also includes laws passed by local governments, such as ordinances passed by cities. So, from the Constitution of the United States to city ordinances, laws created by the legislative branches of the federal, state, and local governments constitute statutory law.

Statutes often empower executive/regulatory agencies to promulgate rules and regulations that carry out the statutes. These rules and regulations are categorized as *regulatory law*.

For example, the Clean Air Act, enacted by the U.S. Congress (legislative branch), directs the Environmental Protection Agency (EPA) (a federal regulatory agency, part of the executive branch) to promulgate rules/regulations for controlling emissions from U.S. power plants. The

Clean Air Act is a statute, so it is clearly statutory law. The EPA's rules/regulations implementing the Clean Air Act are regulatory law. (*Note: The same is true when state statutes empower state agencies to implement said statutes via rules/regulations.*)

Agency rules/regulations are not created by the legislative branch, but they add specificity to the statutes passed by the legislative branch. Keeping with the idea of "*branches,*" think of statutes passed by legislatures as the trunk and branches of a tree. Then, think of the rules/regulations promulgated by executive agencies as the leaves filling out the branches. Parts of statutes are often very general, with details worked out later via executive-agency rules/regulations.

Common law is created by the judicial branch. In other words, courts give us common law. Many refer to common law as *case law* (or *unwritten law*). Rooted in the tradition of English common law dating back hundreds of years, many areas of U.S. law are created by court decisions, as opposed to statutes. Most U.S. states are common-law jurisdictions, wherein the law of certain legal areas is formed by court decisions, as opposed to legislation.

For example, contracts is a state-based, common-law doctrine. What this means is in most states, the legislature does not decide what constitutes a valid contract in the state or what constitutes a breach of

a valid contract in the state. Rather, the state's courts provide such answers. Since the inception of state courts, as contracts cases came before the courts of the various states, the rulings of these courts collectively formed the body of contracts law in the various state. Obviously, then, the law of contracts varies among the states. So, what does it take to form a valid contract in Illinois? The contracts cases of the Illinois state courts will tell you; and their rules for contractual formation might be different than those of another state. What remedies are available to a party to a contract formed in Kentucky when the other party to the contract doesn't fulfill his contractual obligations (i.e., a breach of contract)? Kentucky case law will tell you; Contracts law isn't created by state statutes. It is created by state-court decisions. (*Note: Our examination of common law will focus exclusively on state courts. Though there is a very limited body of common law in the federal system, exploring it is beyond our scope.)*

By now, you should have a firm grasp on what *law* means and on different types of law. With this foundation laid, let's start building upon it.

chapter 2
COURTS

© corgarashu, 2014. Used under license from Shutterstock, Inc.

American life and culture are full of courtroom references and imagery. Every day, the news has no shortage of stories about court appearances, about sentences handed down by judges and juries. Our television and movie screens depict courtroom dramas ad nauseam. Phrases like *I'll see you in court* and *judge, jury, and executioner* are part of our national lexicon. Though we are inundated with courts and trials and judges and juries, many of us really don't know much about our nation's court system. What do these courts do? How does one end up in court? What are the differences among courts? Or are they all the same, except for their location? Let's find out.

PURPOSE OF COURTS

Why do we have courts? What purpose do they serve? Whereas the legislative branch enacts laws and the executive branch executes/implements/administers laws, the judicial branch interprets laws. Sometimes the judicial branch is called upon to decide whether a law passed by the legislative branch is constitutional. Most of the time, the judicial branch is called upon to hear cases against criminal defendants and civil defendants and, if warranted, impose punishment. Stated differently, our nation's courts are in place (partly) to decide whether crimes and civil offenses have been committed.

It is important to remember courts do not perform any of the tasks above unless they are asked to do so. In other words, courts do not bring criminal cases against people. Rather, the prosecutor charges people with crimes, and courts hear the prosecutions. Courts do not sue people. Rather, people sue people, and courts hear the lawsuits. Courts don't get involved on their own. They are reactive, not proactive. They don't issue rulings/opinions for the fun of it. They don't decide whether a certain law is constitutional unless a party challenges that law in court. They don't find someone innocent or guilty of a crime, in the absence of a criminal trial brought about by the government prosecutor. They don't adjudicate issues between and among

private parties unless one of those parties takes the other to court. Courts are there to rule on constitutional issues and to adjudicate disputes, but they don't do so without being asked to do so.

CREATION OF COURTS

Given we are a nation of federal laws and state laws, it stands to reason we have federal courts and state courts. Federal courts were created by Congress, via the U.S. Constitution and federal statutes. The Constitution (Article III, Section 1) established the Supreme Court of the United States, which is the supreme authority on federal law, and further empowered Congress to create federal courts inferior to the Supreme Court: *The judicial Power of the United States shall be vested in one supreme Court, and in such inferior Courts as the Congress may from time to time ordain and establish.* Indeed, Congress created inferior courts (see below) and has otherwise altered the makeup of the federal judiciary. For example, Congress has changed the number of Supreme Court justices.

Likewise, states create and amend their court systems via state constitutions and statutes. For example, the Kansas Constitution (ratified in 1861) established the Supreme Court of Kansas (the supreme authority on Kansas law) and district courts (the trial courts). In 1895, the Kansas Legislature created via statute Kansas' Court of Appeals (the level above Kansas district courts but below the Kansas Supreme Court), in response to the large caseloads that were increasingly burdensome to the existing courts. The statute included a sunset provision that ended the Court of Appeals in 1901, and the Kansas Legislature re-established the Court of Appeals in 1977. Other changes to the Kansas judiciary (e.g., number of Supreme Court justices, manner of selecting justices) have occurred throughout the years via statute. So, via state constitutions and state statutes, the various state legislatures have power to create and amend their respective judicial branches.

Kansas Capitol

FEDERAL COURT SYSTEM

The United States has one federal court system. Its three-level pyramid structure is made up of a base of trial courts (the level with the most courts), a middle level of appellate courts, and a top level, consisting of one court of last resort. I will flesh this out as we proceed, but for now, the basic setup is as follows:

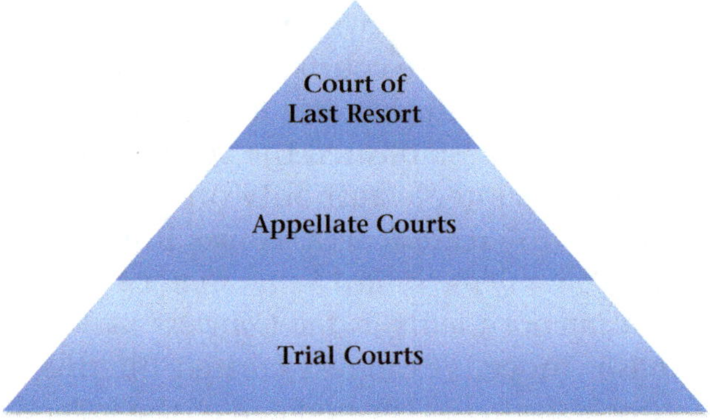

Using this basic pyramid layout as our skeleton, let's put some meat on the bones, so to speak. Because there is only one federal court system, we can easily and quickly add the names of the courts at each level.

BOTTOM LEVEL: TRIAL COURTS

The courts in the bottom level are the trial courts and are called United States District Courts. The country is divided geographically into federal districts. Each state has at least one district, and each district has at least one trial court. For example, Alabama is divided into three districts: Northern, Middle, and Southern. As such, Alabama is home to the U.S. District Court for the Northern District of Alabama, the U.S. District Court for the Middle District of Alabama, and the U.S. District Court for the Southern District of Alabama. California, Texas, & New York each have four federal districts, the most among the states. In all, there are 94 federal districts in the U.S., including districts in the District of Columbia and Puerto Rico and in the U.S. territories of Guam, the Virgin Islands, and the Northern Mariana Islands.

U.S. District Courts have the power to hear most types of cases in the federal system. As such, we should think of these courts as federal trial courts of general jurisdiction. Meanwhile, certain cases involving specialized subject matter (e.g., bankruptcy) are heard in separate trial courts. Let's think of these specialty courts as federal trial courts of limited jurisdiction. More on this later.

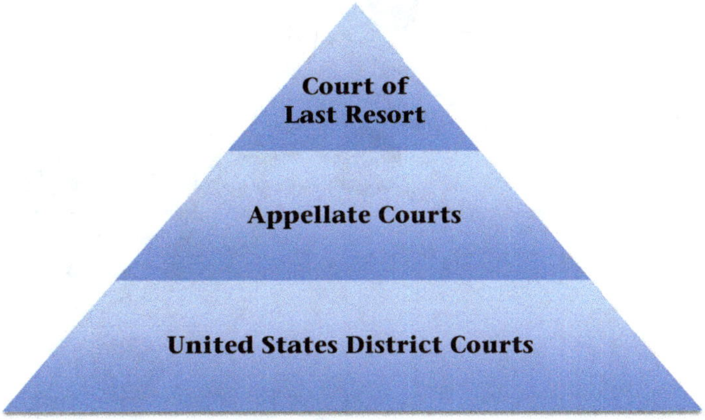

MIDDLE LEVEL: APPELLATE COURTS

The middle level of our pyramid chart is comprised of the first level of federal appellate courts, called United States Courts of Appeals, or United States Circuit Courts. Just as the country is divided into federal districts, the country is divided into federal circuits. There are 13 federal circuits: 11 numbered circuits (First Circuit, Second Circuit. . . Eleventh Circuit), the D.C. Circuit, and the Federal Circuit.

The circuit courts in each numbered circuit hear appeals from the U.S. District Courts within their circuit. For example, the Ninth Circuit, the largest of all the circuits, is comprised of all of the districts within Hawaii, Alaska, Washington, Oregon, Idaho, Montana, California, Arizona, and Nevada. Moreover, the Ninth Circuit includes the U.S. territories of Guam and the Northern Mariana Islands. The Ninth Circuit hears appeals at the federal courthouses in San Francisco (headquarters of the Ninth Circuit), Pasadena, Portland, and Seattle.

The United States Court of Appeals for the District of Columbia Circuit, the smallest circuit, hears appeals from the U.S. District Court for the District of Columbia, as well as appeals from hearings of various federal administrative agencies.

The United States Court of Appeals for the Federal Circuit hears appeals from throughout the country in various subject matters, such as patents, veterans' benefits, and international trade. Moreover, like the

http://www.uscourts.gov/uscourts/images/CircuitMap.pdf

Geographic Boundaries

of United States Courts of Appeals and United States District Courts

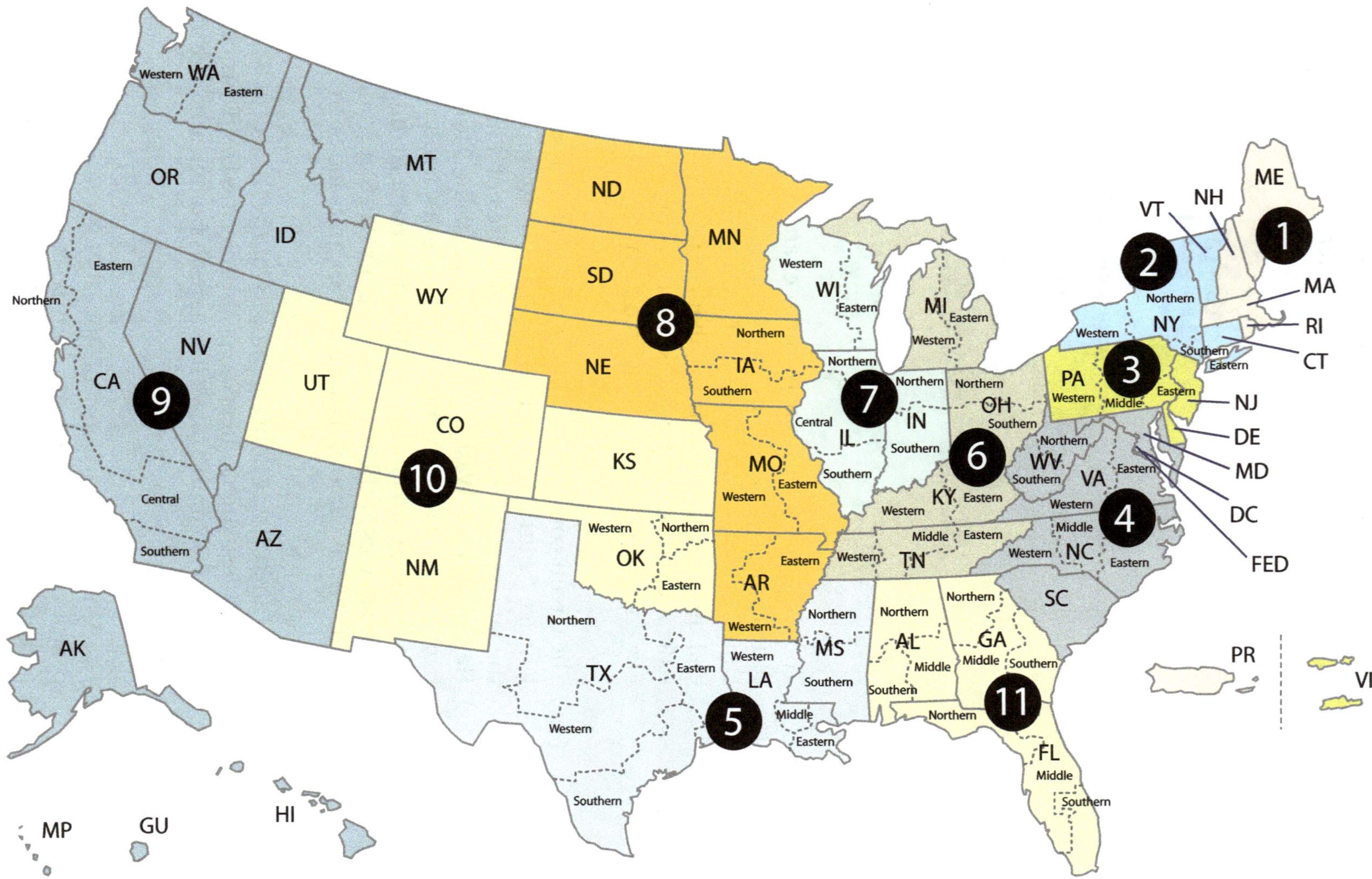

The map above shows the federal circuits, as well as the federal districts within each circuit.

D.C. Circuit, the Federal Circuit hears appeals from the decisions of certain federal administrative agencies.

No trials take place in the U.S. Circuit Courts. These courts' jurisdiction (power) is appellate in nature only. The judges who serve on these courts are known as *federal judges*. Because the federal judiciary was created by Article III of the U.S. Constitution, these judges are also referred to as *Article III judges*. They are appointed by the President of the United States and confirmed by the U.S. Senate. Their appointment is for life (i.e. not term-based).

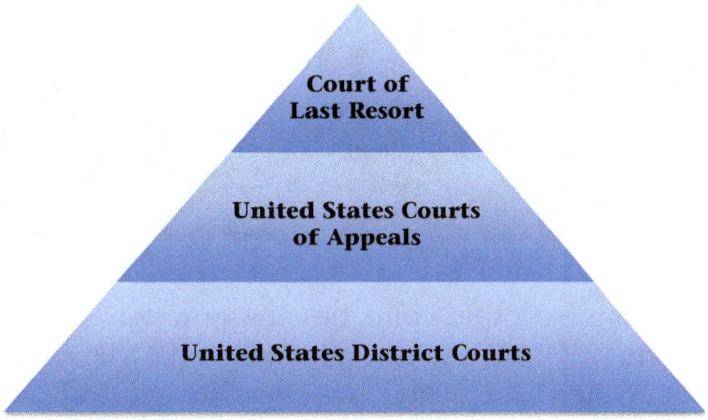

TOP LEVEL: COURT OF LAST RESORT

The Supreme Court of the United States (SCOTUS) is the highest federal court in the country. It is the supreme authority on federal law and is the only court specifically created in the U.S. Constitution. SCOTUS can be referred to as the "*high court*" or the "*court of last resort*" because it is as far (high) as a case can possibly go in the federal court system. It is the second and last possible appeal, and it hears appeals from all 13 federal circuits. SCOTUS can also hear appeals from the various state courts of last resort (stay tuned). Regardless of how a case gets before SCOTUS (and only a small number of all cases appealed to SCOTUS do), there is nowhere higher for a case to go.

While SCOTUS is primarily a court of appellate jurisdiction, the U.S. Constitution (Article III, Section 2) grants SCOTUS original jurisdiction over certain types of cases, meaning the power to hear certain cases before any appeal(s). Per federal statute (28 U.S.C. §1251), SCOTUS' original jurisdiction is either exclusive or non-exclusive. Exclusive

© Orhan Cam, 2014. Used under license from Shutterstock, Inc.

jurisdiction means no other court has the power to hear such cases. §1251(a) grants SCOTUS exclusive jurisdiction over cases between/among states, while §1251(b) grants non-exclusive jurisdiction over the following types of cases: *(1) All actions or proceedings to which ambassadors, other public ministers, consuls, or vice consuls of foreign states are parties; (2) All controversies between the United States and a State; (3) All actions or proceedings by a State against the citizens of another State or against aliens.*

SCOTUS is made up of nine justices who, like all federal judges, are appointed by the President, confirmed by the Senate, and appointed for life.

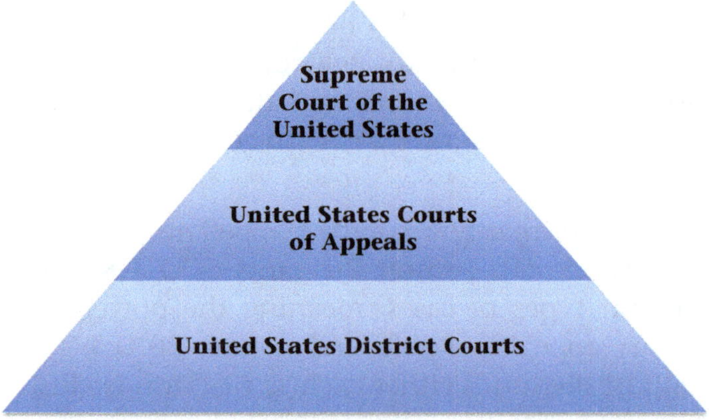

STATE COURT SYSTEMS

While there is one federal court system, there are 50 state court systems. Luckily for us, the basic structure of most of the state court systems is the same as that of the federal court system: trial courts (of general jurisdiction and limited jurisdiction) at the bottom, appellate courts in the middle, court of last resort at the top. As such, a firm grasp of the federal court system will help you understand the makeup of the various state court systems. Even when a state court system is not structured like the federal system, the difference is slight.

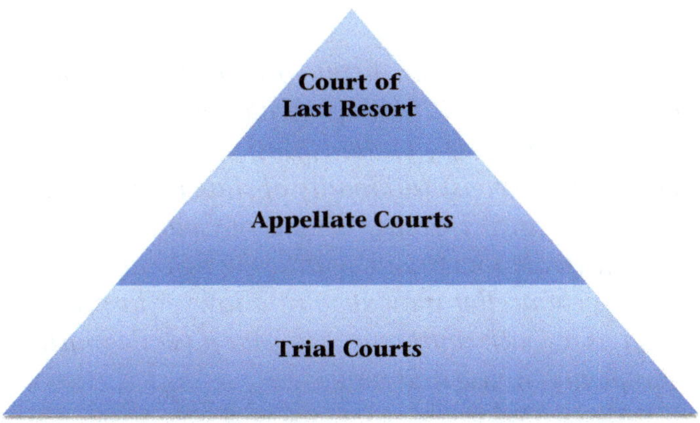

Each state controls the makeup of its court system, but it's not just the structure of state judiciaries that states control. They also control such decisions as the number of state judges/justices, the manner of selecting judges/justices, and the number of jury members for each type of state case. As a result, each state's court system is unique. Now, a closer look at the three court levels common among the state court systems. . .

BOTTOM LEVEL: TRIAL COURTS

As is the case in the federal system, states divide trial courts into trial courts of general jurisdiction (like U.S. District Courts) and/or trial courts of limited jurisdiction (like specialty federal trial courts).

Courts of general jurisdiction have the power to hear cases not assigned by statute to the courts of limited jurisdiction. The names for the general-jurisdiction trial courts differ among the states. For example, Montana has District Courts, while Oregon has Circuit Courts. Some states have more than 1 type of general-jurisdiction trial court. For example, Mississippi has 2 types: Circuit Courts and Chancery Courts. Each type has power over certain types of cases. According to the website of the State Judiciary of Mississippi (http://courts.ms.gov/aboutcourts/circuitcourt_about.html):

> *Circuit Courts hear felony criminal prosecutions and civil lawsuits. Circuit Courts hear appeals from County, Justice and Municipal courts and from administrative boards and commissions such as the Workers' Compensation Commission and the Mississippi Department of Employment Security.*
>
> *Chancery Courts have jurisdiction over disputes in matters involving equity; domestic matters including adoptions, custody disputes and divorces; guardianships; sanity hearings; wills; and challenges to constitutionality of state laws. Land records are filed in Chancery Court. Chancery Courts have jurisdiction over juvenile matters in counties which have no County Court. The chancellor may appoint a lawyer in private practice to sit as a youth court referee to hear juvenile matters such as delinquency, abuse and neglect.*

Although it is rare, some state trial courts of general jurisdiction even have some appellate authority, as well. For example, in Montana, the general-jurisdiction trial courts *"have limited appellate jurisdiction over cases arising in the Courts of Limited Jurisdiction in their respective districts as may be prescribed by law and consistent with the Constitution."* (http://courts.mt.gov/dcourt/default.mcpx)

As for the state trial courts of limited jurisdiction, just as federal statutes are the sources of these specialty trial courts in the federal system, state statutes are the sources of specialty trial courts in the state systems. In Mississippi, there are three limited-jurisdiction trial courts, each with unique authority: County Courts, Justice Courts, and Municipal Courts. Again, according to the website of the State Judiciary of Mississippi (http://courts.ms.gov/aboutcourts/circuitcourt_about.html):

> *County Courts have exclusive jurisdiction over eminent domain proceedings and juvenile matters, among other things. In counties which have a County Court, a County Court judge*

also serves as the Youth Court judge. County Courts share jurisdiction with Circuit and Chancery Courts in some civil matters. The jurisdictional limit of County Courts is up to $200,000. County Courts may handle non-capital felony cases transferred from Circuit Court. County Court judges may issue search warrants, set bond and preside over preliminary hearings. County Courts have concurrent jurisdiction with Justice Courts in all matters, civil and criminal.

Justice Courts have jurisdiction over small claims civil cases involving amounts of $3,500 or less, misdemeanor criminal cases and any traffic offense that occurs outside a municipality. Justice Court judges may conduct bond hearings and preliminary hearings in felony criminal cases and may issue search warrants.

Municipal courts have jurisdiction over misdemeanor crimes, municipal ordinances and city traffic violations. Municipal judges may conduct initial appearances in which defendants are advised of the charges being filed, as well as bond hearings and preliminary hearings.

To muddy the waters even more, Mississippi has two additional specialty courts it doesn't categorize with the three aforementioned limited-jurisdiction trial courts. These courts are Drug Courts and Youth Courts. Once more, according to the website of the State Judiciary of Mississippi (http://courts.ms.gov/aboutcourts/circuitcourt_about.html):

A drug court is a special court given the responsibility to handle cases involving drug-using offenders through comprehensive supervision, drug testing, treatment services and immediate sanctions and incentives.

The Youth Courts deal with matters involving abuse and neglect of juveniles, as well as offenses committed by juveniles. Young people who have not reached the age of 18 may be subject to the Youth Court, although there are some exceptions. Some offenses which would be treated as crimes if committed by adults are known as delinquent acts when they involve juveniles.

The Mississippi example is but one. As previously stated, each state has its own way of organizing and classifying its trial courts. (Check out the websites of the state judicial branches to learn how the states do so.) That said, the gist of each state's bottom level of courts is the same: it is where cases begin. It is where trials happen. Whether general jurisdiction or limited jurisdiction in nature, trial courts are where criminal and civil actions commence.

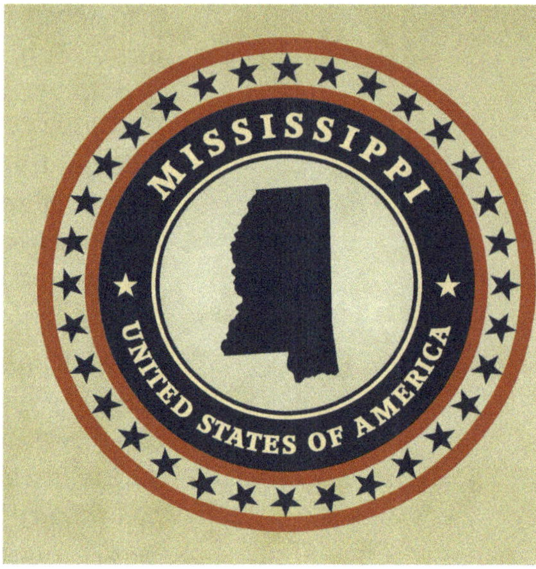

MIDDLE LEVEL: APPELLATE COURTS

Like the federal judiciary, the typical state court system has intermediate (i.e., middle level in our three-level pyramid structure) courts of appeals. These courts are less numerous than trial courts but more numerous than the court of last resort. These courts are higher in the vertical chain than the trial courts but lower than the court of last resort. The function of this middle level of courts is to hear appeals from the trial courts below.

Just as the federal courts of appeals take appeals only from trial courts in their respective judicial circuit, state appellate courts hear appeals from certain (if not all) trial courts in their respective state judicial area (usually called *"circuits,"* as well). States differ on what they call these courts. Most states, such as Indiana, refer to this level of courts as their courts of appeals. These courts typically hear most types of appeals from the various state trial courts, and a common manner of hearing such appeals is by a three-judge panel. (This is also the manner of hearing most appeals in the federal circuit courts.) According to the website of the Indiana Judicial Branch (http://www.in.gov/judiciary/appeals/2336.htm):

> *As the second-highest court in Indiana, the Court of Appeals hears appeals from the state's trial courts. The Court does not preside over trials and must accept all appeals sent to it, with the exception of:*
>
> - *Cases in which the death penalty or life-without-parole is rendered (appealed directly to the Indiana Supreme Court);*

- *Cases in which statutes are declared unconstitutional by a trial court (automatically appealed to the Supreme Court);*
- *Attorney disciplinary cases (which also go to the Supreme Court); and,*
- *Cases involving taxation (which go to the Indiana Tax Court).*

As a result, the 15 members of the Court issue approximately 2,500 written opinions each year. A decision of the Court of Appeals of Indiana is final unless granted further review by the Indiana Supreme Court.

The Court hears cases only in three-judge panels. All panels have statewide jurisdiction and rotate three times per year. Cases are randomly assigned. In addition, there is no deadline for the Court to reach a decision in each case; however, the Court strives to issue decisions within four months of receiving an appeal. Opinions are often issued earlier.

The Indiana Court of Appeals was not created in the Indiana Constitution, as was the Indiana Supreme Court. Rather, to deal with the burden of an increasingly large number of appeals, the Indiana

Indiana Statehouse

Legislature created the Court of Appeals by state statute. This was a common scenario among the various states, which expanded and modified their judiciaries to accommodate their growing populations.

TOP LEVEL: COURT OF LAST RESORT

The top level of our pyramid state-court structure is made up of the highest state court(s) in each state. These courts are to their respective state laws what the Supreme Court of the United States is to federal law: the highest authority. The final say-so. These are courts of last resort, meaning there are no possible appeals beyond these courts on matters of state law.

All but two states (Texas and Oklahoma) have one court at this level. Most states call these courts their *"Supreme Court."* In an odd deviation, New York calls its general-jurisdiction trial courts *Supreme Courts* and its court of last resort the *Court of Appeals*. Texas and Oklahoma have two courts at the top level: a court of last resort for criminal appeals and a court of last resort for civil appeals. In Texas, the Court of Criminal Appeals is the court of last resort for criminal appeals, while the Supreme Court of Texas is the court of last resort for civil appeals. The same is true in Oklahoma: the Court of Criminal Appeals is the court of last resort for criminal appeals, while the Oklahoma Supreme Court is the court of last resort for civil appeals.

Though state constitutions generally create states' highest courts, state statutes have often modified the high courts. For example, the Washington Constitution calls for a supreme court made up of five judges, but the Washington Legislature subsequently upped the number of high-court judges to nine.

New York Court of Appeals

As is the case with the Supreme Court of the United States, state courts of last resort are primarily courts of appellate jurisdiction but also possess certain areas of original jurisdiction, as granted by state constitutions and/or statutes. For example, the Washington Constitution (Article IV, Section 4) grants the Washington Supreme Court original jurisdiction over petitions against state officers:

The supreme court shall have original jurisdiction in habeas corpus, and quo warranto and mandamus as to all state officers. . .

Interestingly, the sentence quoted above goes on to state when the Washington Supreme Court does *not* have appellate jurisdiction, stating that the Court's appellate power applies

in all actions and proceedings, excepting that its appellate jurisdiction shall not extend to civil actions at law for the recovery of money or personal property when the original amount in controversy, or the value of the property does not exceed the sum of two hundred dollars ($200) unless the action involves the legality of a tax, impost, assessment, toll, municipal fine, or the validity of a statute.

The section above is one of many times where an exception to an exception is found in the law: the Washington Supreme Court has power over appeals from the trial courts *except* when the amount in controversy is no more than $200 *except* when such low-dollar cases involve the legality or validity of a Washington state law. If this frustrates you, find a way to cope with it, because the law is riddled with exceptions and exceptions to exceptions! In math, 1 + 1 = 2. In law, rarely do you find such black-and-white rules. Why do you think this is? (Great idea for classroom discussion, teachers!)

chapter 3 JURISDICTION

In the previous chapter, we learned about the courts of the federal judiciary and state judiciaries. But simply knowing which courts comprise each system does not tell us which cases and which parties end up in these courts.

Imagine you are driving in Madison, Wisconsin. You notice flashing lights in your rear-view mirror, immediately noticing that sick feeling one feels when being pulled over by the police. You pull over and await the cop's arrival at your car. When the officer arrives at your car and asks you for your license and registration, you notice his uniform is that of the Mexico City, Mexico, police. He tells you he was just passing through, on his road trip from Mexico to Canada, and thought you were swerving, so he pulled you over. What might many people in the driver's position say to the Mexico City cop? Perhaps, *"You can't pull me over, because you're out of your jurisdiction."* (Respectfully, no doubt.) Telling the cop he is out of his jurisdiction is, in effect, telling him what? That he doesn't have the authority to pull you over and issue you a ticket. You are telling him he doesn't have power over you. Jurisdiction is about power.

For any court to have legal power over you — meaning the authority to issue a binding judgment upon you, either against you personally or against your property — that court must have proper jurisdiction. This is true in the federal court system and the various state court systems; and this is true for actions against people (criminal trials and civil trials) and actions against property.

There are several types of jurisdiction. We will examine three of them: subject-matter jurisdiction, personal jurisdiction, and in rem jurisdiction. To do so, we need to learn the difference between in-personam cases and in-rem cases.

IN-PERSONAM JURISDICTION

Trials involve defendants. In criminal trials, the government prosecutes a criminal defendant. In civil trials, a plaintiff sues a civil defendant. In both cases, people are involved in a dispute heard by a court, and people stand to lose. Such cases are known as *in-personam* cases. They are actions against people. An in-personam case is one with a possible judgment against someone to be handed down by the court, from life without parole to one night in jail to imposition of a fine

or community service. In such cases, two types of jurisdiction are required, before a court may issue a legally-binding ruling: subject-matter jurisdiction and personal jurisdiction. *Subject-matter jurisdiction* is power over the type of case, while *personal jurisdiction* is power over the persons (parties) in a case. Let's look at each.

SUBJECT-MATTER JURISDICTION (SMJ)

One type of power any court needs in order to render judgment against a person is power over the particular type of case. Such power is subject-matter jurisdiction. For a federal court to have power to hear a case, it must have power over that type of case. For a state court to have power to hear a case, it must have power over that type of case. Stated simply, SMJ is about whether a case belongs in the federal court system or in a state court system. Restated: Should a trial (criminal or civil) begin in a federal trial court or a state trial court?

Recall both the federal judiciary and the various state judiciaries have trial courts of limited jurisdiction. These specialty trial courts are the ones hearing cases of the type assigned to them by federal and state statutes, respectively. Given statutes tell us the types of cases that go to these limited-jurisdiction trial courts, let's put aside these courts and focus on which types of cases go to the general-jurisdiction trial courts in the federal system (called U.S. District Courts) and in the various state systems. Let's also put aside the cases for which the U.S. Constitution grants the U.S. Supreme Court original jurisdiction. Our focus is on the federal and state trial courts of general jurisdiction; and our focus is on civil actions (power over criminal actions necessarily involve issues of criminal law and procedure, and this book's focus is chiefly on civil matters). Make sense? We want to know which lawsuits the federal district courts have the power to hear and which ones they do not. We want to know which lawsuits the state trial courts of general jurisdiction have the power to hear and which ones they do not. Let's start with the federal district courts.

FEDERAL SMJ

Generally (anytime I use *"generally,"* I'm indicating the rule I'm stating has one or more exceptions), there are two routes to federal trial court. Stated differently, there are two major types of cases that can be heard by U.S. District Courts. One has to do with federal law, and the other has to do with state law.

FEDERAL QUESTION

The first type of case that can be brought in federal district court is one involving a *federal question*. The U.S. Constitution (Article III, Section 2) states that the federal courts can hear *"all cases, in law and equity, arising under this Constitution, [and] the laws of the United States."* SCOTUS has interpreted the U.S. Constitution's language granting federal courts power to hear cases arising under federal law as the power to hear any case in which federal law *"forms an ingredient of the original cause." See Osborn v. Bank of the United States*, 22 U.S. 738 (1824). This means federal courts have power over a lawsuit if either party (plaintiff or defendant) asserts a federal issue.

But recall SCOTUS is the only federal court created by the Constitution. Via federal statute, the U.S. Congress created federal district courts (and federal appellate courts); and federal statutes give these courts power to hear certain types of cases. The statute authorizing federal district courts to hear federal-question cases, 28 USC §1331, is more limiting than the Constitution's grant of authority. Stated differently, just because a lawsuit contains a federal ingredient, the lawsuit might not be able to be brought in federal district court. The reason: federal district courts must have Constitutional *and* statutory authority to hear a case. §1331 states, *"The district courts shall have original jurisdiction of all civil actions arising under the Constitution, laws, or treaties of the United States."*

So, if a plaintiff is suing for an alleged violation of the U.S. Constitution, a federal statute, or federal treaty, the case is a federal-question case. For example, if Larry sues Moe and Curly for discriminating against him, in violation of the U.S. Constitution, the lawsuit involves a federal issue; and the federal district courts (all of them) have authority to hear the case, on federal-question grounds. Federal courts have power to hear cases based on federal law(s). This makes complete sense, right?

But there is more beneath the surface. For example, for federal-question jurisdiction to exist (and thus give the federal courts power to hear the case), a federal issue must be raised by the plaintiff, in his initial complaint. This requirement rules out federal-question jurisdiction for cases in which the plaintiff does not raise a federal issue but in which the defendant's answer (to the plaintiff's complaint) raises a federal issue (*even an exclusive federal question, which you will learn about shortly; see Holmes Group, Inc. v. Vornado Air Circulation Systems, Inc.,* 535 U.S. 826 (2002)). The same is true for cases in which the plaintiff does not raise a federal issue but in which he/she anticipates a federal-issue in response from the defendant. In *Louisville & Nashville Railroad Co. v. Mottley*, 211 U.S. 149 (1908), SCOTUS writes,

> *[a] suit arises under the Constitution and laws of the United States only when the plaintiff's statement of his own cause of action shows that it is based upon those laws or that Constitution. It is not enough that the plaintiff alleges some anticipated defense to his cause of action, and asserts that the defense is invalidated by some provision of the Constitution of the United States.*

So, a federal issue must be present (i.e., stated) from the beginning of the action. For purposes of establishing federal SMJ, it is the plaintiff's complaint that matters. This is referred to as the *Well-Pleaded Complaint Rule.*

So, for purposes of SMJ, a federal district court focuses on a plaintiff's complaint and decides if the plaintiff's claim *"arises under"* federal law. But even determining what *"arises under"* means has been complicated. A test that works almost all of the time is referred to as *The Holmes Test.* The test is named after SCOTUS Justice Oliver Wendell Holmes, who wrote in *American Well Works Co. v. Layne & Bowler Co.*, 241 U.S. 257 (1916): *"A suit arises under the law that creates the cause of action."* In addition to most cases (I write *"most"* because rare exceptions exist) whose claims are created by federal law that can be heard by federal district courts, federal district courts may also hear certain cases in which a federal issue is *"embedded"* in the plaintiff's complaint, even though the claim is not created by federal law. What this means is even a state-law claim (which could not get into federal court on its own) can be brought in federal district court if a substantial federal issue must be resolved, in order for the court to rule on the merits of the plaintiff's (state-law) claim. In *Franchise Tax Board of the State of California v. Construction Laborers Vacation Trust of Southern California,* 463 U.S 1 (1983), SCOTUS writes,

> *Even though state law creates appellant's causes of action, its case might still "arise under" the laws of the United States if a well-pleaded complaint established that its right to relief under state law requires resolution of a substantial question of federal law in dispute between the parties.*

Note not all cases arising under federal law can begin in federal district court. Recall our earlier look at the makeup of the federal court system. We learned SCOTUS has the power to hear a few types of lawsuits from the get-go. Such original jurisdiction means SCOTUS can hear the case before any appeals. Stated differently, these types of cases *can* begin at SCOTUS, as opposed to reaching SCOTUS on appeal from the lower federal courts, as most cases that reach SCOTUS do; and even one type of case (suits between/among states) *must* begin at SCOTUS.

Oliver Wendell Holmes

However, just because a lawsuit arises under federal law and is not reserved solely for SCOTUS does not mean the case will always be heard by a federal court. The reason is there are two types of federal questions: exclusive federal questions and non-exclusive federal questions. Exclusive federal questions (EFQs) are ones that can only be heard by a federal court, as they are federal issues that are exclusively reserved for the federal courts. Examples of EFQs are bankruptcy cases (28 USC §1334), patent, copyright, and trademark cases (28 USC §1338), and cases specified in Article 3, Section 2, of the U.S. Constitution, such as cases involving ambassadors and admiralty cases.

Contrast that with non-exclusive federal questions (NEFQs), which *can* be brought in federal court but which do not *have* to be brought in federal court. Most federal issues are non-exclusive in nature, meaning they are ones both the federal courts and state courts have power to hear. This shared authority is referred to as *concurrent jurisdiction*. In such cases, the plaintiff has the option to file his lawsuit in federal trial court or an appropriate state trial court (but not both). Whether filed in federal court or state court, the court hearing the case applies the relevant *federal* law.

Let's dive deeper. We just learned a lawsuit that raises (from the beginning) a federal issue can be brought in federal court. But what if, for example, a plaintiff's complaint raises an issue of federal law *and* an issue of state law? What happens then? Can the federal issue still be heard in federal court? What about the state issue? The answer is it depends. If the two issues are related in nature, by which I mean they arise from the same set of circumstances, the federal system has power to hear *both* issues. Such power is referred to as *pendent jurisdiction*, a type of *supplemental jurisdiction*. It is as if the state issue rides the coattails of the federal issue into federal court. If, however, the federal issue and state issue are not related in nature (if, say, the plaintiff's two claims have nothing to do with one another, but he wanted to save time, so he filed them together), the state issue cannot get into federal court on grounds of pendent jurisdiction (which is a form of federal-question jurisdiction). So, to recap, if a plaintiff files a lawsuit with two or more *related* claims that are a combination of federal- and state-law issues, federal-question jurisdiction exists for both/all claims.

DIVERSITY OF CITIZENSHIP

The second type of lawsuit that can be heard in federal court has to do with state law (as opposed to federal-question jurisdiction, which has to do with federal law), and it is referred to as *diversity of citizenship (DOC)*. These are special types of state-law actions allowed to be heard by federal district courts. Without DOC, a state-law claim could not, on its own merits, be heard by federal trial courts, since state-law claim does not arise under federal law. Without DOC, the only way a state question could be heard in federal court would be via pendent jurisdiction. In such case, the state question would not get into federal court on its own merits but rather by virtue of its connection/relation to the federal question(s) raised in the lawsuit.

The DOC statute, 28 USC §1332, begins:

> *(a) The district courts shall have original jurisdiction of all civil actions where the matter in controversy exceeds the sum or value of $75,000, exclusive of interest and costs, and is between—*
>
> *(1) citizens of different States;*

From this, we see DOC has two requirements. One has to do with the dollar amount of the lawsuit. For now, table that one. The other DOC requirement is that the parties to the lawsuit be "*citizens of different States.*" This is referred to as *complete diversity*. (It is the parties' states of citizenship *at the time of the lawsuit's filing* that is controlling.) For example, a case whose plaintiff is an Arkansas citizen and whose defendant is an Oregon citizen would meet the complete-diversity requirement, whereas a case whose plaintiff is an Arkansas citizen and whose defendant is an Arkansas citizen would not meet the complete-diversity requirement.

And what makes one a *citizen* of a state? This is often a complicated question. Citizenship is based on one's domicile. How to determine one's domicile varies among the federal courts. The rule in most is one's domicile is the state where she intends to remain indefinitely. Let's keep it simple (while remembering that the issue can be much more involved): one is a citizen of the state where her primary residence is. If she lives in Oklahoma but owns a vacation home in Florida, she is a citizen of Oklahoma, not Florida.

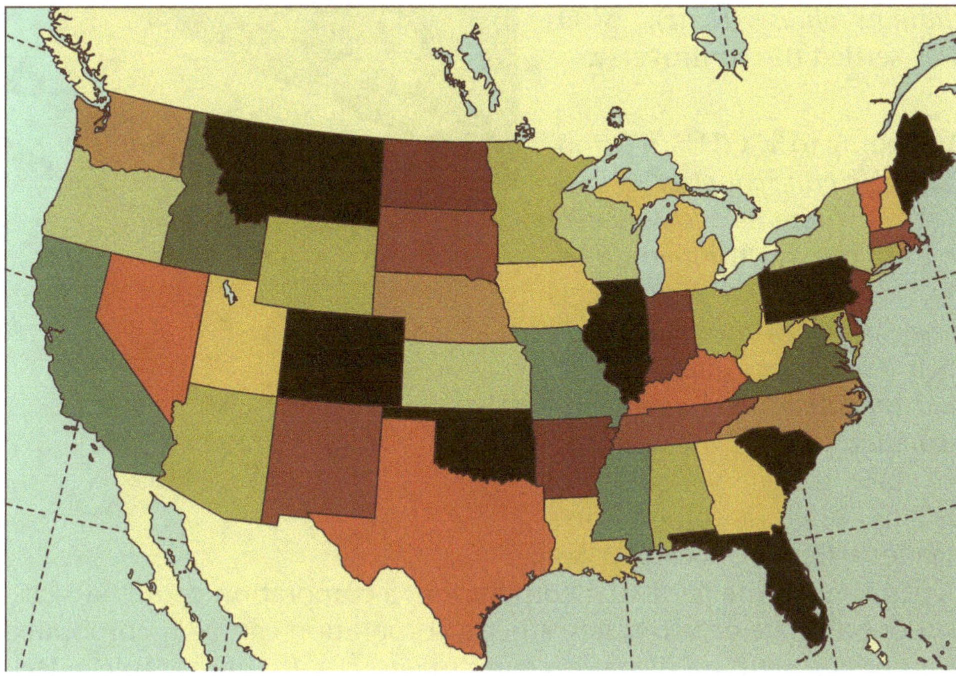

In addition to controversies between/among citizens of different states, DOC also applies to the following, per 28 USC §1332 (a)(2-4):

> (2) *citizens of a State and citizens or subjects of a foreign state, except that the district courts shall not have original jurisdiction under this subsection of an action between citizens of a State and citizens or subjects of a foreign state who are lawfully admitted for permanent residence in the United States and are domiciled in the same State;*
> (3) *citizens of different States and in which citizens or subjects of a foreign state are additional parties; and*
> (4) *a foreign state, defined in section 1603 (a) of this title, as plaintiff and citizens of a State or of different States.*

Corporations, too, are deemed citizens, for purposes of diversity of citizenship. But unlike persons, corporations might be considered citizens of more than one state. A corporation is a citizen of the state where it was incorporated (became a business entity); and a corporation is a citizen of the state where its *"principal place of business"* is located (28 USC §1332(c)(1)). Prior to *Hertz Corp. v. Friend* (No. 08–1107), a February 2010 SCOTUS decision, the federal appellate courts were divided on the question of what constituted the *"principal place of business"* of a corporation. *"In an effort to find a single, more uniform interpretation of the statutory phrase* (Hertz)," SCOTUS settled the controversy.

According to SCOTUS, a corporation's "*principal place of business*" is where its "*nerve center*" is located; and the nerve center, according to SCOTUS, is "*the place where the corporation's high level officers direct, control, and coordinate the corporation's activities.*" (SCOTUS went on to state the nerve center is usually where a corporation's headquarters are located.) So, depending on the particular corporation, a corporation could be a citizen of one state or two states, since a corporation can be incorporated in one state yet have its nerve center in another. If, for example, a Delaware citizen sues a corporation incorporated in Delaware but with its nerve center in New Mexico, there is no complete diversity and, thus, no diversity of citizenship.

Now, let's add a layer: What about a case with two plaintiffs and one defendant? One plaintiff is an Arkansas citizen, and the other plaintiff is a Kansas citizen. The defendant is an Oregon citizen. Complete diversity? Yes! The reason is there is no state common to the plaintiff's side and the defendant's side. Let's keep going. Same case, but now the plaintiffs from Arkansas and Kansas sue two defendants, both citizens of Oregon. Complete diversity? Still yes! Maybe you're wondering how this can be, since we have two parties who are citizens of the same state. The reason is, again, there is no state common to the plaintiff's side and the defendant's side. Restated: No plaintiff is a citizen of the same state as that of any defendant.

Complete diversity does not fail if you see two or more parties with the same state of citizenship on the same side of the case (plaintiff or defendant.) Complete diversity only fails if you see two or more parties with the same state of citizenship on the opposite side of the case! Got it? Just to be safe, when examining a case for complete diversity, draw a vertical line down the middle of a piece of paper. To the left of the line, write the state of citizenship of each plaintiff. To the right, write the state of citizenship for each defendant. If you see any one state on BOTH sides of the line, there is no complete diversity. If there is no state on the left also on the right, there is complete diversity.

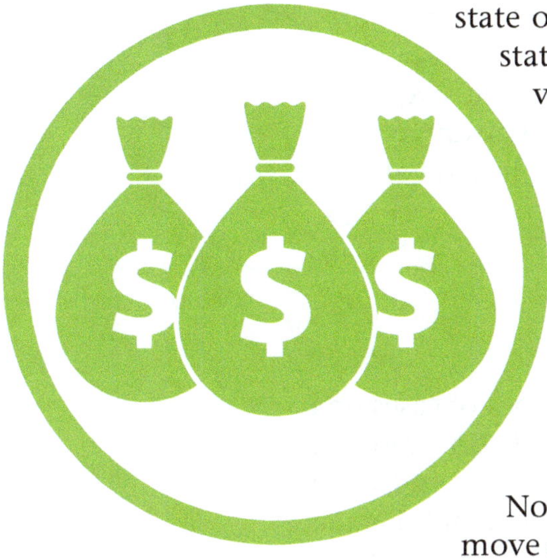

Before leaving the topic of complete diversity, note a few types of state-law cases with less than complete diversity are allowed to go to federal court (e.g. certain class-action lawsuits). We won't explore these types of cases, but mentioning this is a good reminder that law is full of exceptions.

Now that we understand complete diversity, we can move on to the other DOC requirement: lawsuits with complete diversity must also be ones in which the amount in controversy is greater than $75,000 (exclusive of interest and costs). So, if a Louisiana citizen sues a New Jersey citizen for breach of contract (a state-law claim) for $90,000, diversity of citizenship jurisdiction exists. As is the case with determining one's state of citizenship, there is more to learn about the amount-in-controversy requirement.

For example, a plaintiff meets the requirement if she brings a lawsuit with multiple claims (even unrelated ones), and the total dollar amount she sues for exceeds $75,000. In other words, the plaintiff is allowed to aggregate her claims against a common defendant, in order to meet the dollar requirement. Meanwhile, multiple plaintiffs may not aggregate their claims in order to meet the requirement. So, if Bob and Dave each have a $40,000 state-law claim against Terry, they cannot combine their lawsuits in order to meet the amount-in-controversy requirement. There are other layers to peel, but let's move on.

So, what does *"diversity of citizenship jurisdiction exists"* mean? We've learned what DOC is, but what is the effect of its application to a lawsuit? Think back to our look at federal-question jurisdiction. You should recall federal questions are either exclusive in nature or non-exclusive (concurrent) in nature. EFQs can be heard by federal courts only, while NEFQs can be heard by federal courts or state courts. Now, what about DOC? Are DOC suits exclusive or non-exclusive? All DOC claims are non-exclusive in nature, meaning the plaintiff may file his DOC action in federal trial court or state trial court. This should make sense. Since DOC actions involve state laws and not federal law, then DOC claims certainly can be heard by state courts. And DOC actions can be heard by federal courts, too, for as previously mentioned, DOC actions are a special type of state-law-based claim that are allowed to be brought in federal court. Whereas federal questions create either exclusive (federal) or concurrent (federal and state) jurisdiction, DOC is always concurrent. As with NEFQs, plaintiffs have the option to file in federal court or state court.

STATE SMJ

While U.S. District Courts can hear (mostly) *just* two types of cases (federal question & DOC), state trial courts of general jurisdiction can hear *all but* two types of cases. We've already encountered both types. Do you recall what they are? Need a hint? Think back to our pyramid diagram of the typical state court system, and think back to the section above regarding federal SMJ. Is it coming to you now? If not, keep reading.

The two types of lawsuits that cannot be filed in a state trial court of general jurisdiction are (1) one in which the plaintiff's complaint raises an EFQ and (2) one based on a state-law issue a state statute assigns to a state trial court of limited jurisdiction. EFQs can be heard by federal courts only (unless they are asserted not by the plaintiff in her complaint but by the defendant in his answer to the plaintiff's complaint). And each state's specialty trial courts handle certain types of cases not heard by the state's general-jurisdiction trial courts. Other than these two types of lawsuits, state trial courts of general jurisdiction have the authority to hear any type of lawsuit.

REMOVAL

We've now learned which types of cases can be heard by federal courts and by state courts. Before we leave the topic of SMJ, we need to examine the topic of removal jurisdiction. Removal is the process by which certain actions filed in state trial court can be removed, at the defendant's option, to federal trial court. When is removal a possibility, and how does it work?

Removal is a possibility when a plaintiff's claim creates concurrent jurisdiction. There are two types of such claims, and we've learned both: (1) NEFQs & (2) DOC. Actions of these types can be heard by federal trial courts or state trial courts. The plaintiff in such actions chooses whether to file in federal court or state court. If the plaintiff chooses to file in state court, removal to federal court (in the same state where the lawsuit was filed in state court) might be available to the defendant(s), and if it is available, it is available for a limited time, per court rules. Let's learn when removal is and is not available.

Keep in mind removal is the process of moving a case from state court to federal court. Removal does not operate to move cases from federal court to state court. Once a case is properly in federal court, it's there to stay. Since removal allows a certain case to be sent from state court to federal court, the statutes governing removal are federal statutes. The general removal statute is 28 U.S.C. §1441, which states, in part,

> *(a) Generally.—Except as otherwise expressly provided by Act of Congress, any civil action brought in a State court of which the district courts of the United States have original jurisdiction, may be removed by the defendant or the defendants, to the district court of the United States for the district and division embracing the place where such action is pending.*
>
> *(b) Removal Based on Diversity of Citizenship.—*
>
> *(1) In determining whether a civil action is removable on the basis of the jurisdiction under section 1332(a) of this title, the citizenship of defendants sued under fictitious names shall be disregarded.*
>
> *(2) A civil action otherwise removable solely on the basis of the jurisdiction under section 1332(a) of this title may not be removed if any of the parties in interest properly joined and served as defendants is a citizen of the State in which such action is brought.*

What do we learn from these subsections of §1441? First, Subsection (a) reveals when a plaintiff files a NEFQ lawsuit in state court, the defendant may always remove to federal court (provided he does so within the period of time in which the court allows removal[1]).[2] This stands to reason: NEFQs are types of federal laws, and federal courts certainly have the power to hear every federal question. Therefore, if a defendant is sued over a NEFQ, he has the right to have a federal court hear the federal-issue lawsuit, just as the plaintiff had the right to file his NEFQ claim in federal court.

Meanwhile, Subsection (b) reveals when a plaintiff files a DOC lawsuit in state court, the answer is less straightforward: a defendant *might* be able to remove. The general rule is a defendant can remove a DOC lawsuit from state court to federal court; but the exception to the rule is removal is not allowed if the defendant is sued in his own state.

Consider these two contrasting scenarios: (1) Patrick, a Pennsylvania citizen, sues Daniel, a Delaware citizen, in a Pennsylvania state trial court. Patrick's claim is based on state law, and Patrick seeks $100,000. May Daniel remove the case to federal district court in Pennsylvania? Yes. (2) Patrick, a Pennsylvania citizen, sues Daniel, a Delaware citizen, in a Delaware state trial court. Patrick's claim is based on state law, and Patrick seeks $100,000. May Daniel remove the case to federal district

1. The defendant has 30 days to remove the case, per 28 U.S.C. §1446(b): "Requirements; Generally.—(1) The notice of removal of a civil action or proceeding shall be filed within 30 days after the receipt by the defendant, through service or otherwise, of a copy of the initial pleading setting forth the claim for relief upon which such action or proceeding is based, or within 30 days after the service of summons upon the defendant if such initial pleading has then been filed in court and is not required to be served on the defendant, whichever period is shorter."

2. To remove a removable case, the defendant files a notice of removal with the federal court in the district where the relevant state court (i.e., the state court where the plaintiff filed her claim) is located. See §1446(a): "(a) Generally.—A defendant or defendants desiring to remove any civil action from a State court shall file in the district court of the United States for the district and division within which such action is pending a notice of removal signed pursuant to Rule 11 of the Federal Rules of Civil Procedure and containing a short and plain statement of the grounds for removal, together with a copy of all process, pleadings, and orders served upon such defendant or defendants in such action." Note that a plaintiff has a limited period of time in which she can object to removal. A federal court can't hear a case for which it lacks SMJ, but it can hear a case that was improperly removed to it. (Remember: to be removable, the federal district court must have first possessed SMJ over the claim.) See 28 U.S.C. §1447(c): "A motion to remand the case on the basis of any defect other than lack of subject matter jurisdiction must be made within 30 days after the filing of the notice of removal under section 1446(a). If at any time before final judgment it appears that the district court lacks subject matter jurisdiction, the case shall be remanded. An order remanding the case may require payment of just costs and any actual expenses, including attorney fees, incurred as a result of the removal. A certified copy of the order of remand shall be mailed by the clerk to the clerk of the State court. The State court may thereupon proceed with such case."

court in Delaware? No. Why not? Because Patrick filed his DOC lawsuit against Daniel in Daniel's state.

What if there is more than one defendant? What if Patrick sued Daniel and Vinnie? Is removal possible? And, if it is, can any one of the two defendants have a case removed, or must both defendants agree to remove? First, when there are multiple defendants, removal is allowed if the plaintiff files his DOC lawsuit in a state in which no defendant is a citizen. If the plaintiff files his action in a state home to even one of the multiple defendants, removal is not allowed.

Consider these two contrasting scenarios: (1) Patrick, a Pennsylvania citizen, sues Daniel, a Delaware citizen, and Vinnie, a Vermont citizen, in a Pennsylvania state trial court. Patrick's claim is based on state law, and Patrick seeks $100,000. May Daniel and Vinnie remove the case to federal district court in Pennsylvania? Yes. Why? Because neither Daniel nor Vinnie is a citizen of Pennsylvania. (2) Patrick, a Pennsylvania citizen, sues Daniel, a Delaware citizen, and Vinnie, a Vermont citizen, in a Delaware state trial court. Patrick's claim is based on state law, and Patrick seeks $100,000. May Daniel and Vinnie remove the case to federal district court in Delaware? No. Why? Because Daniel is a citizen of Delaware. Finally, if removal is allowed, the choice to remove must be unanimous between/among all defendants.[3]

3. 28 U.S.C. §1446(2)(A): *"When a civil action is removed solely under section 1441(a), all*

Remember: removal is a one-way street: state to federal. If a plaintiff files a concurrent-jurisdiction action in federal court, it stays in federal court. There is no such thing as removal from federal court to state court. Once you're properly in federal court, you're there to stay. So, settle in, and get comfortable!

PERSONAL JURISDICTION (PJ)

Whereas subject-matter jurisdiction is power over the type of case, personal jurisdiction is power over the parties in a case: plaintiff(s) and defendant(s). For a given court to have power to adjudicate an in-personam case, SMJ and PJ must be established. Our examination of PJ is focused chiefly on the defendant. The reason is PJ is established over the plaintiff(s) by virtue of the filing of the lawsuit. If someone files a lawsuit, he is, in essence, asking a court to settle a dispute with the defendant(s). By filing the lawsuit, the plaintiff freely submits to the court's power over him. So, our focus is really on the defendant. And how does a court obtain PJ over the defendant(s) in a given case? There are multiple ways. Any one of the ways is sufficient.

defendants who have been properly joined and served must join in or consent to the removal of the action."

The three ways for a court to obtain PJ over a defendant are as follows: (1) legal appearance by the defendant, (2) service of summons, and (3) long-arm statute. The first two ways apply to both in-state and out-of-state defendants. An in-state defendant is a citizen of the state where the lawsuit is filed. (The state where the lawsuit is filed is referred to as *the forum state*.) For purposes of PJ, a corporation conducting business in the state where the lawsuit is filed is considered an in-state defendant. Those who live in or operate a business in a given state open themselves up to the power of the courts in that state. An out-of-state defendant is not a citizen of the state where the lawsuit is filed. The third way to obtain PJ applies to out-of-state defendants only. Procedurally, it is much easier to obtain PJ over an in-state defendant. Moreover, you will soon learn the first route to PJ involves action by the defendant allowing bypass of the other two routes, each of which is predicated upon the defendant's having contact(s) with the forum state sufficient to justify the exercise of PJ. Stay tuned.

Before explaining each route to establishing PJ, note PJ is about due process and fairness. To have the power over people, courts must ensure the exercise of that power is constitutional. The exercise of PJ over a person must be warranted. SCOTUS, in *International Shoe v. State of Washington* (326 U.S. 310), wrote that *"due process requires only that, in order to subject a defendant to a judgment in personam, if he be not present within the territory of the forum, he have certain minimum contacts with it such that the maintenance of the suit does not offend 'traditional notions of fair play and substantial justice.'"* In other words, the exercise of PJ over a person must be fair and reasonable. Keep this in mind, as we examine the options. See if each of the routes seems fair and reasonable to you.

ROUTE 1: LEGAL APPEARANCE BY THE DEFENDANT

If a defendant formally defends himself against a lawsuit, he surrenders to the court's power over him. Any formal step to defend oneself (i.e., filing an answer to the plaintiff's complaint or filing any number of possible motions) is referred to as a *legal appearance*. A legal appearance need not mean an actual/physical appearance before the court. Just as a plaintiff freely submits to PJ by filing a lawsuit, so, too, does a defendant freely submit to the court's power by legally appearing in

© trekandshoot, 2014. Used under license from Shutterstock, Inc.

the lawsuit. When a defendant takes formal steps (i.e., to the court) to defend himself against a lawsuit, he loses the right to challenge PJ later. However, there is one exception to this rule. It is referred to as a *special appearance*.

A defendant makes a special appearance if the sole reason he appears before the court is to challenge (object to) the court's PJ over him. (A special appearance may also be made to challenge the sufficiency of the service of summons. Service of summons will be examined shortly.) If the court determines the defendant has sufficient contacts (also referred to as *minimum contacts*) with the forum state, the court will rule PJ has been established. In such case, the defendant may appeal the court's finding. A general appearance waives the defendant's right to appeal PJ, but a special appearance does not.

ROUTE 2: SERVICE OF SUMMONS

A summons is the formal notice from a court a lawsuit has been filed. Attached to the summons is a copy of the plaintiff's complaint, informing the defendant he is being sued and of the particular claim(s) filed against him. The purpose, again, is to notify the defendant, to make him aware of the lawsuit. Due process requires notice. If a person being sued is not notified and given the opportunity to be heard, the process is unfair. If the summons is properly served upon the defendant, PJ attaches. (Service of summons is also referred to as *service of process*.) So, what counts as proper service of summons? Well, it depends on whether the lawsuit is against an in-state or out-of-state defendant.

There are several options for serving a summons (issued by the state court where the lawsuit was filed) upon an in-state defendant, as outlined by each state's rules of civil procedure. As stated above, if you live in or operate a business in a state, you open yourself up to the power of that state's courts over you. The nature of your presence within a state means it is fair for courts in that state to have authority over you. *Plaintiffs: If you want the least amount of hassle regarding PJ, sue someone in his own state.* So, there is no big hurdle here. The plaintiff just needs to use one of the state's methods for service of summons. The preferred method for service of summons is personal delivery to the defendant. Personal delivery is referred to as *actual service*.

States vary on issues like when (which days) service of summons may be attempted and who is authorized to serve a summons. In Kansas, *"The sheriff of the county in which the action is filed shall serve any process by any method authorized by this section, or as otherwise provided by law, unless a party, either personally or through an attorney, elects to undertake responsibility for service and so notifies the clerk."* Kansas Statutes Annotated 60-303(b). In Oregon, *"The sheriff of the county in which the action is filed shall serve any process by any method authorized by this section, or as otherwise provided by law, unless a party, either personally or through an attorney, elects to undertake responsibility for service and so notifies the clerk."*

Oregon Rules of Civil Procedure, Rule 7E. Consult each state's rules of civil procedure, to learn their requirements for serving a summons upon an in-state defendant.

For out-of-state defendants (i.e., those who do not reside in the forum or operate a business in the forum state), the only option for service of summons is personal (actual) service of summons while the defendant is in the forum state. If an out-of-state defendant is present in a state where he is being sued, he subjects himself to service of process in that state. For example, if an Idaho resident is sued in West Virginia, the plaintiff may obtain a summons from the particular West Virginia court and personally (by personally, I mean via a qualified person, not necessarily via the plaintiff) serve the summons upon the defendant if the defendant is present in West Virginia. A summons from an West Virginia court may not be served on a defendant outside of West Virginia. Thus, if a defendant wishes to avoid a summons, he should remain outside of the forum state for so long as the forum gives the plaintiff to serve summons. State laws vary on how long a plaintiff has to serve a summons. Nebraska law states that a summons must be served within 6 months of the filing of the lawsuit: "*[a]n action is dismissed by operation of law as to any defendant who is named and who is not served with process within 6 months after the complaint is filed.*" Nebraska Revised Statute 25-217. Montana gives plaintiffs 3 years to serve a summons: "*A plaintiff shall have 3 years after filing a complaint to have a summons issued and accomplish service. Unless appearance has been made by the defendant(s), the court, upon motion or on its own initiative, shall dismiss an action without prejudice if a plaintiff fails to either have the summons issued or fails to accomplish service within 3 years from the date of the filing of a complaint.*" Montana Code Annotated, Title 25, Rule 4(E).

Methods other than actual service vary among the states, but some common methods include sending the summons via certified mail or leaving the summons at the defendant's home or place of business with a person qualified to receive a summons. Many states allow for service via publication in a general-circulation newspaper in the area where the defendant resides (or operates a business). In North Carolina, for example,

> *A party that cannot with due diligence be served by personal delivery, registered or certified mail, or by a designated delivery service authorized pursuant to 26 U.S.C. § 7502(f)(2) may be served by publication. Except in actions involving*

jurisdiction in rem or quasi in rem as provided in section (k), service of process by publication shall consist of publishing a notice of service of process by publication once a week for three successive weeks in a newspaper that is qualified for legal advertising in accordance with G.S. 1-597 and G.S. 1-598 and circulated in the area where the party to be served is believed by the serving party to be located, or if there is no reliable information concerning the location of the party then in a newspaper circulated in the county where the action is pending. North Carolina General Statutes, Chapter 1A, Article 2, Rule 4(j1).

States differ on whether actual service must be attempted before any other method may be attempted.

Before leaving this topic, let's look at the rules for serving a summons issued by a *federal* court, since our preceding examination was focused on summonses issued by state courts. The federal rules are stated in Rule 4 of the Federal Rules of Civil Procedure (FRCP). But before examining the rules for serving a summons, note the FRCP allow a defendant to waive service, in order to avoid the monetary costs of service that will be incurred should they choose not to waive. Subsection (d)(1) states, *"An individual, corporation, or association that is subject to service under Rule 4(e), (f), or (h) has a duty to avoid unnecessary expenses of serving the summons. The plaintiff may notify such a defendant that an action has been commenced and request that the defendant waive service of a summons."* There are pros and cons to waiving service, as outlined in Subsection (d)(2-5):

> *(2) Failure to Waive. If a defendant located within the United States fails, without good cause, to sign and return a waiver requested by a plaintiff located within the United States, the court must impose on the defendant:*
> *(A) the expenses later incurred in making service; and*
> *(B) the reasonable expenses, including attorney's fees, of any motion required to collect those service expenses.*

> (3) *Time to Answer After a Waiver. A defendant who, before being served with process, timely returns a waiver need not serve an answer to the complaint until 60 days after the request was sent—or until 90 days after it was sent to the defendant outside any judicial district of the United States.*
>
> (4) *Results of Filing a Waiver. When the plaintiff files a waiver, proof of service is not required and these rules apply as if a summons and complaint had been served at the time of filing the waiver.*
>
> (5) *Jurisdiction and Venue Not Waived. Waiving service of a summons does not waive any objection to personal jurisdiction or to venue.*

Did you catch that last part? Waiving service of summons does not mean a defendant gives up the right to object to a federal court's PJ over him. Interesting, right?

Now, we proceed to a few of the rules for serving a summons issued by a federal court. Subsection (c)(2) states, "*Any person who is at least 18 years old and not a party may serve a summons and complaint.*" And where may a defendant be served? Subsections (e) and (f) tell us:

> (e) *Serving an Individual Within a Judicial District of the United States. Unless federal law provides otherwise, an individual—other than a minor, an incompetent person, or a person whose waiver has been filed—may be served in a judicial district of the United States by:*
>
> *(1) following state law for serving a summons in an action brought in courts of general jurisdiction in the state where the district court is located or where service is made; or*
>
> *(2) doing any of the following:*
>
> *(A) delivering a copy of the summons and of the complaint to the individual personally;*
>
> *(B) leaving a copy of each at the individual's dwelling or usual place of abode with someone of suitable age and discretion who resides there; or*
>
> *(C) delivering a copy of each to an agent authorized by appointment or by law to receive service of process.*
>
> (f) *Serving an Individual in a Foreign Country. Unless federal law provides otherwise, an individual—other than a minor, an incompetent person, or a person whose waiver*

has been filed—may be served at a place not within any judicial district of the United States:

(1) by any internationally agreed means of service that is reasonably calculated to give notice, such as those authorized by the Hague Convention on the Service Abroad of Judicial and Extrajudicial Documents;

(2) if there is no internationally agreed means, or if an international agreement allows but does not specify other means, by a method that is reasonably calculated to give notice:

(A) as prescribed by the foreign country's law for service in that country in an action in its courts of general jurisdiction;

(B) as the foreign authority directs in response to a letter rogatory or letter of request; or

(C) unless prohibited by the foreign country's law, by:

(i) delivering a copy of the summons and of the complaint to the individual personally; or

(ii) using any form of mail that the clerk addresses and sends to the individual and that requires a signed receipt; or

(3)by other means not prohibited by international agreement, as the court orders.

So, we know where individuals may be served, but what about corporate defendants? Look no further than Subsection (h):

(h) Serving a Corporation, Partnership, or Association. Unless federal law provides otherwise or the defendant's waiver has been filed, a domestic or foreign corporation, or a partnership or other unincorporated association that is subject to suit under a common name, must be served:

(1) in a judicial district of the United States:

(A) in the manner prescribed by Rule 4(e)(1) for serving an individual; or

(B) by delivering a copy of the summons and of the complaint to an officer, a managing or general agent, or any other agent authorized by appointment or by law to receive service of process and—if the agent is one authorized by statute and the statute so requires—by also mailing a copy of each to the defendant; or

> (2) *at a place not within any judicial district of the United States, in any manner prescribed by Rule 4(f) for serving an individual, except personal delivery under (f)(2)(C)(i).*

You should notice these selections from the state and federal rules of civil procedure often reference other sections/subsections, which explain the relevant rules and procedures in more detail and/or which provide exceptions to the rules and procedures. Obviously, to get the most complete picture of the rules for serving a summons in a given jurisdiction (federal or state), you should read, in full, the relevant rules of civil procedure for that jurisdiction.

ROUTE 3: LONG-ARM STATUTES

Previously, we learned two ways a court can acquire PJ over in-state and out-of-state defendants: legal appearance by defendant and proper service of summons. But what if neither of those happens in the case of an out-of-state defendant? In such a scenario, there is one route remaining for acquiring PJ: Within the limits of the U.S. Constitution's Due Process Clause, states may obtain PJ over out-of-state defendants via procedures authorized by state statutes. I refer to all of these statutes, generally, as *long-arm statutes*. Section 1 of the Fourteenth Amendment to the Constitution reads, in full:

> *All persons born or naturalized in the United States, and subject to the jurisdiction thereof, are citizens of the United States and of the state wherein they reside. No state shall make or enforce any law which shall abridge the privileges or immunities of citizens of the United States; nor shall any state deprive any person of life, liberty, or property, without due process of law; nor deny to any person within its jurisdiction the equal protection of the laws.*

In *International Shoe*, SCOTUS stated the Due Process Clause requires an out-of-state defendant to have minimum contacts with the forum state, in order for it to be fair for the defendant to face lawsuit in the forum state. In response, states began passing legislation setting forth the requirements for the courts of their states to acquire PJ over out-of-state defendants. (Each state has passed at least one long-arm statute[4], as has the District of Columbia.) These pieces of legislation authorize service of summons outside the forum state. Figuratively, the forum court reaches with a long arm and grabs control of the out-of-state defendant. Without the ability to reach out-of-state defendants, courts would have PJ over such defendants via the other two routes (general appearance by the out-of-state defendant and service of summons while the out-of-state defendant is physically within the forum state) only.

So, what do these long-arm statutes say? Are they all the same? Let's explore. Remember what SCOTUS said in *International Shoe*: *"due process requires only that, in order to subject a defendant to a judgment in personam, if he be not present within the territory of the forum, he have certain minimum contacts with it such that the maintenance of the suit does not offend 'traditional notions of fair play and substantial justice.'"* So, SCOTUS set the minimum requirements for acquiring PJ over out-of-state citizens. As states drafted their respective long-arm statutes, they had to do so with SCOTUS' words in mind. At a Constitutional minimum, long-arm statutes had to provide out-of-state defendants with the level of due process mandated by *International Shoe*. More specifically, states must ensure the out-of-state defendants their long-arm statutes have power over, are ones with a minimum level of contact with the forum state. Beyond this, states were free to draft their rules as they saw fit.

As a result, not all long-arm statutes are the same. States vary on what constitutes *"minimum contacts,"* with some states granting more latitude to their courts than other states. Let's compare a few of them. We will begin with Illinois, since Illinois was the first state to enact a long-arm statute.

In part, Illinois' long-arm statute reads as follows:

> *(735 ILCS 5/2-209) (from Ch. 110, par. 2-209)*
>
> *Sec. 2-209. Act submitting to jurisdiction – Process.*
>
> *(a) Any person, whether or not a citizen or resident of this State, who in person or through an agent does any of the acts hereinafter enumerated, thereby submits such*

4. Some states have a general long-arm statute and one or more statutes applying to specific types of claims.

person, and, if an individual, his or her personal representative, to the jurisdiction of the courts of this State as to any cause of action arising from the doing of any of such acts:

(1) The transaction of any business within this State;

(2) The commission of a tortious act within this State;

(3) The ownership, use, or possession of any real estate situated in this State;

(4) Contracting to insure any person, property or risk located within this State at the time of contracting;

(5) With respect to actions of dissolution of marriage, declaration of invalidity of marriage and legal separation, the maintenance in this State of a matrimonial domicile at the time this cause of action arose or the commission in this State of any act giving rise to the cause of action;

(6) With respect to actions brought under the Illinois Parentage Act of 1984, as now or hereafter amended, the performance of an act of sexual intercourse within this State during the possible period of conception;

(7) The making or performance of any contract or promise substantially connected with this State;

(8) The performance of sexual intercourse within this State which is claimed to have resulted in the conception of a child who resides in this State;

(9) The failure to support a child, spouse or former spouse who has continued to reside in this State since the person either formerly resided with them in this State or directed them to reside in this State;

(10) The acquisition of ownership, possession or control of any asset or thing of value present within this State when ownership, possession or control was acquired;

(11) The breach of any fiduciary duty within this State;

(12) The performance of duties as a director or officer of a corporation organized under the laws of this State or having its principal place of business within this State;

(13) The ownership of an interest in any trust administered within this State; or

(14) The exercise of powers granted under the authority of this State as a fiduciary.

(b) *A court may exercise jurisdiction in any action arising within or without this State against any person who:*
   (1) *Is a natural person present within this State when served;*
   (2) *Is a natural person domiciled or resident within this State when the cause of action arose, the action was commenced, or process was served;*
   (3) *Is a corporation organized under the laws of this State; or*
   (4) *Is a natural person or corporation doing business within this State.*

As you can see, the reach of Illinois' long-arm statute is quite broad. Other states list fewer specific justifications for PJ but with a general statement meant to reach those whose contacts are not specifically listed but upon whom it would be fair and reasonable (in accordance with the due process required by SCOTUS) to exercise PJ. For example, Nebraska's long-arm statute states (Nebraska Revised Statutes, Chapter 25, Section 536):

25-536. Jurisdiction over a person.

A court may exercise personal jurisdiction over a person:

(1) *Who acts directly or by an agent, as to a cause of action arising from the person:*
   (a) *Transacting any business in this state;*
   (b) *Contracting to supply services or things in this state;*
   (c) *Causing tortious injury by an act or omission in this state;*
   (d) *Causing tortious injury in this state by an act or omission outside this state if the person regularly does or solicits business, engages in any other persistent course of conduct, or derives substantial revenue from goods used or consumed or services rendered, in this state;*
   (e) *Having an interest in, using, or possessing real property in this state; or*
   (f) *Contracting to insure any person, property, or risk located within this state at the time of contracting; or*
(2) *Who has any other contact with or maintains any other relation to this state to afford a basis for the exercise of personal jurisdiction consistent with the Constitution of the United States.*

Finally, California's is not specific at all. Rather, it is simply a short statement akin to the general statement that concludes Nebraska's long-arm statute. California's long-arm statute (California Code of Civil Procedure, Section 410.10) states:

> *A court of this state may exercise jurisdiction on any basis not inconsistent with the Constitution of this state or of the United States.*

So, while some states statutorily carve out specific authority permitted by the broader authority granted by the Constitution, states like California grant their state courts as much latitude as the Constitution will allow. Whether lengthy and detailed or short and general, and whether granting authority less than or as much as the Constitution permits, state long-arm statutes are meant to grant their respective courts power over out-of-state defendants in such a way that Constitutional guarantees of due process are met. Restated, states must ensure exercising PJ over out-of-state defendants is fair and reasonable.

We now know how the various state courts can acquire PJ over out-of-state defendants, but what about the federal courts? How do they do so? The federal long-arm statute is Rule 4(k) of the Federal Rules of Civil Procedure. The rule states, in full:

> *(k) Territorial Limits of Effective Service.*
> *(1) In General. Serving a summons or filing a waiver of service establishes personal jurisdiction over a defendant:*
> *(A) who is subject to the jurisdiction of a court of general jurisdiction in the state where the district court is located;*
> *(B) who is a party joined under Rule 14 or 19 and is served within a judicial district of the United States and not more than 100 miles from where the summons was issued; or*
> *(C) when authorized by a federal statute.*
> *(2) Federal Claim Outside State-Court Jurisdiction. For a claim that arises under federal law, serving a summons or filing a waiver of service establishes personal jurisdiction over a defendant if:*
> *(A) the defendant is not subject to jurisdiction in any state's courts of general jurisdiction; and*
> *(B) exercising jurisdiction is consistent with the United States Constitution and laws.*

bloggers beware

Florida's long-arm statute reaches nonresidents who post material online
Judith M. Mercier and Gennifer B. Powell

The Florida Supreme Court recently ruled that the state's long-arm statute applied to a nonresident who posted allegedly defamatory material to an out-of-state website about a corporation in Florida.

Even though the ruling requires proof of publication within the state, Florida is the fifth jurisdiction in recent months to take a broad view of jurisdiction arising out of web postings about their residents. Courts in Illinois, Indiana, Kansas, New Mexico and Ohio all recently have held that nonresidents who allegedly defamed a resident online expressly directed their statements to audiences in those states and therefore meet the minimum contacts standard.

However, courts in Arizona, Minnesota, Missouri, New Jersey, New York and West Virginia take the opposite view. They continue to hold that without specific evidence that web posters have directed their comments toward audiences in their states, their respective long-arm statutes are not satisfied merely when a nonresident posts allegedly defamatory material about one of their residents online.

In the Florida case, a blogger from Washington state posted accusations to her website that an employment and recruiting company in Florida was engaged in ongoing criminal activity. The website did not specifically mention any Florida consumers, but it did list the Florida addresses of the company and its affiliates. A number of third parties, including several individuals who stated that they were from Florida, posted comments on the website about the accusations.

The company filed a diversity action in federal court, alleging defamation. The blogger moved to dismiss for lack of personal jurisdiction, arguing that she did

continued on next page...

not commit a tortious act in Florida for purposes of satisfying the applicable section of Florida's long-arm statute, and that even if long-arm statute was satisfied, subjecting her to Florida's jurisdiction would violate due process.

The district court agreed with the blogger, finding that although she did not sufficiently rebut the company's claims that a tort was committed in Florida, the exercise of personal jurisdiction would violate due process. The court reasoned that there was no evidence that the blogger specifically targeted Florida residents by posting the allegedly defamatory material on her website, which was accessible everywhere.

On appeal, the Eleventh Circuit recognized that under Florida law, a person does not have to be physically present in Florida to commit a tortious act in the state. For example, a nonresident defendant could commit a tortious act within Florida for purposes of meeting the long-arm statute when that defendant sent "telephonic, electronic, or written communications into Florida" and the cause of action arose from those communications.

The Eleventh Circuit noted, however, that the Florida Supreme Court had not yet addressed whether postings to an out-of-state website about a company in Florida constituted "electronic communications into Florida" for purposes of satisfying the long-arm statute and certified that question to the Florida Supreme Court.

The Florida Supreme Court affirmatively answered the certified question and held that the long-arm statute is satisfied when allegedly defamatory material about a Florida resident is placed on the Web and accessed or "published" in Florida. Internet Solutions Corp. v. Tabatha Marshall, No. SC09-272, 2010 WL 2400390 (June 17, 2010). The Court rejected the idea that sending "electronic communications into Florida" requires that a poster of online material must target specific Florida residents. Rather, the Court reasoned that someone posting material online directs the communication to potential readers within Florida because the poster makes the information available everywhere, including in Florida.

The implications of this decision, and the others like it, are extremely broad. Although this decision raises practical considerations about how a plaintiff will establish that a Florida resident has accessed the information, conceivably, anyone who posts allegedly defamatory material about a Florida resident to a website can be hauled into court in Florida. The Florida Supreme Court, however, expressly declined to address the due process implications of its ruling, leaving open the possibility that defendants might avoid the reach of Florida's long-arm statute by raising constitutional concerns.

The basic and most-used section of Rule 4(k) is Subsection (1)(a). It tells us a federal court in a given state has PJ over a defendant if the state courts of that state would have PJ, per that state's long-arm statute. In other words, the U.S. District Court for the Northern District of Alabama will have PJ over a defendant if Alabama's long-arm statute authorizes an Alabama state court to exercise PJ over that defendant. Subsections (1)(b) and (1)(c) authorize broader authority for certain types of cases. Subsection 2 tells us any federal court has PJ over a foreign defendant in a federal-question case, provided such exercise of PJ is Constitutional. (The Fifth Amendment to the U.S. Constitution states that no person shall *"be deprived of life, liberty, or property, without due process of law."*) More specifically, federal courts have PJ over a non-U.S. defendant in federal-question cases, so long as exercising PJ is fair and reasonable, given the defendant's contact with the United States.

IN REM JURISDICTION

To recap what we learned above, in order for a court to have power over in-personam cases (both over the type of the case and the parties in the case), a court must have SMJ and PJ. But what about cases that are not actions against people/corporations? Legal actions/proceedings involving the status of property are known as *in rem* proceedings.

In-rem proceedings are not about legal offenses. They are not actions that might result in personal judgment/penalty. Rather, they are about the status of property. They are actions against things, not people. For example, if there is no clear titleholder to a piece of land, a court might be called upon to declare the status of ownership of the property. Such an action would be an action in rem. The process of foreclosing a mortgage is an action in rem. Actions about the disposition of property validly seized by the government are actions in rem. To conduct such proceedings, a court needs SMJ and in rem jurisdiction.

Courts inherently have power over property (physical or otherwise, meaning tangible or intangible) located within their respective states. Whether the power belongs to federal courts or state courts in the state where the property is located (i.e., SMJ) depends upon the type of property whose status is at issue. For example, federal courts' power typically extends to asset-forfeiture actions involving large pieces of property, such as vessels, whereas states typically have power over marital status and over the real or personal property within their state.

Regardless of which system (federal or state) has power over the type of property, the court must properly exercise its in-rem jurisdiction. To do so, the court must ensure all interested parties (such as parties who bring the action before the court) and the public in general (near where the property is located) are given proper notice of the in-rem proceeding. For federal courts, the rules for maritime claims are provided in Rule C(4) of the FRCP, which states, in full:

> *(4) Notice. No notice other than execution of process is required when the property that is the subject of the action has been released under Rule E(5). If the property is not released within 14 days after execution, the plaintiff must promptly—or within the time that the court allows—give public notice of the action and arrest in a newspaper designated by court order and having general circulation in the district, but publication may be terminated if the property is released before publication is completed. The notice must specify the time under Rule C(6) to file a statement of interest in or right against the seized property and to answer. This rule does not affect the notice requirements in an action to foreclose a preferred ship mortgage under 46 U.S.C. §§31301 et seq., as amended.*

As for forfeiture actions arising from a federal statute, the rules are laid out in Rule G(4) of the FRCP, which states, in full:

> *(4) Notice.*
> *(a) Notice by Publication.*
> *(i) When Publication Is Required. A judgment of forfeiture may be entered only if the government has published notice of the action within a reasonable time after filing the complaint or at a time the court orders. But notice need not be published if:*
> *(A) the defendant property is worth less than $1,000 and direct notice is sent under Rule G(4)(b) to every person the government can reasonably identify as a potential claimant; or*
> *(B) the court finds that the cost of publication exceeds the property's value and that other means of notice would satisfy due process.*

© lmeleca (Leonid Meleca), 2014. Used under license from Shutterstock, Inc.

(ii) Content of the Notice. Unless the court orders otherwise, the notice must:

(A) describe the property with reasonable particularity;

(B) state the times under Rule G(5) to file a claim and to answer; and

(C) name the government attorney to be served with the claim and answer.

(iii) Frequency of Publication. Published notice must appear:

(A) once a week for three consecutive weeks; or

(B) only once if, before the action was filed, notice of nonjudicial forfeiture of the same property was published on an official Internet government forfeiture site for at least 30 consecutive days, or in a newspaper of general circulation for three consecutive weeks in a district where publication is authorized under Rule G(4)(a)(iv).

(iv) Means of Publication. The government should select from the following options a means of publication reasonably calculated to notify potential claimants of the action:

(A) if the property is in the United States, publication in a newspaper generally circulated in the district where the action is filed, where the

property was seized, or where property that was not seized is located;

(B) if the property is outside the United States, publication in a newspaper generally circulated in a district where the action is filed, in a newspaper generally circulated in the country where the property is located, or in legal notices published and generally circulated in the country where the property is located; or

(C) instead of (A) or (B), posting a notice on an official Internet government forfeiture site for at least 30 consecutive days.

(b) Notice to Known Potential Claimants.

(i) Direct Notice Required. The government must send notice of the action and a copy of the complaint to any person who reasonably appears to be a potential claimant on the facts known to the government before the end of the time for filing a claim under Rule G(5)(a)(ii)(B).

(ii) Content of the Notice. The notice must state:

(A) the date when the notice is sent;

(B) a deadline for filing a claim, at least 35 days after the notice is sent;

(C) that an answer or a motion under Rule 12 must be filed no later than 21 days after filing the claim; and

(D) the name of the government attorney to be served with the claim and answer.

(iii) Sending Notice.

(A) The notice must be sent by means reasonably calculated to reach the potential claimant.

(B) Notice may be sent to the potential claimant or to the attorney representing the potential claimant with respect to the seizure of the property or in a related investigation, administrative forfeiture proceeding, or criminal case.

(C) Notice sent to a potential claimant who is incarcerated must be sent to the place of incarceration.

(D) Notice to a person arrested in connection with an offense giving rise to the forfeiture who is

not incarcerated when notice is sent may be sent to the address that person last gave to the agency that arrested or released the person.

(E) Notice to a person from whom the property was seized who is not incarcerated when notice is sent may be sent to the last address that person gave to the agency that seized the property.

(iv) When Notice Is Sent. Notice by the following means is sent on the date when it is placed in the mail, delivered to a commercial carrier, or sent by electronic mail.

(v) Actual Notice. A potential claimant who had actual notice of a forfeiture action may not oppose or seek relief from forfeiture because of the government's failure to send the required notice.

As for state courts, each state has its own rules regarding proper notice of in-rem proceedings within the state. New Jersey's rules (New Jersey Court Rules, Part IV) are as follows:

4:4-5. Summons; Service on Absent Defendants; In Rem or Quasi In Rem Jurisdiction

(a) Methods of Obtaining In Rem Jurisdiction. Whenever, in actions affecting specific property, or any interest therein, or any res within the jurisdiction of the court, or in matrimonial actions over which the court has jurisdiction, wherein it shall appear by affidavit of the plaintiff's attorney or other person having knowledge of the facts, that a defendant cannot, after diligent inquiry as required by this rule, be served within the State, service may, consistent with due process of law, be made by any of the following four methods:

(1) personal service outside this State as prescribed by R. 4:4-4(b)(1)(A) and (B); or

(2) service by mail as prescribed by R. 4:4-4(b)(1)(C); or

(3) by publication of a notice to absent defendants once in a newspaper published or of general circulation in the county in which the venue is laid; and also by mailing, within 7 days after publication, a copy of the notice as herein provided and the complaint to

the defendant, prepaid, to the defendant's residence or the place where the defendant usually receives mail, unless it shall appear by affidavit that such residence or place is unknown, and cannot be ascertained after inquiry as herein provided or unless the defendants are proceeded against as unknown owners or claimants pursuant to R. 4:26-5(c). If defendants are proceeded against pursuant to R. 4:26-5(c), a copy of the notice shall be posted upon the lands affected by the action within 7 days after publication. The notice of publication to absent defendants required by this rule shall be in the form of a summons, without a caption. The top of the notice shall include the docket number of the action, the court, and county of venue. The notice shall state briefly:

(A) the object of the action, the name of the plaintiff and defendant followed by et al., if there are additional parties, the name of the person or persons to whom the notice is addressed, and the basis for joining such person as a defendant; and

(B) if the action concerns real estate, the municipality in which the property is located, its street address, if improved, or the street on which it is located, if unimproved, and its tax map lot and block numbers; and

(C) if the action is to foreclose a mortgage, tax sale certificate, or lien of a condominium or homeowners association, the parties to the instrument and the date thereof, and the recording date and book and page of a recorded instrument; and

(D) the information required by R. 4:4-2 regarding the availability of Legal Services and Lawyer Referral Services together with telephone numbers of the pertinent offices in the vicinage in which the action is pending or the property is located; or

(4) as may be provided by court order.

The notice rules for state courts vary among the states. Moreover, even within a given state, the rules can vary depending on the type of in-rem proceeding. However, the common method for proper notice of an in-rem proceeding is notice by publication in a general-circulation newspaper. The content and frequency of such publication, again, varies among and even within states. Some states even allow state courts at the local (i.e., county) level to devise their own notice rules, subject to approval by the state.

If a court has proper power, it's time to start the case, right? Not so fast. Just because a court has proper power to hear a case does not mean it's the proper place (the proper court) to hear the case. In other words, for a given case, we have the case in the proper system (SMJ: federal or state) in a proper state (PJ or in rem). Now, we need to figure out which court within that system within that state is the right place to hear the case. Read on.

chapter 4
VENUE

In the last chapter, we explored our nation's federal and state courts. We learned differences among the courts, and we learned about the power of the courts to hear cases — power over the type of case and power over the parties in a case. But just because a court has proper *power* to hear a certain case, it does not mean the court is the proper *place* to hear a case. Venue is about finding the right place for a case. Of the courts with the authority to hear a lawsuit, which one (or more) is (are) the right place to hear the lawsuit?

We know how to determine whether the court where a lawsuit is filed has proper jurisdiction, both SMJ and PJ. But consider this: if the court where the lawsuit is filed has proper jurisdiction, every other court (in the same system: federal or state) in the state has proper jurisdiction, too. If a U.S. District Court in California has proper jurisdiction, so does every other U.S. District Court in California. If a state trial court of general jurisdiction in one Texas county has proper jurisdiction, so does the state trial court of general jurisdiction in every other Texas county.

Do you understand why this is true? Think about it. Pick any state, and then pick federal courts or state courts. If a federal court in that state has SMJ over a case, the case raises a federal question, or it's a diversity-of-citizenship case. The type of case does not change from court to court. If the same case had been filed in a separate federal district, that district would also have SMJ. The same is true for a lawsuit filed in a state trial court of general jurisdiction, which hears state-law cases (other than ones assigned by statute to state trial courts of limited jurisdiction) and cases involving non-exclusive federal questions. No matter in which county (or municipality) the plaintiff files his case, the subject matter of the lawsuit remains the same, and the court will have SMJ. As for PJ, whether federal court or state court, if a court in the state has proper jurisdiction over the parties, every other court will, as well. Remember that PJ is about whether a defendant is sufficiently

connected to a *state*. If due process allows a defendant to face lawsuit in a given state, PJ applies to the defendant for any court (federal or state) in that state. Make sense?

So, now we understand why every federal/state court in the state has jurisdiction if any federal/state court has jurisdiction. But that doesn't mean every U.S. district in the state is the right place to hear a lawsuit in federal court. It doesn't mean every county in the state is the right place to hear a lawsuit in state court. We need to narrow the districts/counties down to the ones that are proper places, or *venues*, to hear the case.

Statutes are our guides. Federal statutes specify which federal districts are appropriate venues, and state statutes specify which counties are appropriate venues. Let's start with the federal.

28 U.S.C. §1391 is the federal law that governs venue, generally. It reads, in full:

> *§1391. Venue generally*
>
> *(a) Applicability of Section.—Except as otherwise provided by law—*
> *(1) this section shall govern the venue of all civil actions brought in district courts of the United States; and*
> *(2) the proper venue for a civil action shall be determined without regard to whether the action is local or transitory in nature.*
>
> *(b) Venue in General.—A civil action may be brought in—*
> *(1) a judicial district in which any defendant resides, if all defendants are residents of the State in which the district is located;*
> *(2) a judicial district in which a substantial part of the events or omissions giving rise to the claim occurred, or a substantial part of property that is the subject of the action is situated; or*
> *(3) if there is no district in which an action may otherwise be brought as provided in this section, any judicial district in which any defendant is subject to the court's personal jurisdiction with respect to such action.*

Subsection (b) gives us the common venue rules. Part (b)(1) tells us if all of the defendants are residents of the same state, any federal district in which any of the defendants resides is a proper venue. Part (b)(2) tells us a federal district is a proper venue if it is where a substantial part of the reason/basis for the cause of action took place. (Not surprisingly, what counts as "*substantial*" is often not so easy to determine, but we can save that discussion for another time.) For example, in a trespass case, the district where a trespass occurred is a proper venue. In a case about whether a valid contract exists between the parties, the district where the contract was allegedly formed is a proper venue. Furthermore, if the subject of the lawsuit is a piece of property, the district where the property is located is a proper venue. Part (b)(3) tells us, in the rare event neither (b)(1) nor (b)(2) provides any U.S. district that is a proper venue (e.g., a tort committed in a foreign country by two defendants who are not residents of the same state), any district in which PJ attaches to any defendant is a proper venue. Such a district is commonly referred to as a *fallback venue*. The venue for most lawsuits will be determined without resorting to (b)(3).

Subsection (b) refers to where a defendant "*resides*," but what does that mean? What counts as a person's residence? What about a corporation? Back to §1391. Subsection (c) provides residency rules, for purposes of determining venue.

> *(c) Residency.—For all venue purposes—*
> *(1) a natural person, including an alien lawfully admitted for permanent residence in the United States, shall be deemed to reside in the judicial district in which that person is domiciled;*
> *(2) an entity with the capacity to sue and be sued in its common name under applicable law, whether or not incorporated, shall be deemed to reside, if a defendant, in any judicial district in which such defendant is subject to the court's personal jurisdiction with respect to the civil action in question and, if a plaintiff, only in the judicial district in which it maintains its principal place of business; and*
> *(3) a defendant not resident in the United States may be sued in any judicial district, and the joinder of such a defendant shall be disregarded in determining where the action may be brought with respect to other defendants.*

> (d) *Residency of Corporations in States With Multiple Districts.—For purposes of venue under this chapter, in a State which has more than one judicial district and in which a defendant that is a corporation is subject to personal jurisdiction at the time an action is commenced, such corporation shall be deemed to reside in any district in that State within which its contacts would be sufficient to subject it to personal jurisdiction if that district were a separate State, and, if there is no such district, the corporation shall be deemed to reside in the district within which it has the most significant contacts.*

Part (c)(1) tells us a person is deemed a resident of the federal district in which he is domiciled (i.e., district of permanent residence). Part (c)(2) tells us, in part, if a defendant is a business, whether incorporated or unincorporated, any district with PJ over the business is a proper venue. Part (c)(3) tells us a defendant who doesn't reside in the U.S. may be sued in any federal district. Part (d), which we need not dive into, examines proper venues when a state with more than one district has PJ over a corporate defendant.

Now that we know how to determine proper venue(s), it is worth noting if a party files a lawsuit in an improper venue, a defendant may make a motion to dismiss the case. 28 U.S.C. §1406 authorizes the court where the lawsuit was (improperly) filed to dismiss the case or transfer the case to a court in a proper venue. Note, however, if the defendant doesn't file such motion in a timely manner, he is deemed to have waived his right to object to the venue. *See* FRCP 12(b) and 12(h)(1).

Before moving on to state venue statutes, recall my mentioning 28 U.S.C. §1391 is the federal law governing venue, *generally*. Thus, the language at the very beginning of the statute: *(a) Applicability of Section.—Except as otherwise provided by law—*. "*Except as otherwise provided by law*" lets us know other federal laws sometime trump the general venue statute. More specifically, there are other federal venue statutes that apply to certain types of claims. (For example, 28 U.S.C. §1400 applies to patents, copyrights, and exclusive rights in mask works or designs.) Obviously, for these types of claims, §1391 is not the applicable venue statute.

And what about proper venue in state courts? You have to look at the laws of each state to learn which counties are appropriate venues for lawsuits in the state. Generally, what we see in the federal law is what we see in state law: appropriate venues include the county where the defendant resides, the county where the cause of action accrued and the county where property that is the subject of the lawsuit is located.

Some states' venue rules are more detailed than others. For example, Florida's venue statutes read, in part:

> ***47.011 Where actions may be begun.***—*Actions shall be brought only in the county where the defendant resides, where the cause of action accrued, or where the property in litigation is located. This section shall not apply to actions against nonresidents.*
>
> ***47.021 Actions against defendants residing in different counties.***—*Actions against two or more defendants residing in different counties may be brought in any county in which any defendant resides.*
>
> ***47.025 Actions against contractors.***—*Any venue provision in a contract for improvement to real property which requires legal action involving a resident contractor, subcontractor, sub-subcontractor, or materialman, as defined in [1]part I of chapter 713, to be brought outside this state is void as a matter of public policy. To the extent that the venue provision in the contract is void under this section, any legal action arising out of that contract shall be brought only in this state in the county where the defendant resides, where the cause of action accrued, or where the property in litigation is located, unless, after the dispute arises, the parties stipulate to another venue.*
>
> ***47.031 Venue of receiverships when property in more than one circuit.***—*When an application is made for a receiver of property and it is located in more than one judicial circuit, the court appointing the receiver has jurisdiction over the entire property for the purposes of that action but the application for the receiver must be made to the circuit court in which the principal place of business, residence or office of defendant is located.*

> ***47.041 Actions on several causes of action.***—*Actions on several causes of action may be brought in any county where any of the causes of action arose. When two or more causes of action joined arose in different counties, venue may be laid in any of such counties, but the court may order separate trials if expedient.*
>
> ***47.051 Actions against corporations.***—*Actions against domestic corporations shall be brought only in the county where such corporation has, or usually keeps, an office for transaction of its customary business, where the cause of action accrued, or where the property in litigation is located. Actions against foreign corporations doing business in this state shall be brought in a county where such corporation has an agent or other representative, where the cause of action accrued, or where the property in litigation is located.*
>
> ***47.061 Action on promissory notes.***—*Actions on unsecured negotiable or nonnegotiable promissory notes shall be brought only in the county in which such notes were signed by the maker or one of the makers or in which the maker or one of the makers resides. When any such note was signed by the makers in more than one county, action may be brought thereon in any such county. This section shall be liberally construed in favor of the makers of such notes.*

Alabama's venue rules read (Alabama Rules of Civil Procedure, Rule 82), in part:

> *(1) AGAINST RESIDENT INDIVIDUALS. Actions against an individual or individuals having a permanent residence in this state:*
>
> *(A) Must be brought in the county where the defendant or any material defendant resides at the commencement of the action, except that if the action is a personal action other than an action on a contract, it may be brought either in the county where the act or omission complained of occurred, or in the county of the permanent residence of the defendant or one of them;*

(B) Must, if the subject matter of the action is real estate, whether or not exclusively, or if it is for recovery or the possession thereof or trespass thereto, be brought in the county where the real estate or a material portion thereof is situated.

(2) AGAINST NONRESIDENT INDIVIDUALS. Actions against nonresident individuals may be brought in any county of the state where such nonresident is found, or in the county where the subject of the action or portion of the same was when the claim for relief arose or the act on which the action is founded occurred or was to be performed.

So, we've learned how to determine whether a court has proper power. We've learned how to determine whether a court is located in a proper venue. If the court where the lawsuit is filed has jurisdiction and is a proper venue, then we're ready to begin the case, right? Not necessarily.

Just because a court has power and is a proper place doesn't mean it will hear the case. One of the parties to a case might make a motion to transfer venue. The party making such motion is usually the defendant, given the plaintiff chose the venue via filing the lawsuit.

Recall if any court has power to hear a case, all courts in the same state and same system (federal or state) have such power. In the federal system, 28 U.S.C. §1404 authorizes such transfer of venue. Section (a) reads: *"For the convenience of parties and witnesses, in the interest of justice, a district court may transfer any civil action to any other district or division where it might have been brought or to any district or division to which all parties have consented."* If a federal court feels another district (or division[1]) in the state (or even a court in another state with proper PJ) is a more convenient venue for a case, the court might transfer the case to such venue. In the state-court systems, state statutes govern transfers from a state court in a given state to another state-court in the same state. A federal court can't transfer a case to a state court, and a state court can't transfer to a federal court. (Don't confuse venue transfer with removal jurisdiction, which we examined in Chapter 3.) Moreover, a state court can't transfer venue to an out-of-state court.[2]

Notice I wrote *"transfer"* of venue. §1404 deals with transfer of venue. No federal statute gives a court with proper jurisdiction and in a proper venue the power to dismiss the case outright. However, courts do, per the common-law doctrine of *forum non conveniens*. In such cases, when a proper-venue court dismisses the case, the plaintiff is free to file her claim with a court in another proper venue. At its discretion, a court can exercise *forum non conveniens* on its own (i.e., *sua sponte*) or in response to the defendant's invoking the doctrine. However, a judge's decision to exercise *forum non conveniens* is appealable, so judges have good reason not to abuse the power. Moreover, for several reasons, dismissal of the case is more burdensome than transfer of venue to the plaintiff. As such, venue transfer is preferable and more common.

What makes another venue more convenient? What makes another court better suited to hear a case? Several private- and public-interest factors can apply, so the reasons vary. Perhaps the lawsuit is filed with an overburdened court, and the court feels another court can hear

1. Some larger federal districts are divided into smaller districts, with a federal district court located in each district.
2. Though you probably assume so, no U.S. court (federal or state) can transfer a case to a court in another country.

the case in a more timely manner. Or perhaps a lawsuit is filed where the defendant resides but the court feels the case is better suited to be heard in the area where the events occurred that led to the lawsuit. Venue rules are meant to land a case in a venue that doesn't inconvenience the parties and/or the witnesses and is in the interest of justice.

Whether the court where the lawsuit is filed — the court with proper power and in a proper venue — keeps the case, transfers the case, or dismisses the case (after which the plaintiff files in another appropriate venue), at some point, the lawsuit finds a home. Whichever court it is, the court has proper jurisdiction and is a proper venue, so we are ready to begin the case.

chapter 5 LITIGATION

DEFINITION AND PURPOSE OF LITIGATION

In the previous chapters, we learned of the makeup of courts and the power of courts. We also learned which courts are the right places to hear cases. With that knowledge, we can turn our attention to the topic of litigation, the process of addressing legal disputes in an appropriate court system.

Litigation refers to a *legal action* or *civil action*. When one sues another, litigation commences. The purpose of litigation is to resolve a legal dispute. Recall from Chapter 1 that, for criminal matters, the government can prosecute someone in court. For civil matters, one can take another to court via lawsuit. Litigation is about lawsuits.

We will learn the basic steps of litigation, from start to finish. How far a given lawsuit proceeds depends on a range of factors and is not our concern. Most lawsuits do not proceed past the early stages. In fact,

most lawsuits never reach trial. Nevertheless, we will move through litigation, stage by stage. Obviously, some litigation is more complex than others. We won't exhaust every possible occurrence, but we will hit the high points. Doing so should give you a good understanding of the basic process of resolving a legal dispute via lawsuit.

RULES GOVERNING LITIGATION

Lawsuits must follow procedural rules. Lawsuits are civil actions (not criminal ones), so these rules are referred to as *rule of civil procedure*. The Federal Rules of Civil Procedure (FRCP) apply to actions in U.S. District Court.[1] Meanwhile, the various states have rules of civil procedure that apply to actions in the trial courts of their respective state-court systems. Note, however, most states' rules mirror those of the FRCP, so we will focus chiefly on the FRCP.

1. The foreword of the FRCP states, "This document contains the Federal Rules of Civil Procedure together with forms, as amended to December 1, 2013. The rules and forms have been promulgated and amended by the United States Supreme Court pursuant to law, and further amended by Acts of Congress." Foreword, Federal Rules of Civil Procedure, December 1, 2013. The FRCP were adopted by the Supreme Court of the United States in 1937: "The original rules, pursuant to act of June 19, 1934, were adopted by order of the Court on December 20, 1937, transmitted to Congress by the Attorney General on January 3, 1938, and became effective September 16, 1938 (308 U.S. 645; Cong. Rec., vol. 83, pt. 1, p. 13, Exec. Comm. 905; H. Doc. 460 and H. Doc. 588, 75th Cong.)." Historical Note, Federal Rules of Civil Procedure, December 1, 2013.

STAGES OF LITIGATION

Before examining the basic stages of a lawsuit, it is helpful to introduce the procedural device referred to as a *motion*. A motion is the means by which a party asks the court to rule on a specific issue. The party who makes the motion is referred to as the *moving party* or *movant*.

It might be helpful to think of a motion as a sideshow. At whatever point a given motion is made, the motion is heard and ruled on by the judge, before the lawsuit proceeds. A judge either grants or denies the motion, after hearing arguments (written and/or oral) from the moving party and the non-moving party. Several types of motions are ones that, if granted by the judge, end the lawsuit. If a motion is denied, the case simply reverts back to where it was when the motion was filed, and the case proceeds. There are several possible motions that can be made by one/either party at various stages of litigation. We will examine a few of them. Now, let's learn the stages of a lawsuit.

The typical stages of a lawsuit are as follows:

1. Pleadings
2. Discovery
3. Trial
4. Appeal
5. Final Judgment

Let's learn a bit about each stage and some possible motions throughout. Keep in mind a lawsuit does not formally begin until both SMJ and PJ have been established.

STAGE 1: PLEADINGS

The pleadings stage of a lawsuit is the period in which the parties to the lawsuit submit required papers (pleadings) to the court. The purpose of the pleadings is to inform the court of the parties to the lawsuit and their respective claims and defenses.

The first pleading is the complaint, and the plaintiff files it. The plaintiff is the one choosing to sue, and she does so by filing a complaint with the court. The plaintiff's complaint lists the plaintiff's claim(s) against the defendant(s), lays out the plaintiff's supporting facts for each claim, and requests a remedy for each claim. For example, perhaps Harry and Sally have a contract requiring Sally to wash Harry's car, in exchange for $50 from Harry. Sally washes the car exactly as required by the contract, but Harry refuses to pay. If Sally wishes to sue Harry for breach of contract, her complaint would list breach of contract as the claim, would list Harry as the defendant, would state the relevant facts (e.g., existence of valid contract, Sally washed car, Harry refused to pay), and would request money damages to compensate her for the breach of contract.

In response to the plaintiff's complaint, a defendant has two options: file an answer or a motion to dismiss. The answer is the defendant's responsive pleading. It is the defendant's direct response to the plaintiff's complaint. An answer either admits or denies whatever is claimed in the plaintiff's complaint. So, for the example above, Harry either admits or denies breaching his contract with Sally. The defendant is not required to disprove the plaintiff's claim. In fact, he is not required to offer any fact(s) disputing the claim. He need only admit or deny it. If admitted, the plaintiff wins the claim, and the court will rule on damages. If denied, the claim remains, and the burden of proving the claim rests on the plaintiff.

The answer is the pleading in which a defendant admits or denies each of the plaintiff's claims, but it is also the pleading in which a defendant can raise matters of his own. For our purposes, two types of these matters merit mentioning. First, a defendant might wish to assert one or more affirmative defenses, which we can simply refer to as *defenses*. Defenses, if proved by the defendant, lessen or relieve altogether a defendant's liability, should a plaintiff prove her claim against the defendant. If Harry has evidence Sally released him of his liability to pay prior to performance of the contract (prior to Sally's washing the car), the answer is the place to assert such evidence. Second, a defendant might also wish to assert claims of his own against the plaintiff. Such claims are referred to as *counterclaims*. For example, if Sally assaulted Harry after she washed the car, Harry would use the answer to assert a counterclaim against Sally for assault. Don't get these two matters confused: a defense is a defendant's direct response to the plaintiff's claim, while a counterclaim is a separate claim the defendant makes against the plaintiff. If a court requires one, a plaintiff will file another pleading, called a *reply,* to respond to (admit or deny) the defendant's counterclaim(s).

In lieu of an answer, a defendant might choose to file a *motion to dismiss* (MTD). The MTD is a request by the defendant for the court to dismiss the case. There are several possible reasons for filing a MTD. For example, the defendant believes the court lacks SMJ or PJ, or the defendant believes the law does not recognize the claim asserted against him (i.e., a claim that, even if proved, cannot result in civil liability because it is not something the law regards as a legal offense). If the judge grants a MTD claim, the claim is, obviously, dismissed, and the defendant need not defend himself against it. If a MTD claim is denied, the defendant must file an answer to the claim. (Note: A plaintiff can file a MTD, as well, as a means of dropping one or more of the lawsuit's claims.)

If a defendant does not file a timely[2] answer or motion to dismiss, the defendant fails to appear, and the court will enter a default judgment against the defendant. In essence, the defendant had his chance to defend himself but didn't. Thus, defendant loses, and the court will turn to the issue of damages.

Any claims remaining after the pleadings have been filed are the ones that move forward. Speaking of moving forward, on to the next stage of litigation. . .

STAGE 2: DISCOVERY

Once the pleadings stage has concluded, the lawsuit moves to the discovery stage. This is the information-gathering phase of the lawsuit. This is the time when both parties gather their evidence, in preparation for trial. Discovery is the process by which each side not only gathers its own facts but also learns of the facts gathered by the other side. Each side puts its factual cards on the table. The two sides do not have to share trial strategies, but they do have to share their

2. The FRCP and the various state rules on pleadings specify deadlines for filing pleadings. Title III (Rules 7-13) of the FRCP governs pleadings in the federal system. Rule 12(a)(1)(A) states, "(1) In General. Unless another time is specified by this rule or a federal statute, the time for serving a responsive pleading is as follows: (A) A defendant must serve an answer: (i) within 21 days after being served with the summons and complaint; or (ii) if it has timely waived service under Rule 4(d), within 60 days after the request for a waiver was sent, or within 90 days after it was sent to the defendant outside any judicial district of the United States." States, meanwhile, vary on the deadlines for filing various pleadings in state trial courts. For example, in Tennessee, "A defendant shall serve an answer within thirty (30) days after the service of the summons and complaint upon him." Tennessee Rules of Civil Procedure, Rule 12.01. In West Virginia, "A defendant shall serve an answer within 20 days after the service of the summons, unless before the expiration of that period the defendant files with the court and serves on the plaintiff a notice that the defendant has a bona fide defense, and then an answer shall be served within 30 days after the defendant was served." West Virginia Rules of Civil Procedure, Rule 12(a).

respective pieces of evidence. Can you imagine why this is the case? Why does each side have to turn over its evidence to the opposing side? Ponder and discuss!

How, specifically, does each side obtain the other side's evidence? The federal rules of discovery and the various state rules of discovery tell us. Title V (Rules 26-37) of the FRCP lists the federal system's discovery rules. Rule 26 states, in part,

> *(a) Required Disclosures.*
> *(1) Initial Disclosure.*
> *(A) In General. Except as exempted by Rule 26(a)(1)(B) or as otherwise stipulated or ordered by the court, a party must, without awaiting a discovery request, provide to the other parties:*
> *(i) the name and, if known, the address and telephone number of each individual likely to have discoverable information—along with the subjects of that information—that the disclosing party may use to support its claims or defenses, unless the use would be solely for impeachment;*
> *(ii) a copy—or a description by category and location—of all documents, electronically stored information, and tangible things that the disclosing party has in its possession, custody, or control and may use to support its claims or defenses, unless the use would be solely for impeachment;*
> *(2) Disclosure of Expert Testimony.*
> *(A) In General. In addition to the disclosures required by Rule 26(a)(1), a party must disclose to the other parties the identity of any witness it may use at trial to present evidence under Federal Rule of Evidence 702, 703, or 705.*
> *(3) Pretrial Disclosures.*
> *(A) In General. In addition to the disclosures required by Rule 26(a)(1) and (2), a party must provide to the other parties and promptly file the following information about the evidence that it may present at trial other than solely for impeachment:*
> *(i) the name and, if not previously provided, the address and telephone number of each witness—separately identifying those the party*

expects to present and those it may call if the need arises;

(ii) the designation of those witnesses whose testimony the party expects to present by deposition and, if not taken stenographically, a transcript of the pertinent parts of the deposition; and

(iii) an identification of each document or other exhibit, including summaries of other evidence—separately identifying those items the party expects to offer and those it may offer if the need arises.

Beyond the rules' requirements regarding general disclosures, as the discovery phase unfolds, each side might desire additional information. What information is fair game (i.e., discoverable)? Rule 26(b)(1) states, in full,

> *(b) Discovery Scope and Limits.*
>
> *(1) Scope in General. Unless otherwise limited by court order, the scope of discovery is as follows: Parties may obtain discovery regarding any nonprivileged matter that is relevant to any party's claim or defense—including the existence, description, nature, custody, condition, and location of any documents or other tangible things and the identity and location of persons who know of any discoverable matter. For good cause, the court may order discovery of any matter relevant to the subject matter involved in the action. Relevant information need not be admissible at the trial if the discovery appears reasonably calculated to lead to the discovery of admissible evidence. All discovery is subject to the limitations imposed by Rule 26(b)(2)(C).*

If a certain piece of information is fair game, how does a party obtain the information from the opposing side? Several means of acquisition are available. We refer to these means as *tools of discovery*. As examples, a party may conduct a deposition (the taking of sworn testimony outside of court), send the other side an interrogatory (a list of questions for the opposing side to answer, under oath), request the other side to produce certain documents, and/or request physical and/or mental examination of a party whose physical and/or mental condition is in dispute. Title V of the FRCP lays out detailed rules for each of the tools of discovery.

During the discovery process, each party must operate in good faith, in accordance with FRCP Rule 37. If the court feels a party is not operating in good faith (e.g., willfully refusing to comply with an opponent's legitimate discovery request), the court can penalize the bad-faith party. Penalties can range from monetary fines to contempt of court to default judgment against the bad-faith party. Rule 37 outlines, in detail, the possible penalties for the various forms of non-compliance with the rules of discovery.

At the end of the discovery phase, either party is free to make a *motion for summary judgment* (MSJ). After reviewing its own evidence and the opponent's evidence, a party might feel there is enough evidence for a court to decide a claim, without proceeding to trial. Such party will make a MSJ. FRCP Rule 56 governs motions for summary judgment. Rule 56 states, in part,

> *(a) Motion for Summary Judgment or Partial Summary Judgment. A party may move for summary judgment, identifying each claim or defense — or the part of each claim or defense — on which summary judgment is sought. The court shall grant summary judgment if the movant shows that there is no genuine dispute as to any material fact and the movant is entitled to judgment as a matter of law. The court should state on the record the reasons for granting or denying the motion.*

(b) *Time to File a Motion. Unless a different time is set by local rule or the court orders otherwise, a party may file a motion for summary judgment at any time until 30 days after the close of all discovery.*

Let's try to make some sense of section (a), which tells us a court will grant a MSJ if the moving party "*shows that there is no genuine dispute as to any material fact and the movant is entitled to judgment as a matter of law.*" What does this mean? To be sure, summary judgment is a complicated issue. For our purposes, the gist of a MSJ is the moving party does not feel a claim deserves to go to trial. Rather, the moving party believes the court has enough information to rule on the claim. FRCP Rule 50 states a court can rule against a party if said party "*has been fully heard on an issue during a jury trial and the court finds that a reasonable jury would not have a legally sufficient evidentiary basis to find for the party on that issue.*" This is referred to as *judgment as a matter of law*. In essence, a judge believes sending the claim to trial is a waste of time, since she believes she can deliver the same outcome (as would occur at a trial with a reasonable jury) now, given the evidence produced during discovery and presented on MSJ.

Either side — plaintiff or defendant — can move for summary judgment. However, to win a MSJ, a plaintiff bears a heavier burden. Translation: a plaintiff has to do more than a defendant to win a MSJ. It is not too difficult to understand why this is the case.

A legal claim is comprised of elements, by which I mean material facts that must be proved in order to prove the claim. For example, if a certain claim has three elements (per the common law of the relevant jurisdiction), the plaintiff is required to prove each of the three elements by a preponderance of the evidence. If the plaintiff cannot prove even one of the elements, he will lose the claim. Moreover, even if the plaintiff proves each of the elements, a defendant might be able to avoid or lessen liability via proving a valid defense. With this in mind, we can understand the different MSJ burdens of proof plaintiffs and defendants bear.

Let's say a plaintiff sues a defendant for just one claim, and the claim is comprised of three elements. If the plaintiff makes a MSJ, in order to win the motion, she must prove *each* of the three elements, and the defendant must offer no valid defense to the claim. This is a tough burden, because if a defendant offers evidence of a valid defense, a genuine dispute exists, and a claim involving genuine disputes (as opposed to a claim in which *"there is no genuine dispute as to any material fact"*) is exactly the type of claim that should proceed to trial.

By contrast, for a defendant to win his MSJ on the plaintiff's claim, he need only show the court there is *one* element the plaintiff cannot prove. This makes sense, right? If the claim were to go to trial, the plaintiff would have to prove *each* element, in order to meet his burden of proof. Therefore, if the defendant can prove that the plaintiff will not be able to prove *even one* of the claim's elements, the plaintiff cannot prove the claim at trial. And if the plaintiff cannot prove the claim at trial, the claim has no business going to trial, and summary judgment for the defendant is warranted.

The defendant's MSJ we just explored is one in which the defendant attacks the plaintiff's claim. A second type of MSJ the defendant can make occurs when a defendant concedes the plaintiff's claim but asserts a defense to the claim. Such a MSJ is an attempt by the defendant to have the plaintiff's claim dismissed by virtue of proving the defense. For a defendant to win such a MSJ, he must prove *each* element of the defense. The defendant's burden of proof for this MSJ (proving *each* element of a defense) is higher than his burden for the previous MSJ (proving there is *even one* element of the plaintiff's claim the plaintiff cannot prove).

At the end of the day, motions for summary judgments are meant to get rid of claims in which there is no real (genuine) dispute as to any material fact. In other words, the claims that should proceed to trial are ones in which both parties have supporting evidence worth weighing. With those claims identified, it's time to go to trial.

STAGE 3: TRIAL

A trial is where the facts of a case are presented. It is where each side uses its evidence and witnesses to present its case to the fact finder. The role of the fact finder is to decide questions of fact (i.e., Have facts been proven?) and issue a verdict. The fact finder is either a jury or a judge. If the plaintiff's complaint asks for money damages, then either party (plaintiff or defendant) typically has a right to a trial by jury.[3] Either party can request a jury. If neither side requests a

3. In the federal system, the right to a jury in civil cases is protected by the Seventh Amendment to the U.S. Constitution, which states as follows: "In Suits at Common Law, where the value in controversy shall exceed twenty dollars, the right of trial by jury shall be preserved, and no fact tried to a jury, shall be otherwise reexamined in any Court of the United States, than according to the rules of the Common Law." Meanwhile, states' laws dictate when a party has the right to a trial by jury. For example, in Nebraska, "Either party to any case in county court, except criminal cases arising under city or village ordinances, traffic infractions, other infractions, and any matter arising under the Nebraska Probate Code or the Nebraska Uniform Trust Code, may demand a trial by jury." Nebraska Revised Statute 25-2705(1). In South Carolina, "The right of trial by jury as declared by the Constitution or as given by a statute of South Carolina shall be preserved to the parties inviolate. Issues of fact in an action for the recovery of money only or of specific real or personal property must be tried by a jury, unless a jury trial be waived." South Carolina Judicial Department Court Register, Rule 38(a). In Indiana, "In all civil cases, the right of trial by jury shall remain inviolate." Constitution of the State of Indiana, Article I, Section 20. State laws also specify the number of jurors for civil cases, as well as the number of jurors who must agree, in order to reach a verdict. In New Jersey, a civil jury usually consists of 6 jurors: Rule 1:8-2(b) of the Rules Governing the Courts of the State of New Jersey states, "A deliberating jury in a civil action shall consist of six persons unless: (1) for good cause shown the court orders a jury of 12 persons pursuant to a demand made in accordance with R. 1:8-1(b); or (2) fewer than six jurors remain prior to commencement of deliberations and the parties then agree on the record to submit the case to the remaining jurors; or (3) more than six jurors remain prior to the commencement of deliberations and the parties then agree on the record that all remaining jurors shall deliberate." As for the number necessary to reach a verdict, Rule 1:8-2(c) states, "(1) Unless the parties have agreed on the record prior to commencement of deliberations to accept a verdict or finding by a lesser number, the verdict or finding shall be by agreement of five jurors when six jurors deliberate, and by 10 jurors when 12 jurors deliberate. (2) If the parties have agreed on the record to submit the case to fewer than six jurors, pursuant to paragraph (b)(2) of this rule, the verdict or finding shall be unanimous, unless the parties have also agreed on the record prior to commencement of deliberations to a verdict or finding by a lesser number. (3) If the parties have agreed on the record to more than six jurors pursuant to paragraph (b)(3) of this rule, the verdict or finding shall be by agreement of five-sixths of the deliberating jurors, unless the parties have otherwise agreed on the record prior to commencement of deliberations." Rule 48 of the North Carolina Rules of Civil Procedure states, "Except in actions in which a jury is required by statute, the parties may stipulate that the jury will consist of any number less than 12 or that a verdict or a finding of a stated majority of the jurors shall be taken as the verdict or finding of the jury."

jury, a judge will be the fact finder. Whether a jury or a judge is the fact finder, the judge is the one who handles the issues of law. Juries do not make legal rulings. Only judges do.

Before discussing the phases of a trial, note most lawsuits never go to trial. The vast majority of complaints filed are dropped or settled prior to reaching the trial stage.

much celebrated American Trial is Dying in Real Life

The trial is dying, according to a new book by a School of Law professor
by Pat Vaughan Tremmel

The American trial continues to thrive in the nation's imagination through a long succession of films, newspaper accounts and best-selling novels. But in real life, the trial is dying, according to a new book by a Northwestern University School of Law professor.

The decline of such a uniquely American engine of democracy would shock the founding fathers, according to the book's author, Professor Robert Burns.

"The Death of the American Trial" basically is a plea from Burns to resuscitate "an essential part of our Constitution that is embedded in the Fifth, Sixth and Seventh Amendments."

Today, the pre-trial proceedings – taking place behind closed doors – are at the statistical heart of judicial contests. While necessary to the functioning of our legal system, pre-trial proceedings cannot do the job of the trial, the book argues.

A forum like no other, the trial allows ordinary Americans to get to the core of a dispute – rather than distorting the issues and burying them in a legalistic avalanche of details, according to Burns.

The number of cases that go to trial has declined at an alarming rate over the last couple of decades, according to the book.

Overall, for all areas of the law, federal civil trials have declined 60 percent since the mid-1980s. In 2002, less than 2 percent of those cases ended in a trial – down from 12 percent in 1962 and 20 percent in the 1920s. Less than 5 percent of criminal cases go to trial; most result in plea bargains.

The trend away from the trial promotes governance by bureaucracies and the automatic functioning of our economic system without enough human intervention, according to the book.

"Corporate and government decisions are often made behind closed doors," Burns says. "Without the ability of ordinary citizens to carefully evaluate those decisions, we diminish our ability to have democratic governance."

continued on next page...

Burns refers to a quote by a federal judge who eloquently brought home the point with a canary-in-the-mineshaft metaphor. (When the canary died, miners knew that toxic gases were present.) "If our people lose their inherited right to do justice in court, other democratic institutions will lose breath too," the judge said.

The reasons that the trial is dying are complicated and differ depending on the context. Lawyers' fees, judges' procedural rules and other technical steps that must be followed on the way to court make trials more expensive. Long delays in getting to trial make settlements more appealing to plaintiffs. Fewer lawyers have the experience and skills to go to trial. Because of legal developments, judges more regularly dismiss cases in motions and in summary judgments - based solely on papers and affidavits.

Cases decided without a trial are much more formal, and not in a good sense, according to Burns. They are based primarily on documents rather than face-to-face encounters between the parties.

"The cases that never get to court have no opening statements, no presentation of witnesses, no cross-examinations - none of the trial's devices that allow for a careful examination of the real situation involved in the case," he says. "The judge gets to pretty much decide everything on his own without the discipline of trial evidence."

The trial, he said, is perhaps the only American forum where attention to the specifics of factual situations is so highly respected. "The disciplined attention that is focused on the facts of a situation in an American courtroom occurs almost nowhere else in the world," Burns argues.

Most important, the trial allows the other side to be heard - "more than congressional hearings do, more than writing about public affairs does," Burns says. "Each side has an unparalleled opportunity to present its story and to challenge the other side's story in a full airing of the facts."

He disagrees with critics who say the issues that come before courts today are too complex for ordinary citizens to comprehend. The devices of trial - direct examination, cross-examination, presentation of testimony, face-to-face encounters - are not suitable to properly present difficult issues, according to the critics.

Burns insists that good lawyers know how to simplify the issues - in an inspired way that improves deliberations - so that ordinary citizens can make important decisions that affect the country.

He argues that many more cases could go to court and be tried in a reasonable amount of time if judges and lawyers worked to change the culture to favor the trial. "Judges, for example, could limit discovery so that cases don't go on forever at the pre-trial process," he says. "In other words, the pre-trial tail of the dog would no longer wag the dog."

Burns quoted the great political thinker Alexis de Tocqueville, who talked about how the trial instilled a "respect for the matter judged, and the sense of right."

"The trial is a great cultural achievement that scrapes off the rust of private selfishness so that citizens can bring to bear their best judgment on matters of public concern," Burns concludes. "That is especially important in an individualist society like ours."

civil lawsuits
as Fewer Cases Go to Trial

Linda Chiem

The number of new civil lawsuits filed in Hawaii's circuit courts decreased by 9 percent last fiscal year after hitting a nine-year high in fiscal 2010 — a product of the long and deep recession and the subsequent slow recovery.

A total of 4,538 new civil lawsuits were filed in Hawaii's circuit courts in the fiscal year that ended June 30, 2011, according to the latest revised figures from the Hawaii State Judiciary.

By comparison, 5,019 new civil lawsuits were filed in state courts in fiscal 2010 — the most filed in a one-year period since the peak of 5,497 new civil lawsuits in 2001, also during a recession.

Paired with pending cases already in the system, the total number of civil cases sitting on the court dockets at the end of fiscal 2011 climbed to 10,357.

But, much of the past decade has been marked by a downward trend in new civil lawsuits thanks to local and national efforts to push alternative dispute resolution in the form of mediation or arbitration as a means of reducing lengthy and costly court battles.

Meanwhile, Hawaii still is contending with an overburdened judicial system, case backlogs and the vanishing jury trial.

Hawaii had a total of 12 civil jury trials in state courts in fiscal 2011, of which only six resulted in an actual verdict, according to the Judiciary.

By comparison, there were a total of 19 civil jury trials in state courts in fiscal 2010, of which 14 resulted in a verdict.

Those numbers do not include criminal cases or cases or trials in federal court.

"The cost of litigation is a huge deterrent and people don't want to go to trial because it's insanely expensive and they don't want to roll the dice," said Elijah Yip, a partner with the Honolulu law firm Cades Schutte. "Most people who get into litigation have this vision of being in court all the time and that's not quite true. You might do motions and hearings, but trials are just an endangered species and the statistics speak for themselves."

Longtime litigator Paul Alston, a partner with the Honolulu law firm Alston Hunt Floyd & Ing, said business disputes that make up a large part of the civil caseload can be more effectively solved by well-versed arbitrators or mediators who are familiar with the legal system tied to them.

continued on next page...

"Nobody wants their case to go to trial, especially in business disputes, and it doesn't make a lot of sense to invite 12 people off the sidewalk [to decide for you]," he said. "You are better off working with people who are sophisticated in business and can resolve problems than you are asking people who know nothing about your business to come in and decide. It's not always a rational way to do it."

Mediation or arbitration programs such as the Hawaii Judiciary's Court Annexed Arbitration Program, which handles all tort or personal injury cases with a possible jury award value of $150,000 or less, have been more heavily promoted in recent years because most Hawaii business owners don't have access to limitless capital for lengthy legal battles. Cases can sit waiting for trial for as long as 18 months, while the typical mediation or arbitration case may take a few days or weeks.

"We're finding better and more efficient ways to resolve legal conflicts in a legal arena where the formality, expense and delay of it just overwhelms practical needs," said Honolulu mediator and arbitrator Lou Chang.

And many commercial and employment contracts, even credit and insurance agreements, more frequently include mandatory arbitration clauses — which essentially means giving up one's right to trial in any legal dispute. It's a business trend that has contributed to the vanishing or dying jury trial, said Duane R. Miyashiro, a litigation partner with the Honolulu law firm Carlsmith Ball.

If either party requests a jury, how is the jury chosen? What is the process for selecting a jury? From time to time, registered voters and/or licensed drivers will be notified they have been summoned for jury duty. After filling out questionnaires with personal information, potential jurors report to the assigned courthouse for the jury-selection process, known as *voir dire*. Depending on how many jurors the case requires, the lawyers for each party to the case whittle down the pool via strikes, or dismissals from the jury pool. An unlimited number of *strikes for cause*, which are used to dismiss a potential juror found to be unfit to decide the case impartially, are available to each lawyer. (Judges can dismiss for cause, too.) This makes sense, right? Juries should be unbiased. So, if a person is biased, she shouldn't be on the jury. Thus, the number of for-cause (i.e., for-bias) strikes is unlimited. A limited number of not-for-cause strikes, known as *peremptory strikes*, are usually available to each side, as well. Peremptory strikes allow a lawyer to strike someone for a reason other than bias or for no reason at all. Note, however, SCOTUS has ruled a peremptory strike cannot be used to strike a potential juror on account of her race, ethnicity, or gender.[4]

Once the requisite number of jurors have been selected, the case is ready to proceed. Not least because television and movies are inundated with courtroom dramas, I don't desire to go into great detail about all of the possibilities a trial presents. Also, keeping in mind that a judge might be the fact finder, we will proceed as if a jury has been seated for the case. For our purposes, it suffices to note a jury trial follows these typical steps (in order):

1. Opening Statement (Plaintiff)
2. Opening Statement (Defendant)

---

4. On January 21, 2014, the Ninth Circuit Court of Appeals ruled unanimously that it is a violation of the U.S. Constitution to exclude a person from a jury based on his/her sexual orientation. See *SmithKline Beecham Corporation, DBA GlaxoSmithKline v. Abbott Laboratories*, No. 11-17357, http://cdn.ca9.uscourts.gov/datastore/opinions/2014/01/24/11-17357.pdf. The ruling was the first of its kind for a U.S. Court of Appeals. Writing for the unanimous three-judge panel, Judge Stephen Reinhardt wrote, "This appeal's central question is whether equal protection prohibits discrimination based on sexual orientation in jury selection. We must first decide whether classifications based on sexual orientation are subject to a standard higher than rational basis review. We hold that such classifications are subject to heightened scrutiny. We also hold that equal protection prohibits peremptory strikes based on sexual orientation and remand for a new trial."

3. Presentation of Case (Plaintiff)
4. Presentation of Case (Defendant)
5. Closing Statement (Plaintiff)
6. Closing Statement (Defendant)

The opening and closing statements are the introduction and summation, respectively, of each party's case. The presentation of each party's case is the truly substantive portion. It is the stage when each side calls witnesses, who are directly examined (by the lawyer who called the witness) and cross-examined (by the lawyer representing the opposing party). It is the stage when evidence is introduced. It is the stage when the facts of the case are submitted for the fact finder's consideration.

It is also the stage when either side might make a *motion for a directed verdict* (MDV). The MDV is a motion made by a party when the other party has finished presenting its case. The motion is made when the moving party feels the other party has not met its burden of proof. If the defense makes a MDV at the conclusion of the plaintiff's case presentation, it does so because it believes the plaintiff did not sufficiently prove each element of its claim. As is the case with a MTD and a MSJ, a MDV is made on a given claim. So, for each claim for which a lawyer makes a MDV, the judge will decide if the other side met its burden of proof. In essence, a party making a MDV is asking the judge not to proceed with the claim, that there is no reason to send the claim to the jury.

If the judge agrees with the defense that a plaintiff did not meet its burden for a given claim, then the defense does not need to present its case (its defense). Rather, the claim is dismissed. Likewise, after the defense presents its case, the plaintiff can make a MDV on a given claim, asserting that the defense did not present a defense sufficient to overcome the plaintiff's case. (Remember that the defense need not present a defense if the plaintiff doesn't meet its burden in the first place.) If the judge agrees, then the plaintiff wins the claim, and the claim moves straight to the issue of damages.

But what if a claim is not decided after a MDV? What if a claim makes it all the way through the closing statements? In such case, the jury considers each side's case (evidence) and issues a verdict on the claim. Whether the jury rules in favor of the plaintiff or the defendant, the losing party might make one or two motions immediately after hearing the jury's verdict. One of these motions takes issue with the jury. The other takes issue with the judge.

First, if the losing party previously made a MDV the judge denied, the losing party might make a *motion for a judgment notwithstanding the verdict* (MJNV[5]).[6] If a party makes a MJNV, it is asking the judge to set aside the jury's verdict and issue an opposite ruling directly from the bench. As a rule, our judicial systems don't like to set aside juries' verdicts, so granting a MJNV is rare and will occur only if the jury has no justification for its verdict. In other words, only if a jury rules completely against the weight of the evidence will a judge grant a MJNV. If a judge feels a reasonable jury could find as the jury found, he will deny the MJNV, *even if* he would have ruled on the evidence (the facts) differently.

A second and much more common motion the losing party might make is known as a *motion for new trial* (MNT). Here, the moving party takes issue with the judge's legal rulings, not the jury's factual rulings. Recall only a judge can decide questions of law, such as whether a piece of evidence should be admitted as evidence or whether a lawyer's objection to a question of a witness should be sustained or overruled. How a judge rules on these issues of law can impact the outcome of a case. As such, a MNT is made if a party believes a judge committed one or more errors of law that affected the outcome of the case. We refer to such case-altering mistakes as *material errors of law*.

You might already be thinking, "*Wait, you're asking a judge to rule on whether he made a big mistake in the case?*" Exactly. The judge will likely deny the motion, but he might decide he did, in fact, make a material error of law. The MNT gives the judge a chance to correct any material mistakes. If he grants the motion, the case can be retried. If the judge denies the motion, the moving party can appeal the issue. Remember appellate courts exist to decide whether a trial-court judge made a mistake on a legal issue. After trial, the losing party might appeal any material error(s) of law. Let's talk about appeals.

5. A motion for judgment notwithstanding the verdict is referred to as *JNOV*, but let's keep it simpler and refer to it as *MJNV*.
6. In the federal system, a MJNV is known as a *renewed motion for judgment as a matter of law*, since the federal corollary of the MDV is known as a *motion for judgment as a matter of law*. Again, the party is asking the judge to rule in its favor, after the judge previously denied a motion to do so. Hence, *renewed*.

STAGE 4: APPEAL

As just stated, an appeal is the process by which a losing party asks a higher (i.e., appellate) court to decide whether the trial judge committed one or more material errors of law. The party who files the appeal is referred to as the *appellant*, and the other party (the winner at trial) is referred to as the *appellee*. For example, a losing party's lawyer might appeal to an appellate court on the issue of whether the trial judge allowed a line of witness questioning that unduly prejudiced the jury against his client. Or maybe an appeal is filed on the issue of whether the trial judge correctly ruled on the constitutionality of a statute. Federal and state statutes specify how long a party has to file an appeal in the federal and state systems, respectively.

The typical stages of an appeal (whether an appeal to an intermediate appellate court or an appeal to a court of last resort) are as follows:

1. Filing of Appeal
2. Trial Record Sent to Appellate Court
3. Written Briefs
4. Oral Arguments
5. Appellate Decision

Once the losing party (from the trial) files an appeal with the correct appellate court, the appellate court notifies the relevant trial court below an appeal has been filed for the case. The trial court then sends the appellate court the trial record, comprised of all of the relevant documents from trial (e.g., pleadings, motions, trial transcript). The record apprises the appellate court of the details of the case.

Next, each side files with the appellate court a written brief stating their respective positions on the issue(s) appealed. The appellant's brief states why it believes the judge committed one or more material errors of law. The appellee's brief states why it does not believe the judge committed one or more material errors of law.

After the appellate court reviews the written briefs, a date is set for oral arguments. At oral arguments, the parties' lawyers go before the appellate court and orally present the positions outlined in their respective written briefs. The appellate court will ask the lawyers questions about the issue(s) on appeal.

Some time after oral arguments, the appellate court will issue its decision (ruling). If this book were about advanced civil procedure, we would examine all of the possible actions the appellate court might take (e.g., affirm, reverse, remand, etc.). Regardless of the content of the appellate court's decision, the court will publish its ruling, referred to as the *opinion*.

The *formal opinion* is the decision of the court. It is primary law. If, for example, SCOTUS rules 7-2 a certain statute is unconstitutional, the formal opinion is the opinion of the majority of seven. In such case, the formal opinion is the statute is unconstitutional. The *dissenting opinion* in such case is the opinion of the minority of two. It is the opinion disagreeing with the formal opinion. In this case, the dissenting opinion is the statute at issue is not unconstitutional. In unanimous appellate decisions, there is no dissenting opinion. Lastly, for any given ruling, a *concurring opinion* might be issued. A concurring opinion is written by one or more court members who agree with the formal opinion but do so for a different reason. Here, for example, one of the seven might write a concurring opinion, stating his reason for finding the statute unconstitutional is different than the reason specified in the formal opinion.

As alluded to previously, the appellate process we just covered is the same for intermediate courts and courts of last resort. So, an appeal might be made to both courts in a given case. The process of appeal is the same for each appellate court.

Before leaving the appeals process, it is worth noting the number of judges/justices on state appellate courts varies among the states. In the federal-court system, SCOTUS is comprised of nine justices. The federal circuit courts are made up of a number of judges, though most appeals in the federal circuit courts are heard by three-judge panels. So, most decisions by federal circuit courts will be 3-0 or 2-1 decisions.

STAGE 5: FINAL JUDGMENT

At some point, a party does not appeal within the time permitted by statute, or there are no more appeals available. In other words, at some point, the appeals process is over, and a final judgment for the case is entered. The case has ended. There is nowhere else for the case to go. At this point, *res judicata* applies. This means the matter has been adjudicated. The case is closed. The effect is the case (i.e., the claim or claims to which *res judicata* applies) cannot be filed again.

If the final judgment is the plaintiff loses on the claim, the plaintiff can never re-file the same claim. If the final judgment is plaintiff wins and is owed damages, the plaintiff can proceed to attempt to collect the damages owed him. Whether the plaintiff is able to collect money and/or another remedy is a topic for another day. The next chapter, however, provides an overview of the types of remedies available to parties who win at trial.

chapter 6
REMEDIES

In Chapter 5, we learned most lawsuits don't go to trial. Rather, most claims are dropped voluntarily, dismissed by the court, or settled between/among the parties. Even of those claims that reach trial, many are settled before the trial concludes with a verdict.

In this chapter, we will set aside claims dropped, dismissed, and settled.[1] We will also set aside cases in which a plaintiff loses at trial.[2] Instead, we will study claims resulting in a winner and a loser at trial, with the loser penalized, in order to satisfy the winner. We will focus on verdicts ordering a party is owed something from the other party.

1. To be clear, cases settled outside of court, by their nature, involve a remedy. If two sides contractually agree not to continue with a lawsuit, obviously it is because they have reached a mutually-agreeable solution preferable to continuing to a verdict. Parties will have courts sign off on (i.e., enforce) the settlement or simply file notice with a court the case has been dropped. Either way, the settlement ends the matter. Such settlements involve remedies satisfying aggrieved parties, but our focus is on remedies ordered by courts.
2. In such cases (pun intended), the case is over. Plaintiff is owed nothing. Defendant has no liability.

Recall from Chapter 3 a plaintiff, in her complaint, must request a remedy. A court needs to know why a plaintiff has filed a lawsuit. It is not enough she has a grievance. What does she want the court to do about it? Courts in civil cases don't exist to hear disputes. Rather, they exist to hear disputes and issue rulings.[3] In cases with an injured party who wins at trial, they exist to right wrongs. They exist to hand out remedies, which are mechanisms to satisfy the winning party. Remedies impose upon the losing party, to the benefit of the winning party.

This chapter's focus is on civil remedies, but bear in mind courts in criminal cases, likewise, don't exist simply to hear disputes. They are not there simply to listen to the government prosecutor's evidence that a defendant committed a crime. Rather, they are there to order punishment for the defendant, when warranted. So, civilly and criminally, courts don't exist just to provide a forum for two sides to present their case; they exist to resolve the case in favor of one side or the other.

3. Recall from earlier chapters courts without proper jurisdiction cannot issue legally-binding decisions.

TYPES OF REMEDIES

There are multiple types of remedies, and the particular remedy ordered depends on the type of case. Broadly, remedies come in three forms: *legal remedies*, *equitable remedies*, and *declaratory judgments*. Because declaratory judgments do not order remedies but rather state the court's assessments of the parties' rights in a given dispute,[4] our examination is of legal remedies and equitable remedies.

LEGAL REMEDIES

Legal remedies are money damages. Recall from Chapter 5 either party can request a jury, when the plaintiff seeks money damages. So, we know juries are authorized to award money damages. If a trial does not involve a jury, the judge performs the fact-finding function and, if warranted, awards money damages.

The most common type of damages is *compensatory damages*. Compensatory damages compensate a party for his injury. Injury can come in many forms, such as medical bills, lost wages, emotional distress, lost opportunity, and property loss. The goal of compensatory damages is to make the party receiving the damages economically whole. In other words, compensatory damages are meant to put the receiving party in the same economic position he would be in had the injury not occurred.

For example, if a jury finds Bert assaulted and battered Ernie and, as a result, Ernie incurred $5,000 in medical bills and lost wages, the jury will

4. To learn about declaratory judgments issued by federal courts, see 28 U.S.C. §2201 and FRCP Rule 57.

order Bert to pay Ernie $5,000, to compensate him for his loss. Likewise, if a jury determines Zach breached his contract with Melinda and the value of Melinda's contractual injury is $10,000, the jury will order Zach to pay Melinda $10,000 in damages, to compensate her for the opportunity loss his breach caused.

Compensatory damages come in two forms: special damages and general damages. Special damages are injuries of a specific cost. They are injuries that can be calculated and assigned a dollar amount. Ernie's hospital bill (for the injury Bert caused him), for example, is a special damage. By contrast, general damages are ones for which specific dollar amounts are not calculated, such as pain and suffering.

In some cases, a losing party is ordered to pay damages beyond compensatory damages (i.e., beyond what is necessary to compensate the victim for his loss). Such damages are referred to as *punitive damages*. These are punishment damages. They are extra damages. They are reserved for situations calling for harsher penalties than just compensatory damages. Punitive damages are not normally available in contracts cases.[5] They are, however, possible in cases involving intentional torts or gross negligence. So, punitive damages are meant to punish really bad behavior. Juries award punitive damages far more often than judges order them.[6] Additionally, some states have statutes authorizing punitive damages, while other states allow for them via case law.

Before proceeding to equitable remedies, it's worth exposing you to some miscellaneous damages. For example, *nominal damages* are damages of an insignificant amount, such as $1. These minor damages are awarded when a party suffered violation of a right (e.g., breach of

5. Punitive damages are sometimes awarded in contract cases involving fraud.
6. See *Punitive Damages: How Judges and Juries Perform*, Joni Hersch and W. Kip Viscusi, May 2002, http://www.law.harvard.edu/programs/olin_center/papers/pdf/362.pdf.

jury awards
Compensatory Damages in Kid Rock Case

By Associated Press

A suburban Atlanta jury has awarded $40,000 in compensatory damages to a man who says musician Kid Rock and his entourage beat him during a 2007 fight at a Waffle House restaurant.

Harlen Akins sued Kid Rock, whose real name is Robert James Ritchie, and five members of his entourage over the fight. The judge dismissed two of the defendants Thursday.

Akins was seeking $6,000 in medical fees and an unspecified amount in punitive damages. The jury decided Friday not to award punitive damages.

The responsibility for the compensatory damages will be divided among the four remaining defendants based on the level of fault the jury judged for each of them.

The musician pleaded guilty in March 2008 to a misdemeanor charge of simple battery stemming from the fight.

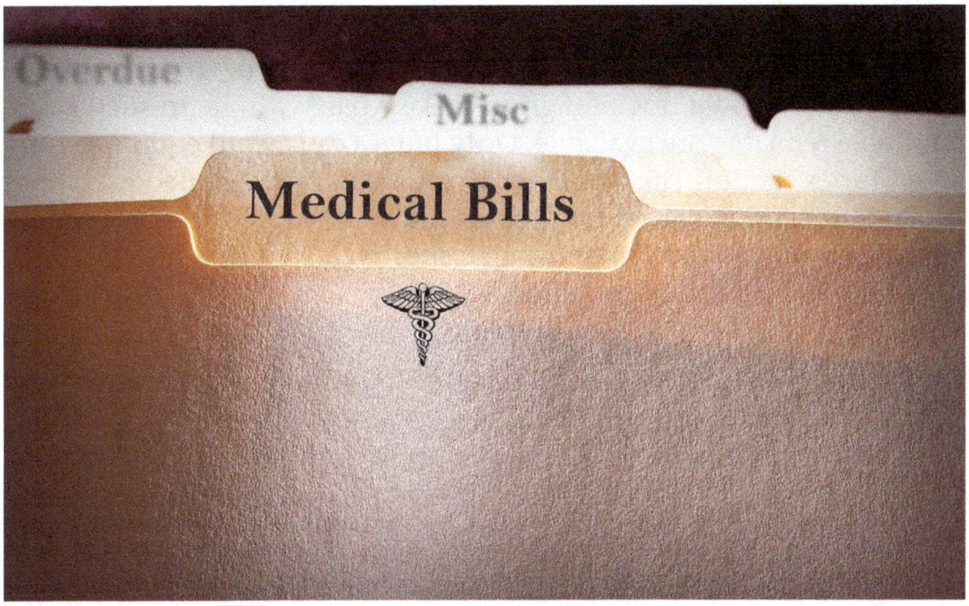

contract) but cannot show his injury was substantial enough to deserve compensation. In essence, the winning party has wasted the court's time. If a court awards you a dollar because you technically won the case, did you really win?

Treble damages triple the amount a jury awards. Statutes mandate that judges triple compensatory damages in certain cases involving intentional violations. So, if a jury awards $10,000 in one of these types of cases, the judge would change the damages to $30,000. Finally, in contract cases, there are several miscellaneous types of damages. For example, *liquidated damages* are pre-determined damages set forth in the parties' contract (and, within limits, honored by courts), *incidental damages* are costs to transport goods or otherwise arrange for alternative sale, following a breach of contract, and *consequential damages* are indirect losses stemming from a breach of contract, such as lost profits.

EQUITABLE REMEDIES

Damages are the preferred remedy in civil cases, so if money can make the winning party whole, only legal remedies will be awarded. However, money is often not enough to make a party whole. In such cases, equitable remedies are available. Only judges can award equitable remedies. Juries cannot. The two most common equitable remedies, *specific performance* and *injunctions*, are court orders for the losing party to do something or not to do something, respectively.[7] So, when might legal remedies be insufficient to redress an injury?

Let's start with contracts cases. Imagine Holly and Derrick have a valid contract for Holly to purchase Derrick's antique dresser. On the day the sale is to take place, Holly shows up with the money, but Derrick

7. There are certain types of money awards that are considered equitable remedies, such as restitution, but we do not explore them here. Furthermore, there are other types of non-monetary equitable remedies, such as replevin, not covered here.

refuses to part ways with the dresser. He refuses to take the money and sends Holly away, without the dresser. Holly sues Derrick for breach of contract. Obviously, if a court orders only that Derrick pay Holly money, Holly is not satisfied. Why? Because she wants the dresser! Here, a legal remedy is insufficient to redress Holly's injury from the breach of contract. Thus, the judge will order Derrick to sell the dresser. Such an order is referred to as an *order of specific performance*. The name should make sense, because the judge is ordering Derrick to perform as specified in the valid contract.

And what about equitable remedies for tort cases? Imagine Julie, who lives in a dense subdivision, plays loud music in her house every day from midnight to 2:00 AM. The loud music wakes her neighbors. The neighbors ask Julie not to blast loud music during the middle of the night, but she refuses. The neighbors sue Julie for nuisance. Will money sufficiently redress the neighbors' injury? Of course not! The neighbors want the music to stop. As such, the judge will issue an *injunction* ordering Julie to stop playing her music so loudly. Note, in tort cases, injunctions can also be orders to do something. For example, if Julie regularly parks her car in her neighbor Ben's driveway without Ben's permission, she is trespassing. Money wouldn't make Ben whole. Ben wants Julie's car off his property. A judge will issue an injunction ordering Julie to remove her car from Ben's property.

In almost all U.S. states, any given trial court is empowered to award legal remedies and/or equitable remedies.[8] An exception is Delaware, which has separate courts of law and courts of equity. Delaware has several types of (trial) courts of law, while Delaware's Court of Chancery is a court of equity.[9]

8. In the early days of English common law, separate courts of law and courts of equity existed. So, the nature of the remedy sought by the plaintiff determined whether a court of law or a court of equity heard the case. In the early years of the United States, several states had separate courts of law and courts of equity. Most states later merged these courts.

9. The jurisdiction of Delaware's Court of Chancery is specified in the Delaware Code, Title 10, Chapter 3, Subchapter III. http://delcode.delaware.gov/title10/c003/sc03/index.shtml

chapter 7 ALTERNATIVE DISPUTE RESOLUTION

To this point, our focus has been on courts: the makeup of courts, the power of courts, court venues, the stages of litigating disputes in court, and remedies one might obtain from a court. But courts are not the only way to resolve disputes. Suing someone is not the only route to a remedy. A number of out-of-court options are available for dealing with a grievance against another. Collectively, these options are referred to as *alternative dispute resolution (ADR)*.

Before learning about several types of ADR, let's consider why a person might choose ADR instead of litigation. Why pursue a legal claim outside of court, when you could pursue one in court? Aside from any personal considerations that might lead one to ADR instead of litigation, ADR is generally a quicker and cheaper way to resolve a dispute. All things being equal, a lawsuit takes more time and more money than any of the various forms of ADR. Additionally, ADR is a privately-controlled process. The parties in dispute decide issues of format and procedure, neither of which they would control in litigation. Moreover, ADR is more private than litigation. Someone who would rather handle a problem outside of the public's view would likely opt for ADR, which is far more closed off to the public than lawsuits, which become part of official court records and publications.

Largely for these reasons, ADR is increasingly popular. These days, more and more people choose ADR over litigation. Again, ADR takes less time, costs less money, gives parties more control, and is more private.

Even law schools increasingly devote time and resources to teaching their students about ADR and training them to facilitate the various forms of ADR. For example, as of this writing, Columbia Law School offers ADR courses and clinics on topics such as "*Introduction to Mediation and Mediation Advocacy*" to "*International Commercial Arbitration*" to "*Native Peacemaking.*"[1] Some law schools have created centers devoted to ADR topics, such as Columbia Law School's Center for International Commercial and Investment Arbitration and the University of Oregon School of Law's Alternative Dispute Resolution Center. You can find law schools offering LL.M. (Master of Laws) programs in ADR, such as The George Washington University Law School's LL.M. in Litigation and Dispute Resolution. Several law schools even have legal journals devoted to ADR topics, such as the *Harvard Negotiation Law Review*, the *University of Missouri Journal of Dispute Resolution*, and the *Rutgers Conflict Resolution Journal*. The teaching of ADR is so prevalent and common among U.S. law schools you can find rankings of the top law schools for ADR training.

1. For a complete list of ADR courses at Columbia Law School, see http://web.law.columbia.edu/courses/browse?id=306.

Okay, you get the general idea. ADR is an alternative to litigation. For many, it is a very attractive alternative. Law schools are ramping up their ADR offerings. But what is ADR, specifically? Let's learn about some of the several types.

TYPES OF ADR

There are many ways to attempt to resolve disputes outside of court. We will examine three very common forms of ADR: negotiation, mediation, and arbitration.

NEGOTIATION

Imagine Larry and his neighbor Jeff have a dispute. Maybe it's a dispute about a tree on Larry's property that is overgrown and hanging over Jeff's property. Maybe it's a dispute about a personal issue that leads to a fight in which Jeff is injured. Whatever the nature of the dispute, if one of the two has a legal grievance against the other (in these cases, Jeff), the former could file a lawsuit against the latter and have their dispute heard by a court. Alternatively, Larry and Jeff could try to solve their problem themselves. They could try to work it out without involving a court or other third party. This process of resolving a dispute privately and without a third party is referred to as *negotiation*.

In negotiation, the parties, you guessed it, attempt to negotiate their way to a mutually-agreeable solution. There is no lawsuit, no pleadings, no motions, no judge, no jury, and no courtroom. It's just Larry and Jeff (and their lawyers, if they choose to involve them). If the two parties can work their way to a solution suiting each of them, they have negotiated their way to resolution. The result is a *negotiated settlement* the parties can then have a court approve. The settlement is a contract between/among the parties. Once approved by a court, the settlement is an enforceable contract protecting the parties against violations of the terms of the settlement.

© Photographee.eu, 2014. Used under license from Shutterstock, Inc.

So, when can the parties attempt to negotiate their way to a settlement? They can, as in the example above, attempt negotiation from the very beginning. Alternatively, they can try negotiation even if they are already involved in a lawsuit. So long as a judgment has not been handed down by a judge/jury, the parties are free to negotiate. Once a verdict has been issued, it is too late to settle the case. So, from the moment a dispute arises until the moment a court judgment is handed down, the parties may attempt to negotiate their way to a settlement.[2] Indeed, some courts even require parties to participate in a *settlement conference*, where they attempt negotiation, before proceeding with litigation.

© NINETY1FOTO, 2014. Used under license from Shutterstock, Inc.

It is worth noting most cases settle outside of court, are dropped by the plaintiff, or are dismissed by a judge. Of all lawsuits filed each year, only a small number reach a judgment in court.

2. In criminal cases, the government prosecutor and criminal defendant are free to settle the criminal case before the case reaches a verdict. Such settlement is referred to as a *plea bargain*.

MEDIATION

Like negotiation, mediation is a form of ADR that can lead two parties to a settlement. Unlike negotiation, however, mediation involves more than the parties in dispute. Using our example above, Larry and Jeff might involve a third party in an effort to resolve their dispute. Such third party is known as a mediator. A mediator's job is to hear the parties' respective positions on the dispute and offer an unbiased opinion about the dispute. Having an unbiased third party weigh in on the merits of the dispute can give the parties a realistic idea of what ruling an unbiased judge or jury might give.

An important characteristic of mediation is it is not legally binding. In other words, the mediator's opinion is just that: an opinion. It is not a legal ruling. It is not a verdict. It has no force of law. Either party is free to disregard the mediator's opinion and proceed with a lawsuit or further ADR.

Mediation need not be formal. If Larry and Jeff negotiate at a coffee shop and ask a nearby patron for an honest opinion on their dispute, the patron is a mediator. Of course, mediation can be much more formal. Parties are free to hire a professional mediator. Either way, the parties choose to involve a third party, in an effort to reach a settlement. If they reach a settlement, the situation is the same as if negotiation led to settlement: the parties have a contract that can be enforced by a court.

mediation fails
for Samsung and Apple

By the Associated Press

Apple and Samsung Electronics have failed to settle their latest patent dispute despite a daylong meeting between top Samsung executives and Apple's chief executive, Timothy D. Cook, hosted by a mediator earlier this month.

The companies detailed the lack of progress in a court filing on Friday. Judge Lucy H. Koh of the United States District Court in San Jose has been pushing the sides to settle the two-year-old case.

While the two sides said they remained willing to work through a mediator, the lack of a settlement points them toward a trial in March.

Apple and Samsung, the world's top two smartphone makers, have waged legal battles over mobile devices since Apple accused Samsung of copying the iPhone and the iPad in 2011. Later, Samsung claimed that Apple had used its technologies without permission, expanding battles to courts in Asia, Europe and North America.

In November, a Silicon Valley jury added $290 million to the damages that a previous jury said Samsung owed Apple for copying vital iPhone and iPad features, bringing the total award to $930 million.

The previous verdict covered 13 older Samsung devices. Samsung has said it would appeal.

The latest trial will consider Apple's claims that Samsung's newest devices, like its Galaxy S3, also copied Apple's technology.

So, we know parties in dispute may choose mediation, but can they be ordered to mediation? Yes. Often, parties to a lawsuit are ordered by the judge in the case to try mediation. Of course, the judge will not physically make the parties attend, but if they do not, they will not be allowed to move forward with litigation. In effect, the judge is saying to the parties, *"If you wish to proceed with your case, give mediation a try."* If the parties give mediation a good-faith effort, they are free to head back to the judge afterward and proceed with the case. Why? Because whether the parties choose mediation on their own or whether a court orders it, mediation is not legally binding.

ARBITRATION

Like mediation, arbitration involves a third party (an arbitrator or panel or arbitrators). Unlike mediation, however, arbitration is legally binding. An arbitration ruling is not an option that either party can disregard. Rather, it is a legally-enforceable ruling (referred to as an *award*). It is as if a judge or jury issued a verdict.

arbitration ruling Intensifies Public-Private School Debate

ERIC SONDHEIMER

If there's one big lesson learned from last week's arbitration victory by four private schools over the CIF Southern Section, it's that the section will no longer decide to move private schools from their sports areas for competitive equity reasons.

Twice the Southern Section has tried to move La Verne Damien and Glendora St. Lucy's, believing its bylaws provided authority to do so. Twice the schools have won legal decisions to stay put.

"There's a message, and we have to accept that message," Southern Section Commissioner Rob Wigod said.

St. Bonaventure, Oaks Christian, Damien and St. Lucy's get to stay in their current sports areas. All the schools in their areas have to meet again and come up with new leagues by April 7.

Wigod said the dispute cost the section $250,000 in legal fees and the price could have been $3 million if the matter had gone to trial instead of arbitration.

Attorney Robert Prata, who represented Damien and St. Lucy's, said his work was pro-bono. But he did get hugs from his two sons who attend Damien and play sports.

Clearly, the battle between private and public schools is heading toward a tipping point. Sending St. Bonaventure and Oaks Christian back into an area loaded with public schools re-ignites the debate whether private and public schools should be separated in the playoffs.

The Southern Section rejected the idea of allowing the powerful St. Bonaventure and Oaks Christian football teams to play only in the Catholic school Mission League while the schools' other teams remained in their current configurement. That would have been the simple solution.

Now in Ventura County, administrators must find some public school participants to join a football league with St. Bonaventure and Oaks Christian. There don't appear to be a whole lot of volunteers other than Westlake, so things could get ugly.

Also, Oaks Christian wants to join the Marmonte League for all sports, and some public schools in the area want none of that.

Wigod said on Saturday he wasn't ready yet to analyze the ramifications of the decision.

"We saw it more as a bylaw challenge," he said. "We believed that we had followed the bylaws that the membership makes. Obviously, those bylaws were challenged and the decision of the arbitrator went against us."

There won't be changes to area placement again until 2018, so there's time to review, reflect and regroup. But the issue of private versus public schools in sports competition isn't going away. The debate is intensifying and the costs are rising.

Somehow, the two sides need to find common ground.

"The concept of separating people has never been something we should work toward," Prata said.

"The kids want to play each other," Oaks Christian Athletic Director Jan Hethcock said. "It's the coaches and administrators that don't want to play."

As for animosity directed at private schools, Hethcock said, "I can't make people like us if they have some preconceived idea we're a big monster that we go out and recruit people. That's absolutely incorrect. We're nice to everybody who comes on our campus. That's what education is about. We have no enemies."

Perhaps this will be a second chance for St. Bonaventure and Oaks Christian to re-introduce themselves to schools in their neighborhood. For at least the next four years and probably longer, they all must get along.

But just as rulings by judges and juries can be overturned, so, too, can an arbitration award be set aside by a court. Courts don't often overturn an arbitration award, but in exceptional cases, they will — for example, if the award resulted from bribery by one of the parties to the dispute or if the arbitrator ruled not on the merits but as a result of duress (threat).

And how do parties end up in arbitration? In most cases, parties in dispute contractually agree to arbitration. Parties can create such contracts (that bind them to arbitration) either before or after a dispute arises. Sales contracts and employment contracts are common examples of pre-dispute agreements to arbitrate. For example, a contract for a cell phone might contain an arbitration clause. If the customer does not want to submit to arbitration of a potential dispute with the seller of the phone, the customer is free not to purchase from that seller. Likewise, an employment contract between a company and its unionized workers might contain an arbitration clause binding the employer and workers to arbitration, should an employment dispute arise. As well, parties are free to agree to arbitration after a dispute has arisen. Perhaps desiring a cheaper and quicker resolution to their dispute, the parties will sign a contract binding them to arbitration.

Parties agreeing to arbitration also choose the arbitrator(s). As is the case with mediation, the parties can be as informal or formal as they desire. A common choice of arbitrator (or mediator, for that matter) is one (or more) certified by the American Arbitration Association (AAA). What does it take to be an AAA-certified arbitrator? From their website:[3]

> *Applicants for membership on the AAA National Roster of Arbitrators must meet or exceed the following requirements:*

3. Reprinted by permission of American Arbitration Association.

1. *QUALIFICATIONS*
    a. *Minimum of 10 years of senior-level business or professional experience or legal practice.*
    b. *Educational degree(s) and/or professional license(s) appropriate to your field of expertise.*
    c. *Honors, awards, and citations indicating leadership in your field.*
    d. *Training or experience in arbitration and/or other forms of dispute resolution.*
    e. *Membership in a professional association(s).*
    f. *Other relevant experience or accomplishments (e.g., published articles).*
2. *NEUTRALITY*
    a. *Freedom from bias and prejudice.*
    b. *Ability to evaluate and apply legal, business, or trade principles.*
3. *JUDICIAL CAPACITY*
    a. *Ability to manage the hearing process.*
    b. *Thorough and impartial evaluation of testimony and other evidence.*

4. *REPUTATION*

   a. *Held in the highest regard by peers for integrity, fairness, and good judgment.*
   b. *Dedicated to upholding the AAA Code of Ethics for Arbitrators and/or Standards of Conduct for Mediators.*

5. *COMMITMENT TO ADR PROCESS*

   a. *Willingness to devote time and effort when selected to serve.*
   b. *Willingness to support efforts of the AAA.*
   c. *Willingness to successfully complete training under the guidelines of the Commercial Arbitration Development Program.*

6. *LETTERS OF RECOMMENDATION**

When requested by the AAA to do so, furnish letters from at least three active professionals in your field, but outside of any firms or professional associations in which you are employed or on which you currently serve as an officer, director, or trustee. Each letter must address the following:

   a. *Nature and duration of the relationship*
   b. *Why the applicant would be qualified to serve Recommended sources for letters:*
      1. *Current AAA Panel member*
      2. *Current or former state or federal judge***
   3. *An attorney who served as your opposing counsel***
   4. *Former employer or client*

** Letters of recommendation must be sent directly to the AAA Vice President from the writers, in sealed envelopes.*

*** Suggested for attorney applicants.*

7. *PERSONAL LETTER*

Submit a letter to your local AAA office explaining why you feel you would like to be included on AAA's Roster of Arbitrators along with a current copy of your personal resumé or CV. Your letter should provide a detailed description of your willingness to commit yourself to serving and representing the Association. Also indicate in the letter whether or not you are currently a neutral with any other ADR agencies. Please feel free to contact your local AAA office should you have any questions.

AAA also certifies mediators, according to the following minimum requirements:[4]

Qualified mediators are the heart of the mediation process and the AAA is committed to offering a Panel of Mediators in which parties can have the utmost confidence. For this reason, we have established the following minimum qualification criteria applicants must meet in order to be considered for acceptance to the AAA's Panel of Mediators.

- *General Experience*

  A minimum of 10 years of senior-level experience in business, industry, or a profession.

- *Education*

  Educational degree(s) and/or professional license(s) appropriate to applicant's field of expertise.

- *Mediator Training and Experience*

  Applicants must meet BOTH of the following minimum requirements:

A. *Training: Applicant must be able to document – by either a certificate of completion or a letter from the training organization – the completion of at least 24 total hours of training in mediation process skills encompassing the following topics: conflict theory, negotiation, dynamics of the mediation process, issues identification, generating options, caucusing, managing party interaction, ethics, impasse strategies, philosophies of mediation and mediator styles, role of the mediator, and simulated mediation role-plays providing performance-based evaluation.*
B. *Experience: Applicant must be able to document* ONE of the following:*
   (i) *Has served as a mediator on at least five mediation cases, in the applicant's primary field of expertise, filed privately, or through a court system over the last three calendar years. OR*

4. *See* http://www.adr.org/aaa/ShowPDF?doc=ADRSTG_003877.

(ii) Has served informally in the role of a mediator on at least four different occasions over the last two calendar years (documentation required). "Informal" mediations are defined as those that are privately arranged but not conducted under the auspices of an ADR provider or assigned through a court mediation program. Examples of informal mediations would be situations such as resolving disputes among business partners, employees, or industry colleagues in the normal course of business.*

- *Membership in at least one business, trade, or professional association.*

**Due to the confidential nature of mediation, the only documentation the AAA requires is the contact information (name and telephone number) of the advocates who appeared before the applicant in the mediations. In cases of self-represented parties, an applicant may use the party's contact information only if the party has waived any applicable provision of confidentiality.*

Various state laws authorize and facilitate different forms of ADR. Among other matters, such laws detail state courts' authority in relation to ADR and the effect of settlements between/among parties. A look at Texas' ADR statutes is instructive here. Texas Civil Practice and Remedies Code Title 7, Chapter 154, states, in part:

Sec. 154.001. DEFINITIONS. In this chapter:

(1) "Court" includes an appellate court, district court, constitutional county court, statutory county court, family law court, probate court, municipal court, or justice of the peace court.
(2) "Dispute resolution organization" means a private profit or nonprofit corporation, political subdivision, or public corporation, or a combination of these, that offers alternative dispute resolution services to the public.

Sec. 154.002. POLICY. It is the policy of this state to encourage the peaceable resolution of disputes, with special consideration given to disputes involving the parent-child relationship, including the mediation of issues involving conservatorship, possession, and support of children, and the early settlement of pending litigation through voluntary settlement procedures.

Sec. 154.021. REFERRAL OF PENDING DISPUTES FOR ALTERNATIVE DISPUTE RESOLUTION PROCEDURE.

(a) A court may, on its own motion or the motion of a party, refer a pending dispute for resolution by an alternative dispute resolution procedure including:

(1) an alternative dispute resolution system established under Chapter 26, Acts of the 68th Legislature, Regular Session, 1983 (Article 2372aa, Vernon's Texas Civil Statutes);

(2) a dispute resolution organization; or

(3) a nonjudicial and informally conducted forum for the voluntary settlement of citizens' disputes through the intervention of an impartial third party, including those alternative dispute resolution procedures described under this subchapter.

(b) The court shall confer with the parties in the determination of the most appropriate alternative dispute resolution procedure.

(c) Except as provided by agreement of the parties, a court may not order mediation in an action that is subject to the Federal Arbitration Act (9 U.S.C. Sections 1-16).

Sec. 154.023. MEDIATION.

(a) Mediation is a forum in which an impartial person, the mediator, facilitates communication between parties to promote reconciliation, settlement, or understanding among them.

(b) A mediator may not impose his own judgment on the issues for that of the parties.

(c) Mediation includes victim-offender mediation by the Texas Department of Criminal Justice described in Article 56.13, Code of Criminal Procedure.

Sec. 154.025. MODERATED SETTLEMENT CONFERENCE.

(a) A moderated settlement conference is a forum for case evaluation and realistic settlement negotiations.

(b) Each party and counsel for the party present the position of the party before a panel of impartial third parties.

(c) The panel may issue an advisory opinion regarding the liability or damages of the parties or both.

(d) The advisory opinion is not binding on the parties.

Sec. 154.027. ARBITRATION.

(a) *Nonbinding arbitration is a forum in which each party and counsel for the party present the position of the party before an impartial third party, who renders a specific award.*
(b) *If the parties stipulate in advance, the award is binding and is enforceable in the same manner as any contract obligation. If the parties do not stipulate in advance that the award is binding, the award is not binding and serves only as a basis for the parties' further settlement negotiations.*

Sec. 154.071. EFFECT OF WRITTEN SETTLEMENT AGREEMENT.

(a) *If the parties reach a settlement and execute a written agreement disposing of the dispute, the agreement is enforceable in the same manner as any other written contract.*
(b) *The court in its discretion may incorporate the terms of the agreement in the court's final decree disposing of the case.*
(c) *A settlement agreement does not affect an outstanding court order unless the terms of the agreement are incorporated into a subsequent decree.*

By now, you should have a good idea of some alternatives to litigation for people involved in a legal dispute. Let's turn our attention to some subject-matter areas where legal disputes are common.

chapter 8 TORTS

What is a *tort*? Consider the following definitions:

> *A wrongful act, not including a breach of contract or trust, that results in injury to another's person, property, reputation, or the like, and for which the injured party is entitled to compensation* – Dictionary.com[1]

> *A wrong that is committed by someone who is legally obligated to provide a certain amount of carefulness in behavior to another and that causes injury to that person, who may seek compensation in a civil suit for damages.* – TheFreeDictionary.com[2]

> *A civil wrong which can be redressed by awarding damages* – Legal Information Institute[3]

> *A wrongful act resulting in injury, for which the injured party is entitled to compensation* – Random House Webster's School & Office Dictionary[4]

1. http://dictionary.reference.com/browse/tort
2. http://www.thefreedictionary.com/tort
3. http://www.law.cornell.edu/wex/tort
4. Random House Webster's School & Office Dictionary, Random House, Inc., 1993.

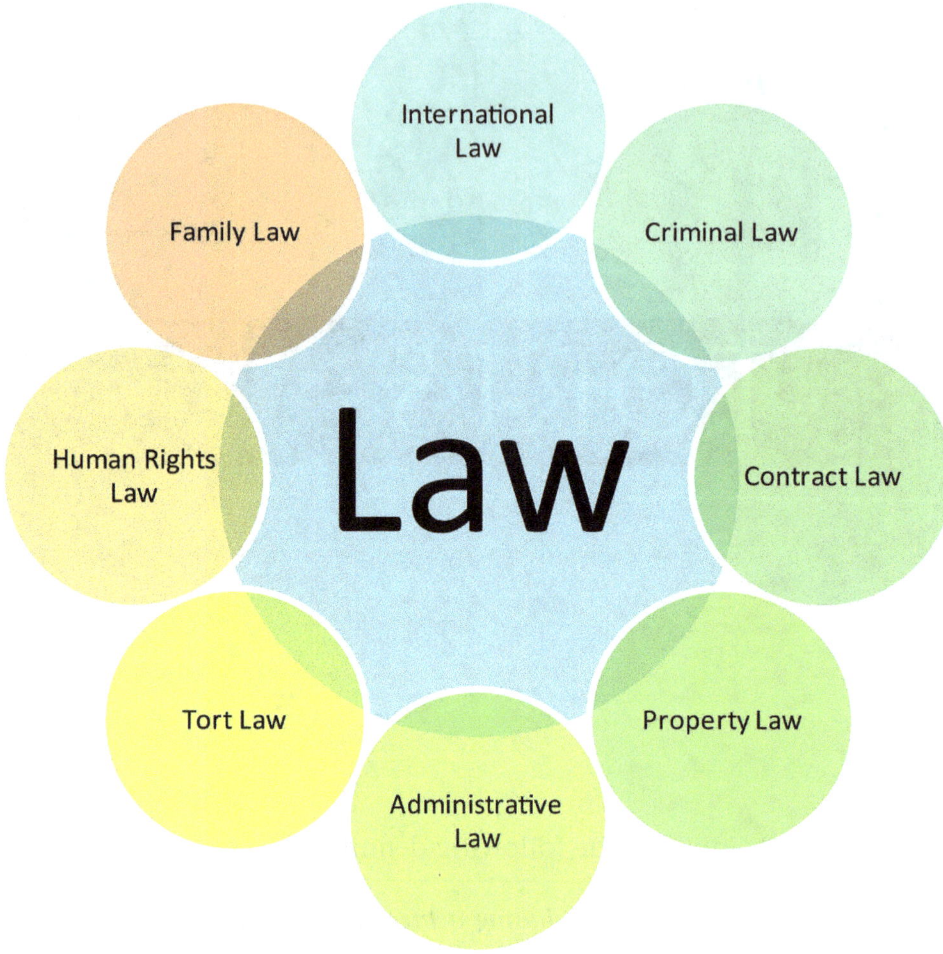

It seems there are as many unique definitions of *tort* as there are sources; but all of the definitions really say the same thing. So, what is it they are saying? Let's get there by establishing what torts are not. First, torts are not crimes. Crimes are criminal wrongs; torts are a branch of civil wrongs. And since civil wrongs are offenses that can lead to lawsuits, we now know torts are something for which one can sue. Secondly, torts are not breaches of contract. So, torts are civil wrongs other than breaches of contract. One can sue another for breach of contract, but such a lawsuit would not be a tort lawsuit.

The source of tort law is common law. Over time, the various states developed case law on tort subjects collectively forming the body of

tort law in each state. So, what constitutes a certain tort in New Mexico is determined by New Mexico state court cases. What constitutes the same tort in Iowa is determined by Iowa state court cases. However, some torts are defined by state statutes, so not all tort law is formed by common law (though most is).

Before learning the categories of torts, note the same action can constitute both a crime *and* a tort. For example, Lisa kills Walt in California. If Lisa's action is considered to be murder, per California's criminal (penal) code, the State of California can prosecute Lisa for murder. Meanwhile, Walt's family might sue Lisa for wrongful death, a tort. Thus, in this case, Lisa can be taken to court for a crime and a tort. The former is a matter of criminal law; the latter a matter of civil law. The former is a prosecution; the latter a lawsuit. The former is taken to court by a government prosecutor; the latter by a private plaintiff. Make sense?

A famous example of this is the case of O.J. Simpson. In 1994, Ronald Goldman and Nicole Brown Simpson, the ex-wife of O.J. Simpson, were murdered in Los Angeles. In 1995, O.J. Simpson was put on trial for their murders. In 1996, O.J. Simpson was sued for wrongful death. The same offense resulted in a criminal trial (for the crime of murder) and a civil trial (for the tort of wrongful death). Criminal offense and civil offense. Prosecution and lawsuit.

We can learn something else from the case of O.J. Simpson. What were the results of the criminal trial and the civil trial? O.J. Simpson was found not guilty in the murder trial, but he was found liable for wrongful death. In other words, he won in the prosecution but lost in the lawsuit. How can this be? The same action was the basis for each trial, so why the disparate outcomes? The reason is criminal trials and lawsuits have different burdens of proof.

Recall from earlier in the book our examination of burden of proof, or the weight of the evidence. How strong the prosecutor's evidence must be to convict a criminal defendant is not the same as how strong a plaintiff's evidence has to be to win a lawsuit. The former is a higher burden. In other words, evidence must be stronger in a criminal trial than in a lawsuit. The criminal burden of proof is *beyond a reasonable doubt.* The civil burden of proof is *by a preponderance of the evidence* (i.e., more than 50%). So, evidence strong enough to prove a tort has been committed might not be strong enough to prove a crime has been committed. This is exactly what happened in the O.J. Simpson cases. The evidence was strong enough to prove O.J. Simpson was civilly liable for the deaths but not strong enough to prove he was criminally liable for the deaths.

Now, what about the categories of torts? Torts can be divided into two broad categories: those one does on purpose and those one does not do on purpose. In other words, torts are either intentional or unintentional. Let's learn about each.

INTENTIONAL TORTS

True to their name, intentional torts are torts one commits intentionally. If someone commits a tort on purpose, he commits an intentional tort. (The person who commits a tort is referred to as a *tortfeasor.*) Whereas unintentional torts share the same name (*negligence*), each intentional tort has its own name. All things being equal, a tort committed on purpose is more egregious in the eyes of the law than one not committed on purpose. As such, there are certain rules of law applicable to intentional torts but not unintentional torts. We will encounter examples shortly.

So, which torts are *named* (my term, not a common term) torts? Let's examine a few of them. As we learn about each, don't forget these are intentional torts. For each tort, the plaintiff bears the burden of proving the defendant meant to do whatever it is the particular tort entails.

Also, bear in mind just because a plaintiff proves the elements of a tort does not always mean she will prevail on her claim. Why not? Because each of these torts has multiple defenses potentially available to the defendant. After explaining each of the torts, I will turn to some defenses. Though I do not list statute of limitations as a defense below, remember every tort has a *statute of limitations* — a time period in which a person with a claim can file a lawsuit for that claim — and if the plaintiff sues after the statute of limitations expires, she sues too late and will not be able to pursue her claim. As such, a defendant who is sued after the statute of limitations has expired will assert as a defense the plaintiff waited too late to sue.

BATTERY

A *battery* is a harmful or offensive touching of another. Notice the word *touching*. For there to be a battery, there must be a touch. The defendant or something the defendant sets in motion must make contact with the plaintiff's person. Alternatively (and less common than the two ways just mentioned), the defendant can intentionally create a situation causing a harmful touch to befall the plaintiff.

For example, imagine Maddox is having lunch at a café. While he is seated at his table, Jody, a stranger, approaches him and punches him in the face. Jody's punch constitutes a battery. A punch is a harmful touch. Easy enough. Now, same scenario except, this time, Jody, seated at a table a few feet from Maddox, throws her plate at Maddox, striking him in the face. Again, a battery has been committed. A plate to the face is a harmful touch. Jody didn't touch Maddox, but something she set in motion — a plate — did.

Let's examine a few more examples tweaking the scenarios above. What if Jody pushes Amanda, a stranger walking past Maddox's table, into Maddox? Battery? You bet. Here, Jody set in motion another person, and the person struck Maddox. New hypothetical: Jody walks up to Maddox and spits in his face or pours hot coffee on him. Battery. She doesn't touch Maddox, but she sets in motion saliva and coffee that touch Maddox in offensive and harmful ways, respectively. Last one: recall a battery usually occurs when the defendant or something the defendant sets in motion touches the plaintiff in a harmful or offensive manner; but I also mentioned a defendant can commit a battery by intentionally creating a situation that causes a harmful touch to befall the plaintiff. For example (our last for battery), Jody is at the café when Maddox arrives. As he approaches his table and just before he sits down, Jody pulls the seat back, unbeknownst to Maddox. Maddox sits down, but there is no chair, so he falls to the floor. This, too, constitutes battery. Jody didn't touch Maddox with herself or with anything she set in motion, but she intentionally set in motion a chain of events causing a harmful touch to befall Maddox.

Now that we have a good idea of what a battery is, let's look at a few defenses to the tort of battery. In other words, if Maddox sues Jody for battery, what might Jody offer the court to escape liability (either partially or altogether)?

First, Jody might punch or kick or make some other harmful contact with Maddox, in order to defend herself from him. If Maddox begins punching Jody for no reason, shouldn't Jody be able to defend herself? Would it make sense for Jody to punch Maddox back and then be sued for battery when she injures Maddox? Of course not. *Self -defense* is a defense to the tort of battery, as is *defense of another*. If Jody sees Maddox beating up Julie, shouldn't Jody be able to come to Julie's aid? Of course. That said, the defenses of self-defense and defense of another are only viable defenses to the extent the self defense or defense of another is reasonable, under the circumstances. If Maddox punches Jody, what are some reasonable responses? It is likely a fact finder would find it reasonable for Jody to push back or kick back or punch back. But what if Maddox pushes Jody one time, as he passes her on the sidewalk, and then proceeds to walk away from her? If Jody turns and stabs him, is that reasonable, under the circumstances? Surely not, right? We can toss around hypotheticals and make our best guesses about the reasonableness of a response, but ultimately the decision is left to the fact finder. So long as the fact finder believes that Jody's response doesn't go too far, Jody will be able to enjoy the defense of self-defense or defense of another.

Another justifiable reason Jody might hit Maddox is Maddox asked her to or told her she could. Thus, *consent* is a defense to the tort of battery. But as was the case with defending oneself or another, consent is a valid defense to an extent: If the person receiving consent exceeds the permission granted her, she no longer enjoys the defense of consent. For example, imagine Maddox asks Jody to slap him one time in the face, because he has never been slapped and wants to know what it feels like. Instead of slapping him once, Jody grabs a golf club and repeatedly strikes Maddox in the face. Jody, of course, would not have a viable defense of consent, should Maddox sue her for battery. *"But Maddox said I could strike him!"* Jody might say to the court. True, but he said you could slap him one time, not hit him multiple times with a golf club, the court would reply. Here, Jody exceeds the limits of the consent and, thus, loses the defense. Before leaving the defense of consent, note players in a sporting event consent to

the normal touches in the sporting event. If a running back for the Green Bay Packers is tackled during a game by a linebacker for the Chicago Bears, has the linebacker committed a battery against the running back? Of course not! Tackles are normal touches in a football game; and, by playing sports, a person consents to the normal touches in the sport.

ASSAULT

With a good grasp on what constitutes a battery, you can understand the tort of assault (since the definition includes the word *battery*). An *assault* is the placing of another in reasonable apprehension of an imminent battery. An assault does not involve a touch (as does a battery). Rather, an assault is making someone reasonably apprehensive of a harmful or offensive touch. Battery is about the body; assault is about the mind.

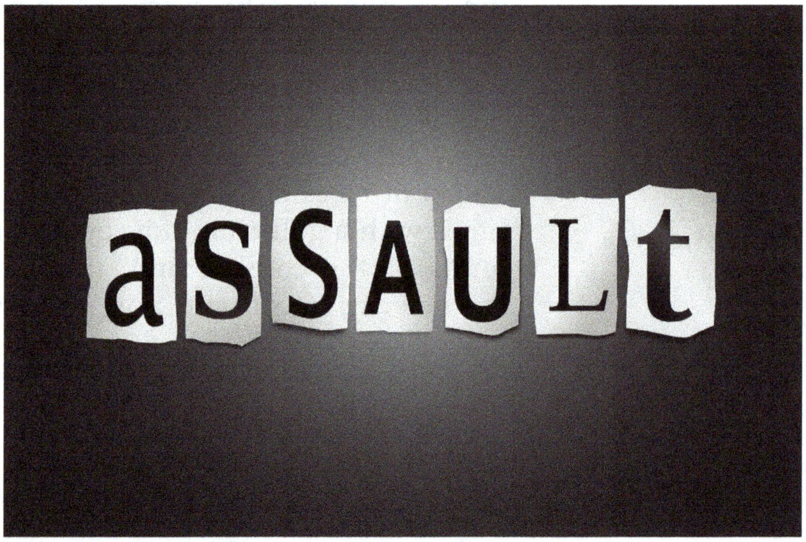

Imagine Jackson raises his clenched fist at Tara. If Tara believes Jackson is about to punch her, an assault has occurred. No touch has taken place. Rather, Tara is in reasonable fear a battery (here, a punch) is imminent. What if Jackson swings a baseball bat at Tara, but she ducks just in time to avoid being struck by the bat? An assault has taken place. Tara ducked, because she reasonably feared she was about to be battered by the baseball bat. No battery, however, occurred. Why not? Because there was no touch! What if Jackson hits Tara, who doesn't know Jackson is behind her, on the back of the head with a baseball bat? A battery has taken place, but an assault has not taken place. Why no assault? Tara was unaware Jackson was swinging a baseball bat toward her, so she was never in fear of an imminent battery. Final scenario: Jackson and Tara are facing each other. Jackson swings a baseball bat toward Tara. Tara tries to duck but doesn't duck quickly enough, so the bat strikes her in the face. What do we have here? Assault and battery.

Let's look a bit closer at two words in the definition of assault: *reasonable* and *imminent*.

First, the plaintiff's apprehension a battery is about to take place must be *reasonable*. Thus, the fear must be legitimate to a reasonable person. Stated differently, the fact finder believes the plaintiff's fear was reasonable under the circumstances. Go back to our first example: Is it reasonable for Tara to fear getting struck by Jackson when he raises his clenched fist to her? Yes, unless the circumstances are such that a reasonable fact finder would find Tara's fear unjustified. If, for example, a reasonable person in Tara's place knew Jackson were joking, Tara's apprehension would not be reasonable. Or how about if Jackson raised his clenched fist while asking, *"Does my fist look weird to you?"* Surely in such a case Tara should not fear getting punched by Jackson.

Play with the scenario however you want. What matters is whether Tara's fear, given all of the relevant factors and circumstances, is reasonable in the eyes of the fact finder. Also, notice my examples do not involve words alone. Words alone are insufficient to constitute assault. Threatening words must be coupled with some physical act, in order to constitute assault. So, a threat with a raised fist or a baseball bat would suffice.

Second, there must be a reasonable apprehension of an *imminent* battery. Imminence is required. Thus, if Jackson says to Tara, *"I'm going to punch*

you twenty years from today!" There is no assault. Why not? Because Tara has no reason to believe the punch is about to take place. By his own words, Jackson makes it clear he intends to punch Tara in twenty years. Thus, there is no imminence. It is not enough (to establish the tort of assault) to have a reasonable fear of a battery at some point in the future. The apprehension must be of a battery that is to occur very soon.

As for defenses, the possible defenses to an assault claim are much the same as those for a battery claim. Perhaps a defendant asserts that the plaintiff consented to the assault. Perhaps the defendant claims that his actions were in an effort to defend himself or another. As was the case with these defenses in the case of a battery, such defenses to a claim of assault are valid only to the extent that (for consent) the defendant's actions didn't exceed the bounds of the consent given and (for self-defense or defense of another) the defendant's action was reasonable, under the circumstances.

TRESPASS (TO LAND)

There is more than one type of trespass, but when you think of a trespass, you probably think about land/property; so, we will focus on the tort of *trespass to land*. An unlawful intrusion on another's property is a trespass to land. Restated, trespass to land is entering another's land without permission or justification.

If I intentionally walk onto property not my own, without permission or some justification (stay tuned), I commit the tort of trespass to land. Even if I think the property is mine, I commit a trespass. Why? Because the land is not mine, and I knowingly entered it unlawfully. Bad intention is not required.

How about this scenario? I walk by a house with a front yard in complete disarray. I have quite the green thumb and a keen eye for outdoor design, so I enter the yard and clean it up. The yard looks so much better than before. I probably even raised the property value! Trespass to land? Absolutely. Good intentions do not make my entry lawful. If the property owner didn't give me permission to clean his yard, my good-intentioned entry is unlawful.

wildlife trooper
with Traps on Private Land Sued for Trespass

Zaz Hollander

An Alaska wildlife trooper has been named the defendant in a lawsuit that claims he and his trapping partner violated the law when they set snares for fox and coyote on private property without permission..

Central Gravel Products owners Nicolene Jordan and Mark Loomis filed the civil lawsuit against Trooper John Cyr for "multiple trespasses and creation of an ongoing nuisance" on land they lease in a suburban area near Colony High School.

The complaint, which Talkeetna attorney Paul Brattan filed Thursday in Palmer Superior Court, also lists as a defendant Rick Ellis, Cyr's trapping partner and a past president of the Alaska Frontier Trappers Association.

Ellis said Friday he hadn't yet been served and declined to comment. Cyr previously instructed a reporter to contact Ellis for any comments. He is a wildlife trooper based out of Palmer.

The lawsuit centers on an incident last month that's sparked a debate about just how far hunters and trappers can go before bumping up against private property rights.

Jordan and Loomis in mid-November discovered at least 38 snares in an old potato field on 160 acres leased for years from landowner Ralph Kircher. Neither they nor Kircher ever gave the trappers permission to enter the property, both said last month.

They also found several moose heads and what looked like the body of a moose calf used as bait, according to the complaint. Boot prints led in and out of the property about 200 feet from a sign marking the entrance to the gravel company.

Cyr's name was on a state permit for the salvaged moose parts.

Loomis pulled the snares and Jordan filed a formal complaint about the trooper's actions with the Department of Public Safety.

A wildlife trooper sergeant came out and investigated the complaint. He found nothing illegal happened because the place the trappers entered the property wasn't posted with a sign prohibiting trespassing or trapping, troopers said at the time.

Under Alaska's criminal trespass statute, property owners must post every road and known access point on their land with signs 144 square inches in size that are inscribed with the landowner or leaseholder's name and contact information.

continued on next page...

There was no sign at the point where the trappers entered, authorities said. But there were other signs on the property.

Even if Jordan and Loomis "attempt to post enough signs to convince every potential passing trapper that they have complied with the strict provisions in the Alaska criminal trespass statute, the frequent gale-force winds in the area will soon blow a goodly portion of these signs away," the complaint says.

Ellis said last month that he and Cyr trapped fox and coyote on the land last year. This year, he set the snares but hadn't started trapping yet.

They never asked for permission, he said, because they didn't have to.

Ellis, in a contention echoed numerous times by the troopers, said the trappers did nothing illegal. That's because the place they entered the property – a pull-out blocked by several logs – wasn't posted.

"Lacking the presence of any signs, anybody can go anywhere they want," he said last month. "They can trap, they can hunt, they can do whatever."

Several attorneys said in interviews that Ellis' assertion is just not true.

Trapping or hunting on private property that's not properly posted may not be a crime but it's also not legal and could lead to civil lawsuits like the one filed this week by Loomis and Jordan, they said.

"It is a civil wrong," said attorney Sam Fortier, a longtime Anchorage attorney who represents 30 village corporations. "What (the troopers) said was true but that's not the whole story. There's kind of an omission. I think it's wrong to omit material facts as much as it to misstate them."

Civil trespass in Alaska is defined much more simply than its criminal counterpart, according to the Alaska Court System's standard jury instructions: "A trespass is an intrusion onto land possessed by another without consent or other privilege. Trespass includes not only entry onto land, but also remaining on land, or causing a third person or thing to enter or remain."

In a civil trespass case, a landowner or lease holder has the right to damages as well as attorney fees if they can prove someone intentionally entered the land when it wasn't an emergency even if no "harm" was done to the property, according to Doug Pope, another Anchorage attorney with decades of practice who's also a former Board of Game chairman.

"The trappers in your story would be classic examples of that," Pope wrote in an email, referring to an earlier Daily News story about the original incident involving the snares.

Troopers can only enforce criminal statutes, spokeswoman Megan Peters said Friday. "We have to go by the criminal definition of the law."

continued on next page...

The complaint against Cyr and Ellis, however, charges that the men also may have violated criminal law.

The document refers to a state statute that defines criminal trespass as "a person who, without intent to commit a crime on the land, enters or remains upon unimproved and apparently unused land."

But the land in this case was clearly not "unimproved and apparently unused," so it was not necessary to post signs, the complaint charges.

"Snares were set within a dozen feet of excavations and gravel storage piles," it says. "Therefore there could have been no question in any reasonable person's mind about the land being 'apparently unused.' "

Cyr had also bought gravel there in the past, according to the complaint.

Even if the court doesn't find that Cyr and Ellis violated criminal law, they are still liable for civil trespass and creating a nuisance with the snares and carcasses, which could draw animals to the site in close proximity to a school, the complaint says.

Jordan and Loomis are seeking damages to be determined at trial, as well as attorney fees.

Superior Court Judge Eric Smith will hear the case. No hearings have been scheduled yet.

Do I have to enter another's property with my own body in order to trespass on the land? Absolutely not. If I set in motion something that enters another's property without permission or justification, I trespass. If I throw a bag of garbage on someone's front yard: trespass. If I push my shopping cart onto someone's driveway: trespass. If I park my car half on my driveway and half on your yard: trespass.

As with any other tort, a plaintiff suing for trespass to land must prove injury, in order to receive money damages. Some states require the trespass to cause actual injury (monetary loss). Others don't require actual injury, just the fact of unlawful entry. That said, if someone steps on your property and then leaves your property, causing no monetary damage, do you think it's a good idea to sue this person for trespass? No. This one-off, unauthorized entry causing no money loss is not worthy of damages. Feel free to sue, but if you prove your case, expect to receive only nominal damages. However, in the case of a repeated or continuing trespass (e.g., a person regularly trespasses or parks his car on your driveway and won't move the car), a trespass lawsuit is certainly warranted. In cases of continuing trespass, the plaintiff will seek injunctive relief from the court. In other words, the plaintiff wants the court to order the defendant to stop trespassing. If the continuing trespass also caused money loss, the plaintiff will also, of course, seek money damages.

So, when is my entry onto the land of another *not* a trespass to land? In other words, what are some defenses to a trespass claim? Let's look at a few.

First, if the owner or rightful possessor of the land grants me *permission* to enter his land, I am an invitee, not a trespasser.

Second, if I enter another's land *not of my own volition*, I am not committing a trespass. For example, if I sleepwalk onto your property: no trespass. Why? Because there is no intentional, affirmative conduct. If I stand by your property line and have a seizure that causes me to fall on your property: no trespass. Again, no intentional, affirmative conduct.

Third, myriad situations create a justification for my entry. For example, an *emergency* will excuse my entry. Imagine I am walking on a sidewalk. As I pass your yard, a car veers off the road and is heading straight at me. If I jump out of the way and land on your yard, I am not trespassing. The need to protect myself from being hit by the car makes my entry (for which I don't have permission) justified. What if I am being chased by a man with a gun who is threatening to shoot me? If I run across your yard in an effort to get to safety, am I trespassing? If crossing your yard is reasonable, under the circumstances, it certainly is not a trespass. How about this? As I walk past your house, I see an unattended toddler crawling toward a swimming pool. If I run onto the property to keep the toddler from falling into the pool, I am not trespassing. In each of these situations, I entered another's land without permission, but the circumstances that caused the entry justify the entry. As such, the entries will be lawful.

NUISANCE

Closely related to the tort of trespass to land is the tort of nuisance. How are the two torts different? Whereas trespass to land is a physical invasion of another's property, *nuisance* is a non-physical (intangible) invasion of another's property. Whereas trespass to land interferes with another's possession of property, nuisance interferes with one's enjoyment of property.

What might intangibly invade, say, your neighbor's property? To name a few, noise, light, and odor. If you and your band mates have band practice in your garage at 2:00 AM, the noise is likely a nuisance for neighbors trying to sleep. If you leave the spotlight on the corner of your house on every night, and the bright light shines toward your neighbor's bedroom, the light might be a nuisance to him, as he tries to sleep. If you pile loads of trash in your backyard, the resulting offensive smell might be a nuisance to your neighbor, who wishes to sit in his backyard in olfactory peace! Nuisance can occur via several other mediums, such as vibrations and temperature.

To determine whether a nuisance claim is worthy of a remedy (money or, if money is inadequate, an injunction), the fact finder will consider a range of factors and decide whether a remedy is warranted, given the relevant circumstances.

Defenses are generally harder to come by with nuisance. As usual, *consent* might be possible. Also, if the particular activity is *authorized* by the zoning laws/regulations of the particular locality, the defendant might have a valid defense. Some, but not most, jurisdictions allow a defense to defendants when the plaintiff moved to his property after the nuisance existed. In essence, this defense is one of *assumption of risk*.

FALSE IMPRISONMENT

Unlawfully confining/restraining another against her will constitutes the tort of *false imprisonment*. Confining/restraining someone can occur in myriad ways, from physically holding the person to tying up the person to threatening the person with physical harm. In whatever form, if someone takes away another's meaningful choice to move as she pleases, the former falsely imprisons the latter. No physical injury is required, in order to have a valid claim. The loss of freedom of movement constitutes sufficient injury.

What are some defenses to the tort of false imprisonment? Obviously, one can *consent* to being held or bound. Also, *self-defense* and *defense of another*, to the extent they are carried out reasonably, are legitimate defenses. If Donald sees Baxter punching Amanda, Donald is justified in intervening and attempting to stop the attack. If Donald holds Baxter

north liberty man
Accused of Assault, False Imprisonment

Lee Hermiston

A North Liberty man is in custody after allegedly choking a woman and threatening her with a knife in November.

According to North Liberty police criminal complaints, on Nov. 16, 2013, 22-year-old Eric M. Washpun got into an argument with a woman at his apartment that turned physical. Police said Washpun used his hands and forearm to choke the woman, who later reported to police that she could not breath during the assault. The woman suffered from red marks, scratches and pain around her neck, police said.

Washpun also allegedly wielded a knife during the assault. Police said Washpun waved the knife in the woman's face while she was cornered into a closet. Police said Washpun wouldn't put the knife down or allow the woman to leave. She later told police that she was afraid Washpun would cut or stab her if she tried to move or leave the closet.

According to jail records, Washpun was booked at the jail Tuesday night. He faces charges of domestic assault - impeding breathing with bodily injury, domestic assault while displaying a weapon and false imprisonment.

From "North Liberty Man Accused of Assault, False Imprisonment" by Lee Hermiston, KCRG.com, April 28, 2014.

until the police arrive, he likely has a valid defense of defense of another. In the criminal-law context, police with *probable cause* to arrest someone have a valid defense of legal right. Additionally, most states have statutes protecting merchants against claims of false imprisonment. The typical statute (commonly referred to as a *shopkeeper's privilege*) states a merchant sued for false imprisonment has a valid defense against such claim if the merchant had probable cause to detain and detained reasonably (in terms of time and manner). As an example, here is North Carolina's shopkeeper's privilege, found in Subsection (c) of N.C.G.S. §14-72.1:[5]

> *A merchant, or the merchant's agent or employee, or a peace officer who detains or causes the arrest of any person shall not be held civilly liable for detention, malicious prosecution, false imprisonment, or false arrest of the person detained or arrested, where such detention is upon the premises of the store or in a reasonable proximity thereto, is in a reasonable manner for a reasonable length of time, and, if in detaining*

5. http://www.ncga.state.nc.us/EnactedLegislation/Statutes/HTML/BySection/Chapter_14/GS_14-72.1.html

or in causing the arrest of such person, the merchant, or the merchant's agent or employee, or the peace officer had at the time of the detention or arrest probable cause to believe that the person committed the offense created by this section. If the person being detained by the merchant, or the merchant's agent or employee, is a minor under the age of 18 years, the merchant or the merchant's agent or employee, shall call or notify, or make a reasonable effort to call or notify the parent or guardian of the minor, during the period of detention. A merchant, or the merchant's agent or employee, who makes a reasonable effort to call or notify the parent or guardian of the minor shall not be held civilly liable for failing to notify the parent or guardian of the minor.

DEFAMATION

Defamation is the tort of communicating a false statement that damages (lowers) another's reputation. To constitute defamation (which covers the common law concepts of libel and slander), the statement must be false, must be a statement of fact (not an opinion), must be a statement of a nature that lowers or injures one's reputation, and must be communicated to at least one third party. Let's flesh out these elements.

First, the statement must be false. If the statement is true, there is no defamation. Second, the statement must be one of fact. In other words, it must be something objectively verifiable. Opinions don't cut it. Stating Joey is ugly is not defamation, because looks are subjective. On the other hand, stating Joey cheats on his tax returns is not opinion. He either cheats on his tax returns or does not cheat on his tax returns. No subjectivity. Next, the content of the statement must be of a nature that injures the reputation (character, standing, esteem) of the person about whom the statement is made. If I tell someone that Madison eats apples when she does not eat apples, there is no defamation. Eating apples is not something that tends to lower Madison's reputation. By contrast, stating Madison regularly uses harmful chemicals to taint the supply of apples at the local grocery is something that would injure Madison's reputation. Lastly, the statement must be communicated to at least one third party. If I tell only Madison she taints the local grocery store's apples, there is no defamation. If no one other than Madison is privy to the statement, her reputation is not injured. Only when I communicate the false and defamatory statement of fact to someone other than Madison do I commit the tort of defamation.

katie holmes sues
Star for Libel over "Drug Shocker" Cover

Christie D'Zurilla

Katie Holmes sued the publishers of Star magazine for $50 million in federal court on Tuesday, accusing the tabloid of implying on a January cover that she is a drug addict.

"Of all the fabricated stories that continue to be published about me, this instance is beyond the pale," Holmes said in a statement. Publisher American Media Inc. "knew this outrageous story was false and printed it anyway to sell magazines," the statement said.

The headline on the Star cover, which featured a picture of a disheveled Holmes, screamed "Addiction Nightmare: Katie DRUG SHOCKER!" and added, "The real reason she *can't* leave Tom."

The "addiction" alleged in the story was to Scientology's e-meter device, the use of which Star said "gives subjects a temporary feeling of euphoria, followed by a crash and a craving for more,"according to Gossip Cop. Scientology followers believe the e-meter can detect mental trauma.

Holmes' lawyer called the cover a "cheap trick on the public."

Star said in a statement that it stands behind its reporting. "The physical effect of the e-meter on its users is a matter of significant public concern and we plan to vigorously defend the suit filed by Ms. Holmes," adding that it could not wait to depose the actress regarding the e-meter.

The lawsuit also states that the implication that Holmes wants to leave husband Cruise is untrue.

About this time last year, **Angelina Jolie** and **Brad Pitt** filed a claim against the British tab News of the World over a story alleging that they had split up.

Brangelina won and donated the settlement money to charity.

Closely related to the tort of defamation are the torts of *injurious falsehood* and *false light*. All three torts require communicating to a third party a false statement about the plaintiff. The difference among the three is in the type of false statement. Whereas defamation is a false statement that damages the plaintiff's reputation, injurious falsehood is a statement about the plaintiff's commercial goods or business activities, and false light is a statement portraying the plaintiff incorrectly, though not in a way lowering her reputation.

If I publish a false story claiming Wally stole money from a local grocery store, I commit the tort of defamation. Falsely stating that Wally is a thief hurts Wally's reputation/character, so the tort of defamation is available to Wally. If I publish a false story that the inventory of boats at Wally's Watercraft are defective and unsafe, I commit the tort of injurious falsehood. Obviously, Wally stands to lose business at Wally's Watercraft, so the law provides a cause of action of injurious falsehood (also referred to as *slander of goods*). If I publish a false story that Wally, who is the nation's foremost expert on chocolate ice cream, doesn't like chocolate ice cream and never eats it, I commit the tort of false light. Why false light and not defamation? Because there is nothing defamatory about saying a person doesn't like chocolate ice cream. Ice cream preference doesn't affect one's reputation/character. But saying the nation's premier expert on chocolate ice cream doesn't eat chocolate ice cream can negatively impact the expert's business dealings related to chocolate ice cream. As such, the law affords the expert a claim of false light.

And what about defenses to the tort of defamation? Obviously, *truth* is an absolute defense. A true statement cannot constitute defamation. No matter how defamatory the content of the statement, if the statement is true, there is no tort of defamation. The law also provides a few types of *privilege* defenses to a claim of defamation. Generally speaking, those who enjoy a certain privilege do so because courts have decided (via common law) to protect the speaker on a topic of public interest. For example, a person committing defamation in the course of a judicial or legislative proceeding has an *absolute privilege* against a defama-

attorney files lawsuit

Over Comments He Says Cast Him as "Tree Mutilator"

Columbia Heart Beat cited for its criticism.

By Andrew Denney

Columbia attorney Aaron Smith has filed a lawsuit against the Columbia Heart Beat, its publisher, Mike Martin, and two people quoted in an op-ed penned by Martin over critical comments about the state of Smith's yard that he claims cast him in a false light as a "tree mutilator."

The lawsuit, filed Jan. 15 in Boone County Circuit Court, says Martin and Columbia residents Sarah Grim and Ruthie Moccia placed Smith in a false light because of their descriptions of Smith's property at 802 W. Stewart Road after he removed trees there.

The comments — one of which said the tree removal made it appear that a "brontosaurus had lunch in the front yard" — were featured in a Jan. 3 op-ed in the Heart Beat with the headline "TREE TRAGEDY: When a falling ax is a good reminder."

"It's the most atrocious, destructive thing I have ever seen," Moccia is quoted as saying about the tree removal in the op-ed.

Smith claims the comments in the op-ed would be considered "highly offensive to a reasonable person" and that they make him look as if he has "no care or compassion for his community or its natural aesthetics."

Since the comments were published, the lawsuits state, there have been online comments that have helped to fuel a neighborhood "rally" against Smith regarding the tree removal and passersby have shouted out "unsolicited, negative" comments about the tree removal. Smith said his damages in the matter exceed $25,000.

"I just think personal attacks like this shouldn't go on in our community," Smith said in an interview. "If someone doesn't stand up and take a stand against it, it's going to continue."

Smith claims Martin did not contact him to find out why the trees were removed or what his future plans are for the property before Martin published the op-ed. He also said Martin did not ask for Smith's consent to publish the article.

Smith submitted comments to the Heart Beat about his reasoning for taking down the trees and his future plans to improve the aesthetics of the property, and those were published on the publication's website on Jan. 14.

According to online court records, neither Martin nor any of the defendants named in the lawsuit had been served with papers as of yesterday. The Tribune sent a Facebook message to the Heart Beat's profile, which is maintained by Martin,

continued on next page...

seeking comment, and Martin replied that he had not heard of the lawsuit before receiving a message from the Tribune.

In the lawsuit, Smith is claiming defamation on the part of Martin and the Heart Beat and "false light invasion of privacy" on the part of all the defendants.

According to the website for the Arlington, Va.-based Reporters Committee for Freedom of the Press, specific requirements to bring a claim of false light invasion of privacy vary across jurisdictions, but generally plaintiffs need to show that the false light in which they have been cast would be "highly offensive to a reasonable person," which the committee considers a vague standard that "potentially chills speech."

Smith said in his lawsuit that the defendants' portrayal of him as a "tree mutilator" is "highly offensive to a reasonable person."

The committee's website states that about two-thirds of U.S. states recognize false light invasion of privacy, while the remaining third either don't recognize it or eventually reject it because of its overlap with defamation.

Sandy Davidson, a Missouri School of Journalism professor who teaches a course in media law, said traditionally Missouri has been one of the states that considers false light invasion of privacy as overlapping with defamation, meaning that a plaintiff has had to show actual malice on the part of a defendant.

tion claim. Careful, though: a witness testifying in court will enjoy an absolute privilege, but when that same witness has finished testifying and then defames someone as he exits the courthouse, there is no longer any privilege (because the latter statement was not made as part of a judicial proceeding). Also, a *qualified privilege* exists for various types of statements. A qualified privilege is not absolute. What this means is the plaintiff, in response to a defendant's assertion of qualified privilege, can overcome (negate/rebut) the defendant's privilege by proving the defendant made the statement maliciously (e.g., proving the defendant knew the statement was false but made the statement anyway). Examples of times when a qualified privilege is likely present are when the media speak/publish on a matter of public interest and when a citizen speaks at a town-hall meeting.

The list of intentional torts we examined above is certainly not exhaustive, but it should give you an idea of the types of intentional torts available throughout the various states.

UNINTENTIONAL TORTS (A.K.A. "NEGLIGENCE")

We just learned some torts requiring intent on the part of the tortfeasor. Obviously, the law holds accountable those who intentionally, unlawfully harm others. But what about times when one injures another but didn't mean to do so? What about injuries resulting from accidents? The law also provides recourse for those who are injured by people who did not intend the harm they caused. This area of law is referred to as *negligence*, the law of unintentional torts.

Negligence law exists to ensure those injured unintentionally can obtain a remedy. Imagine a world where the only people who can be compensated for injury are those who can prove the person committing the harm did so on purpose. Such a world would give a free pass to anyone whose unintentional recklessness/carelessness causes harm. Obviously, this is not the world we live in, and we have negligence law to thank.

Unlike the intentional torts we just learned about, with unique names for each type of tort, the term *negligence* covers a multitude of types of carelessness. Though carelessness/recklessness can occur in so many forms, the term *negligence* covers them all. The tort is negligence, and no matter what form the careless behavior takes, if the elements of the tort are present, the careless behavior is called negligence.

And what are the elements of the tort of negligence? There are four: duty of reasonable care, breach of duty, proximate cause, and injury.

DUTY OF REASONABLE CARE

The first element a plaintiff suing for negligence must prove is the defendant owed her a duty of reasonable care. This element tells us there is a

© Jinga, 2014. Used under license from Shutterstock, Inc.

category of people who are potential plaintiffs: ones who are reasonably foreseeable victims of a defendant's carelessness. Stated differently, the people who could reasonably be injured as a result of a careless act are those to whom the careless actor owes a duty of reasonable care. So, if I'm teaching a class full of students, each student is a reasonably foreseeable victim of any carelessness I might exhibit. If I swing a baseball bat in a circular motion as hard as I can, I put at risk of injury all of the students in my class. If the bat slips out of my hand, it could end up hitting any of the students. Thus, I owe my classroom of students a duty to teach class with reasonable care. (Notice the duty is one of *reasonable* care, not perfect/flawless care. More on this later.)

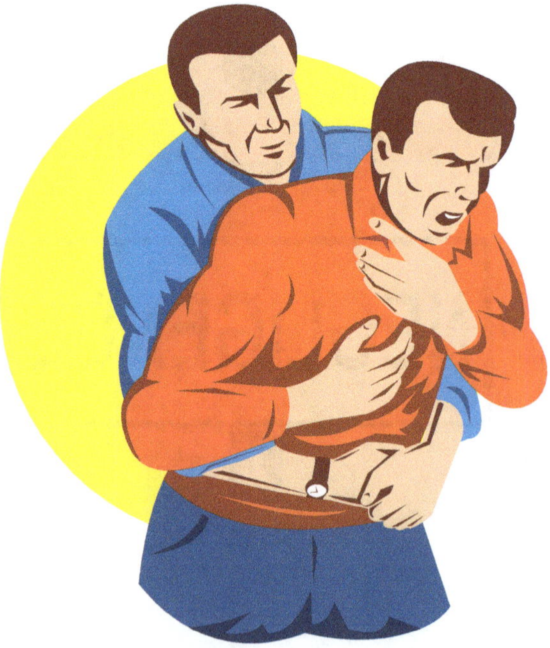

© patrimonio designs ltd, 2014. Used under license from Shutterstock, Inc.

Okay, so, we know we have a duty to act reasonably. Whether teaching class or walking down the sidewalk or boarding an airplane, we owe a duty to do so reasonably to each person who is a reasonable foreseeable victim of any careless behavior on our part. But what about someone in distress/peril? Do we owe that person a duty to intervene? If someone is choking, do we have a duty to attempt the Heimlich maneuver? If someone is on fire, do we have a duty to attempt to douse the fire? The answer: it depends.

grandmother sued Over Dog Bite

at Cottage Hills home

Ann Maher

Dog bite injuries accounted for about one-third of homeowner liability insurance claims paid out in 2012 – costing over $489 million – according to a report released by the Insurance Information Institute (III) in December.

While dog bite lawsuits don't account for that percentage of cases filed in local courts, they are routinely filed.

One of the latest such cases filed in Madison County pits the plaintiff against her grandmother and uncle.

Christie Helminger filed suit against Maria Tidwell and Edward Tidwell on March 18 in Madison County Circuit Court.

Helminger claims she was lawfully on the property of Maria Tidwell at 1338 1st St. in Cottage Hills on March 22, 2012, whereupon opening the garage door a dog charged her, biting her on the calves and causing a permanent scar.

She claims the dog, whose breed was not identified in the suit, was not in the garage during previous visits.

Represented by Joseph R. Reames of Wood River, Helminger is seeking in excess of $50,000 in damages. She claims her grandmother and uncle were in violation of the Animal Control Act which in relevant part provides:

"If a dog or other animal, without provocation, attacks, attempts to attack, or injures any person who is peaceably conducting himself or herself in any place where he or she may lawfully be, the owner of such dog or other animal is liable for civil damages to such person for the full amount of the injury proximately caused thereby."

Helminger claims she endured pain, suffering, mental anguish, loss of normal life, disfigurement, injuries both internal and external and expenditures for the cost of healthcare, past and future, all of which will continue. She claims her grandmother owed her a duty to exercise reasonable care and caution in owning and keeping the dog so as not to cause injury.

According to the III study, dog bite claim value between 2003-2012 increased 51.4 percent, rising from $324.2 million in 2003 to $489.7 million in 2012. The average cost per claim increased 55.3 percent in the same period from $19,162 in 2003 to $29,752 in 2012.

Generally, we have no duty to aid another in distress. So, if I'm at dinner and a nearby patron starts to choke, I can keep eating my Cobb salad, without fear of getting sued by the choker. If I pass by someone aflame, I can keep walking, without fear of getting sued. *But the person is choking! How can you sit there eating a salad? But the person is on fire! How can you just walk on by?* How can this be? Why is this the general rule? Discuss with a classmate.

Though there is no general duty to come to the aid of someone in peril, the law does impose such a duty on certain people. For example, a duty to rescue exists for people who have a special relationship with the one in peril. For example, a parent would have a duty to aid her child in distress. Also, a duty to rescue exists for people who place another in peril. If I set you on fire, I cannot then say, "*Well, I'd put out the fire, but I have no duty to do so.*" I most certainly do have a duty to rescue, since I am the reason you are on fire! There are other limited instances in which a court might impose a duty to rescue, but the duty to aid another in distress is the exception, not the rule.

BREACH OF DUTY

Once a plaintiff proves the defendant owed her a duty of reasonable care, she must prove the defendant failed to live up to that duty. In other words, she must prove the defendant's action was unreasonable, under the circumstances.

Whether a certain act is unreasonable is a more complicated inquiry than you might think. What is unreasonable to you might not be unreasonable to me. What is careless/reckless to you might not be careless/reckless to me. The inquiry is subjective, and the issue is the fact finder's to decide. But how does a jury (if the fact finder is a jury) decide whether a certain act is unreasonable, under the circumstances? Does a judge simply tell the jury, "*Well, it's up to you. Was the defendant's act unreasonable?*" Is that all a jury has as guidance? Certainly not.

Fact finders employ what is referred to as the *reasonable-person test* (RPT): Was the defendant's act something a reasonable person would have done? If so, no breach of duty. If not, breach of duty. Note the test asks whether a *reasonable* person would have committed the act. The test doesn't ask whether a *perfect/flawless* person would have committed the act. The standard is one of reasonable care, not perfect/flawless care. What the defendant did might not have been conducted with utmost care, but so long as his action was reasonable, he did not breach his duty.

The RPT is a test calling for considering any and all relevant factors or circumstances that contributed to the act. Such consideration not only gives the fact finder guidance; it also leads to more just outcomes. Consider this scenario: Wanda is shopping at a crowded grocery store. As she emerges from one of the shopping aisles, she is knocked to the ground by Jim, who was sprinting past the aisle. Okay, pause. RPT: Would a reasonable person sprint through a crowded grocery store? If all we focus on is the act, we would likely say it is not reasonable to sprint through a crowded grocery store.

But the RPT does not just focus on the act. The RPT calls for the fact finder to consider the circumstances surrounding the act. For example, what if the reason Jim was sprinting through the store was that another man was trying to kill him, chasing him with a gun or knife or other weapon? How about the RPT now? Is it reasonable to flee from a person trying to kill you in a crowded grocery store? I venture to say your answer would change, yes? If someone were trying to kill you, you would not stand in the store and say to yourself, *"Well, I'd really like to run away so I can avoid being harmed or killed; but I'd better not, because I'd hate to run into someone and then be sued for negligence."* The emergency created by the would-be attacker is a factor/circumstance for the fact finder to consider. For any breach inquiry, the RPT asks whether the defendant, given all of the relevant factors/circumstances surrounding the act, acted reasonably.

CAUSATION

Once a plaintiff proves the defendant owed her a duty of reasonable care and the defendant failed to live up to that duty, the plaintiff must prove the defendant's unreasonable act legally caused her injury. To do so, a plaintiff must prove *factual (cause-in-fact) causation* and *legal causation*. Let's learn about each.

Depending on the particular jurisdiction, factual causation (also referred to as *actual causation*) can be established by proving either *but-for causation* or *substantial-factor causation*. But-for causation means the plaintiff's injury would not have occurred but for the defendant's carelessness. Stated differently, but for the defendant's breach, plaintiff would not have been injured. Meanwhile, substantial-factor causation requires more than a showing that the injury would not have occurred but for the carelessness; it requires a showing the carelessness was a substantial reason for the injury.

California uses the substantial-factor test. In *Mitchell v. Gonzalez,* 54 Cal. 3d 1041, 819 P.2d 872, 1 Cal. Rptr. 2d 913 (1991), the Supreme Court of California laid down the rule. The following are selections from the Court's opinion:[6]

> *In this case we decide whether BAJI No. 3.75,fn. 1 the so-called proximate cause instruction, which contains a "but for" test of cause in fact, should continue to be given in this state, or whether it should be disapproved in favor of BAJI No. 3.76, the so-called legal cause instruction, which employs the "substantial factor" test of cause in fact.*
>
> *We granted review in this case to determine whether courts should continue to instruct juries on cause in fact using BAJI No. 3.75 in light of the frequent criticism of that instruction. We conclude that the Court of Appeal was correct and that BAJI No. 3.75 should be disapproved.*
>
> *We believe the foregoing authorities properly criticize BAJI No. 3.75 for being conceptually and grammatically deficient. The deficiencies may mislead jurors, causing them, if they can glean the instruction's meaning despite the grammatical flaws, to focus improperly on the cause that is spatially or temporally closest to the harm.*
>
> *[4] In contrast, the "substantial factor" test, incorporated in BAJI No. 3.76 and developed by the Restatement Second of*

6. http://law.justia.com/cases/california/cal3d/54/1041.html

Torts, section 431 (com. to BAJI No. 3.76) has been comparatively free of criticism and has even received praise. "As an instruction submitting the question of causation in fact to the jury in intelligible form, it appears impossible to improve on the Restatement's 'substantial factor [test.]' " (Prosser, Proximate Cause in California, supra, 38 Cal.L.Rev. 369, 421.) It is "sufficiently intelligible to any layman to furnish an adequate guide to the jury, and it is neither possible nor desirable to reduce it to lower terms." (Id., at p. 379.)fn. 7

Moreover, the "substantial factor" test subsumes the "but for" test. "If the conduct which is claimed to have caused the injury had nothing at all to do with the injuries, it could not be said that the conduct was a factor, let alone a substantial factor, in the production of the injuries." (Doupnik v. General Motors Corp. (1990) 225 Cal. App. 3d 849, 861 [275 Cal. Rptr. 715].)

[1c] The continued use of BAJI No. 3.75 as an instruction on cause in fact is unwise. The foregoing amply demonstrates that BAJI No. 3.75 is grammatically confusing and conceptually misleading. Continued use of this instruction will likely cause needless appellate litigation regarding the propriety of the instructions in particular cases. Use of BAJI No. 3.76 will avoid much of the confusion inherent in BAJI No. 3.75. It is intelligible and easily applied. We therefore conclude that BAJI No. 3.75, the so-called proximate cause instruction, should be disapproved and that the court erred when it refused to give BAJI No. 3.76 and instead gave BAJI No. 3.75. (See ante, p. 1052, fn. 7.)

Establishing factual causation (whether but-for or substantial-factor), however, is not enough to establish causation. Can you understand why? Let's look at an example using but-for causation. Imagine I commit a careless act. Now, imagine that my careless act sets in motion a chain of events that, 20 years later, results in an injury to you. Had I not acted carelessly, the chain of events that ultimately led to your injury would not have occurred. Is but-for causation present? Absolutely. Should I be held liable for your injury? Of course not. But-for causation alone does not equal legal causation. If but-for causation were all it took to establish legal causation, each of us would be liable for any carelessness on our part that changes the course of history, so to speak, and eventually results in an injury we, otherwise, have nothing to do with. The law does not hold us accountable for injuries too disconnected or remote from us to qualify as being predominantly our fault.

Therefore, in addition to factual causation, a plaintiff must prove *legal causation*. Given the plaintiff's injury would not have occurred but for the defendant's careless act (or that the carelessness was a substantial factor in producing the injury), should the defendant be held legally liable (responsible) for the plaintiff's injury? This question is what *proximate causation* is all about. Consider this definition of proximate cause, from the Legal Information Institute:

> *An actual cause that is also legally sufficient to support liability. Although many actual causes can exist for an injury (e.g., a pregnancy that led to the defendant's birth), the law does not attach liability to all the actors responsible for those causes. The likelihood of calling something a proximate cause increases as the cause becomes more direct and more necessary for the injury to occur.*[7]

Go back to our example above. I set in motion a chain of events that injures you 20 years later. Yes, you would not have been injured but for my carelessness. But my carelessness is not legally sufficient to justify holding me responsible for your injury. So, factual causation is present, but legal causation is not. Why not? Because the injury 20 years later was not a reasonably-foreseeable injury; and the law does not hold careless actors responsible for injuries not reasonably foreseeable at the time of the careless act. The *reasonably-foreseeable test* is the most common test for establishing proximate causation.

Obviously, the closer the carelessness is to the injury, the more likely causation is present. Imagine I repeatedly swing a baseball bat in a circular motion (I'm trying to stretch my shoulder!). However, I don't notice you are standing nearby. As I swing the bat, I get closer and closer to you and eventually strike you with the swinging bat, injuring you. Here, both factual and legal causation are present. Factual: would you not have been injured but for my careless swinging of the bat? Yes. Legal: is my carelessness close enough to the injury to justify legal liability? Was it reasonably foreseeable to me I might strike someone nearby? Yes.

7. http://www.law.cornell.edu/wex/proximate_cause.

And what about an example using substantial-factor causation? Is it possible to prove the defendant's carelessness was a substantial factor in producing the plaintiff's injury without also proving the injury was reasonably foreseeable? Yes. Consider this: imagine I come home from work and head to my backyard to practice my baseball swing. Unbeknownst to me, while I arrived home, a trespasser climbed the fence of my backyard. When the trespasser saw my car pull into the driveway, he hid in the doghouse in my backyard. While practicing my swing in the backyard, the trespasser decides to emerge from the doghouse, since he is claustrophobic in the tiny doghouse. I have no idea he is in the doghouse. As he climbs out of the doghouse, which is behind me, my practice swing strikes the trespasser, injuring him. Is my swing a substantial reason for his injury? Of course. But should I be held liable? Certainly not, because his injury is not one I should have reasonably anticipated at the time I swung the bat. Get it?

These examples are fairly straightforward. Other scenarios are more difficult. Where to draw the line between holding a defendant liable and not holding a defendant liable is a fact-specific inquiry for the fact finder; and the causation rules fact finders operate under are determined by the particular jurisdiction.

INJURY

In addition to each of the elements listed above, a plaintiff suing for negligence must prove actual injury. All things being equal, this element is much easier to prove. Injury worthy of compensation could be physical injury and/or economic (pecuniary) damage. If I carelessly swing a baseball bat, and the bat hits you and your laptop, I am on the hook for the amount of damage to you and your laptop. A plaintiff can prove the amount of his injury via, for example, a medical bill and laptop-repair bill.

Historically, if a plaintiff also suffered emotional injury, she could recover damages for such emotional injury; a recent trend, however, is to allow (in limited cases) recovery for purely emotional injury. In other words, depending on the law of the respective state, a plaintiff might be able to recover for emotional injury, without proving any physical or economic injury.

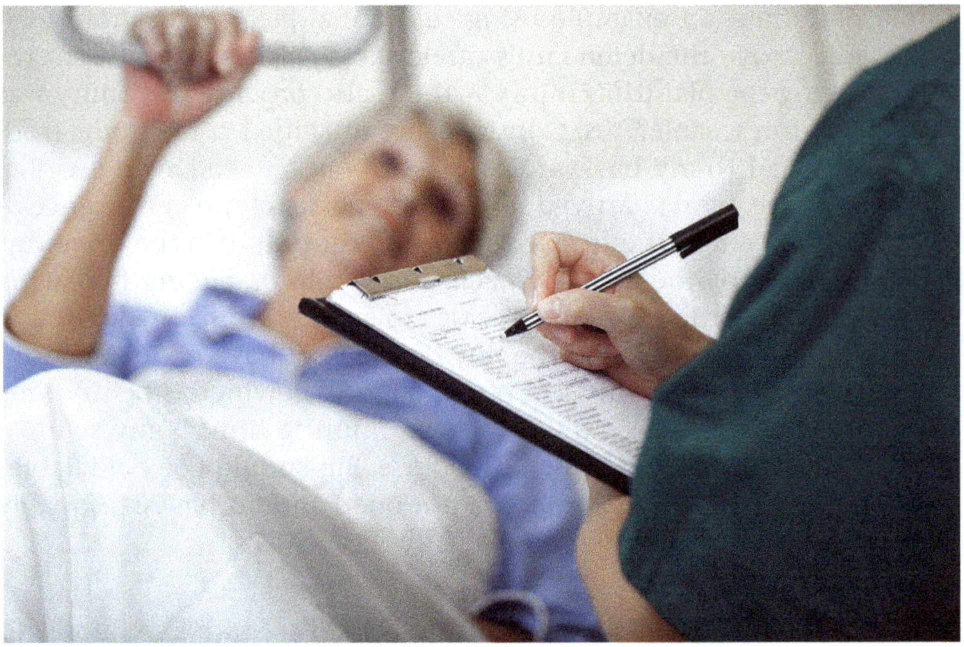

© racorn, 2014. Used under license from Shutterstock, Inc.

DEFENSES TO NEGLIGENCE

Now that we know the elements of the tort of negligence, let's learn some defenses to negligence. Though it might be the case a defendant has nothing with which to counter a plaintiff's negligence lawsuit, sometimes a defendant can respond to a negligence lawsuit with evidence that allows him to avoid liability partially or altogether.

One potential defense is the *statute of limitations* (SOL), which is the time the law of the respective allows one to sue for negligence. If the person doesn't sue before the SOL expires, then she loses the right to sue. In other words, she had her chance to sue, but she waited too long.

The SOL for negligence (and all other torts, for that matter) varies among the states, but the typical SOL for negligence claims is two years. The two-year period begins when the negligence occurs (i.e., when the claim arises). For example, here I go again, wildly swinging my baseball bat. Though I don't mean to, I hit you with the bat, injuring you. If this scenario took place in a state with a two-year SOL for negligence, you have two years from the time I carelessly struck you with the baseball bat to sue me for negligence. If you sue me, say, four years after I hit you with the bat, I will assert SOL as a defense. By doing so, I am not

trying to prove I wasn't negligent; rather, I am asserting you no longer have the legal ability to sue me for such negligence.

Another possible defense arises when the injury to a plaintiff is not entirely the defendant's fault. In cases of *shared liability*, the defendant will defend himself with evidence the plaintiff's injury is partially her own fault. If both parties are partially to blame for the plaintiff's injury, will the plaintiff be able to obtain damages? If so, will she get full damages or just partial damages? The answers depend on where the lawsuit is filed, as states' laws on shared liability vary.

Several rules of shared-liability recovery exist (and even within a state, it is possible that the rule of recovery depends on the type of claim). For our examination, I'll divide the rules into two types.

One type is *contributory negligence* (also referred to as *pure contributory negligence*). Followed by just a handful of jurisdictions,[8] contributory negligence doesn't allow a plaintiff to recover damages if she contributed to her injury. In other words, if a plaintiff was even a little negligent, she cannot recover. Even if the defendant was much more negligent than the plaintiff, the rule of contributory negligence acts as a complete bar to recovery of damages. Most states view this rule as unduly harsh to injured plaintiffs and, as such, eschew this rule.

The other type of recovery rule is *comparative negligence* (also referred to as *comparative fault*). In one form or another, most states follow the rule of comparative negligence, which allows a plaintiff to recover damages but which reduces the damages in proportion to the plaintiff's degree of negligence. In other words, if a plaintiff is 25% responsible for her injury and the defendant 75% responsible, the plaintiff can recover 75% of the amount of her injury. She will not be compensated for the 25% of the damages attributable to her own negligence/fault.

---

8. Alabama, Maryland, North Carolina, Virginia, and the District of Columbia follow the rule of contributory negligence, generally. Meanwhile, Indiana follows the rule of contributory negligence for only certain types of claims.

maryland's highest
Court Upholds Contributory Negligence Law

By Associated Press

Maryland's highest court on Tuesday upheld a law that says people cannot recover damages from an injury in a negligence case if they are found to be partly at fault.

In a 5-2 ruling, the Court of Appeals declined to change the law of contributory negligence. Retired Judge John Eldridge noted that attempts to change the law in the Legislature have failed consistently.

"For this court to change the common law and abrogate the contributory negligence defense in negligence actions, in the face of the General Assembly's repeated refusal to do so, would be totally inconsistent with the court's long-standing jurisprudence," Eldridge wrote.

The law was last reviewed by the Maryland court 30 years ago. From 1966 to 1982, the Maryland General Assembly considered 21 bills seeking to change the contributory negligence standard, and none of the measures were enacted.

Judge Glenn Harrell, writing in dissent along with recently retired Judge Robert Bell, compared the law to "a dinosaur."

"With the force of a modern asteroid strike, this court should render, in the present case, this dinosaur extinct," Harrell wrote.

Harrell noted that only Maryland, Virginia, Alabama, North Carolina and the District of Columbia still have the law. Harrell wrote that 46 states use a comparative negligence system that reduces the damages an injured person can receive in proportion to his or her degree of fault.

"The all-or-nothing consequences of the application of contributory negligence have long been criticized by scholars and commentators," Harrell wrote.

The business community had kept a close eye on the case.

Karen Harned, executive director of the NFIB Small Business Legal Center, praised the ruling. The National Federation of Independent Business filed a brief in the case contending that Maryland's small businesses would be negatively affected at a time when many already are struggling.

"While it is important that businesses take the proper steps to ensure safety on their property, abandoning contributory negligence would have only led to uncertainty, rising insurance premiums and an onslaught of frivolous lawsuits for employers," Harned said in a statement.

The case was brought by a soccer player, James Coleman, who had volunteered to assist in coaching a team of young players in a program of the Soccer Association of Columbia in Howard County.

In 2008, while assisting the coach during practice, he jumped up and grabbed the crossbar of a goal to retrieve a ball. The goal was not anchored, and Coleman fell backward, drawing the weight of the crossbar onto his face. He suffered multiple severe facial fractures. He sued the soccer association. A jury concluded the association was negligent, but it also found that Coleman was negligent, and the trial court entered a judgment in favor of the soccer association.

There are different forms of comparative negligence. Some states (but not most) allow a plaintiff to recover damages even if she is more at fault than the defendant. This rule is referred to as *pure comparative negligence*. For example, if the fact finder determines the plaintiff's injury is 95% her own fault and only 5% the defendant's fault, she can still recover 5% of the damages. Just as most states view contributory negligence as unfair to plaintiffs, most states view pure comparative negligence as unfair to defendants.

Most states strike a balance between contributory negligence and pure comparative negligence. In these states, plaintiffs cannot recover damages if they are more at fault for their own injuries than the defendants they sue. Makes sense, right? If you are more to blame for your injury than I am, why should I have to pay you? Some of these states allow recovery if the defendant is more at fault (e.g., plaintiff 49% responsible, defendant 51% responsible), while others allow recovery if the parties are equally at fault (50/50). Whether the former or the latter, what these states' rules have in common is they do not award damages to a plaintiff more at fault than the defendant.

Another negligence defense — and a nice segue to the next chapter, which covers the law of contracts — is a defense rooted in contract: *assumption of risk*. We'll learn much more in the following chapter; but, for now, suffice it to say a person who is informed of a risk of a particular activity and who nonetheless freely chooses to engage in the activity assumes the risk involved. In essence, the one who assumes a risk consents (via contract) to the possible risks involved in the activity and, therefore, might be barred from recovering for injuries sustained therefrom.

And, with that, let's proceed to the law of contracts.

chapter 9 CONTRACTS

In Chapter 8, we learned about torts, a major area of common law. Another major area of common law is the law of contracts. Like tort law, contracts law varies from state to state. Each state's state courts, over time, have formed a body of common law establishing the laws of contracts in their respective state. Although contracts law is similar among the states, there are variations. So, to learn precisely the laws of contracts in a given state, one must consult the case law of that state.

In this chapter, we will learn how contracts are formed, various ways contracts are terminated, and other rules of contracts law. First, however, we need to understand what a contract is. Consider the following definitions:

An agreement creating obligations enforceable by law – Legal Information Institute[1]

1. http://www.law.cornell.edu/wex/contract

A binding agreement between two or more persons or parties
– Merriam-Webster.com[2]

An agreement enforceable by law – Dictionary.com[3]

Simply defined, a *contract* is a legally binding agreement. Let's examine this three-word definition into two parts: the noun (*agreement*) and the noun's modifiers (*legally binding*). An agreement is a private matter, by which I mean a court is not involved in forming an agreement. By itself, an agreement is not legally binding, meaning it is not something a court will enforce. Once an agreement becomes legally binding, a court is there to enforce the rights of the parties. So, an agreement is a private matter, but once it becomes it becomes legally binding (i.e., becomes a contract), the law is there as security for the parties. So, what constitutes an agreement, and what makes an agreement legally binding? In other words, how does an agreement become a contract? Before we find out, let's learn some important terms and concepts that will serve us well throughout this chapter.

2. http://www.merriam-webster.com/dictionary/contract
3. http://dictionary.reference.com/browse/contract

CONTRACT CLASSIFICATIONS

The classifications below are not formal names. They are my way of explaining certain aspects of contracts. Any given contract will fit into one of the types listed under each classification. In other words, the classifications are not mutually exclusive.

LEGAL STATUS

- **Valid**
  A *valid contract* is one in which all of the contractual-formation elements are present. Later in this chapter, we will learn the four elements typically required to form a contract. A valid contract has all four of these elements present. A valid contract is enforceable against all parties to the contract. Each party is completely bound to the terms of the contract.
- **Void**
  A *void contract* is not a contract, because it is one that does not contain all of the required elements of formation. For example, one of the four required elements is that the contract's purpose be legal. So, a contract to rob a bank would lack the legality element and would, thus, be void. A void contract is not enforceable against either party. No party is bound to the terms of the agreement.
- **Voidable**
  A *voidable contract* is a special type of contract in which a party (or both parties) to the contract is not fully bound. Such a situation will arise when a party to a contract has less-than-full mental capacity to enter a contract, in the eyes of the law (e.g., a child), or when a party to a contract's consent to the contract is not genuine, in the eyes of the law (e.g., consent given under duress). For such parties, the contract entered into is voidable at their option, meaning they have the ability, for a period of time, to walk away from their contractual obligations, without breaching the contract (without legal penalty). Whereas a void contract never exists, a voidable contract exists but with the possibility that, for one or both parties, the contract will end before full performance, without penalty.

- **Unenforceable**
  An *unenforceable contract* starts as a valid contract, but due to some operation of law (e.g., change in law, running of the statute of limitations for breach of contract), the contract is no longer one either party can legally enforce against the other. Neither party can take the other to court, to force the latter to be bound by the contract's terms. For example, Bert and Ernie form a contract on Monday. The contract calls for Bert to pay Ernie $100 to build a windmill in Bert's backyard on Friday. On Tuesday, the day after the contract is formed, the legislature of the state where the contract is formed outlaws the building of personal windmills. On Monday, Bert and Ernie formed a valid contract. On Tuesday, the purpose of the contract (building a windmill) became illegal. Thus, on Tuesday, their valid contract became an unenforceable contract. Each party is freed from his contractual obligations, and neither can take the other to court to have the terms of the contract enforced.

METHOD OF FORMATION

- **Express**
  An *express contract* is formed by the words (oral or written) of the parties. The terms of the parties' agreement are stated upfront and are, thus, known at the time of execution. Inferring an agreement from the conduct of the parties is not required, because the parties expressly agree to bind themselves to one another. An oral contract is an express contract: the parties speak the terms of their agreement. A written contract is an express contract: the parties write the terms of their agreement.
- **Implied (a.k.a. Implied-in-Fact)**
  An *implied contract* is formed not by the express words (oral or written) of the parties but rather by conduct of the parties. In other words, the parties' conduct indicates their mutual intent to be bound to one another. Many everyday errands we run involve implied contracts: eating in a restaurant, getting into a taxi, hopping in a barber's chair for a haircut, etc. In such scenarios, we don't expressly state to the other party we agree to pay for goods supplied or services rendered. Rather, our conduct reveals to the other side (and, if it comes to it, a court) our assent to the transaction. Imagine Connor takes a shirt to his local dry cleaner. He hands his shirt to the worker behind the counter and the worker hands him a claim ticket. Neither

speaks to the other during their interaction. Neither stated any contractual terms. Neither expressly indicated to the other intent to be bound. However, mutual intent can be inferred by the parties' actions toward one another. In *Baltimore & Ohio Railroad Co. v. United States,*[4] the Supreme Court of the United States defined *implied contract* as follows: *[a]n agreement 'implied in fact' founded upon a meeting of minds, which, although not embodied in an express contract, is inferred, as a fact, from conduct of the parties showing, in the light of the surrounding circumstances, their tacit understanding.*[5]

- **Quasi (a.k.a. Implied-in-Law)**
  A *quasi contract* is not a contract formed (expressly or implied) by the parties. Rather, it is a contract created by a court where a contract does not, otherwise, exist. Situations arise where, though a contract was never formed between the parties, a court feels it necessary to impose obligations against one of the parties, in order to be equitable. In other words, a court feels one party is being harmed by the relationship and is worthy of some sort of remedy (e.g., restitution). A party could be harmed by performing services under an oral agreement, when the law of the given state requires such an agreement to be in writing, to be enforceable. The parties, thus, never truly formed a contract, but it would be unfair not to order the non-performing to pay the performing party for services rendered. If payment were not ordered by a court, the non-performing party would be unjustly enriched, at the expense of the other party.

WHEN CONTRACT IS FORMED

- **Bilateral**
  An *offeror* is one who makes an offer. An *offeree* is one to whom an offer is made (and, thus, one who has the choice to accept an offer or not). A *bilateral offer* is one seeking a return promise from an offeree. Thus, a *bilateral contract* is created by an exchange of promises. Restated: a bilateral contract is formed when promises are swapped (when a mutual agreement is made). For example, Granger says to Zoe, *"I agree to pay you $50 if you agree to wash my car at noon tomorrow."* Granger makes a promise to Zoe. Granger seeks a return promise from Zoe. If Zoe

4. *Baltimore & Ohio Railroad Co. v. United States*, 261 U.S. 592 (1923), http://supreme.justia.com/cases/federal/us/261/592/case.html
5. *Id.* at 597.

agrees (accepts Granger's offer), the two have swapped promises. When they do, they obligate themselves to future performance (Granger obligates himself to pay Zoe for washing his car, while Zoe obligates herself to washing Granger's car). They have a contract, even though performance is to occur later. Thus, if Zoe doesn't wash Granger's car at noon tomorrow, she breaches their contract. Likewise, if Zoe washes Granger's car at noon tomorrow and Granger refuses to pay, Granger breaches their contract.

- **Unilateral**
  A *unilateral offer* is not one in which the offeror seeks a return promise from the offeree. And, in fact, an offeree's return promise would not create a contract. Rather, a unilateral offer seeks full performance by the offeree of the act requested by the offeror. So, whereas a bilateral contract is *promise for promise*, a unilateral contract is *promise for performance*. For example, a unilateral offer is made when Granger says to Zoe, *"If you wash my car at noon tomorrow, I will pay you $50."* Granger doesn't want Zoe to agree/promise to wash his car; he wants her to wash his car. As such, if Zoe promises Granger she will wash his car at noon tomorrow, she does not accept his offer. No contract is created. Zoe is not obligated to wash Granger's car. In other words, if Zoe doesn't wash Granger's car at noon tomorrow, Granger cannot sue Zoe for breach of contract. Why not? Because they never formed a contract. To accept a unilateral offer (and, thus, form a contract), the offeree must fully perform the requested act. So, unless Zoe washes Granger's car at noon tomorrow, no contract will be formed. However, if Zoe washes Granger's car at noon tomorrow (which she is not obligated to do, as she was when she accepted a bilateral offer in the example above), she accepts Granger's unilateral offer, and Granger is obligated to pay.

CONTRACT FORMATION

A valid contract is comprised of four elements: *agreement, consideration, legal capacity,* and *legality of purpose.* All four elements must be present, in order to have a legally binding agreement. Let's examine each.

AGREEMENT

An *agreement* is a covenant between or among parties. An agreement is often referred to as a *meeting of the minds,* meaning the parties are in harmony about the nature of their covenant. If the parties' intentions about their dealing are the same, there is a meeting of the minds. There is mutual understanding/agreement.

There are two elements to an agreement: *offer* and *acceptance.* An offer not accepted cannot become an agreement, and one cannot accept something not offered. Thus, both offer and acceptance are required to form an agreement.

An offer is comprised of three elements: (1) apparent, present intent to make an offer; (2) inclusion of material terms; and (3) legal communication to the offeree.

First, the offeror must appear to be genuine in his immediate/present intent to make an offer, in his intent to be bound by the terms of his offer. In other words, the offeror's apparent intent (in the view of a reasonable offeree), not his actual intent, is what matters. So, for example, if Fred writes an offer to Alex, and it reasonably appears Fred is genuinely making Alex an offer, the requisite intent is present, even if Fred actually has no intention to follow through. Perhaps Fred is actually joking, but if it is not reasonably apparent he is joking, Fred's intent to make an offer is valid.

Second, an offer must contain definite material terms. In other words, the major terms must be included, such that the offeree understands what is being offered. For example, if Fred sends Alex an offer stating, *"I hereby make you an offer;"* are the terms of Fred's offer sufficient? No. Why not? Because Alex does not know any specifics of the offer. Alex does not know what it is Fred is offering. By contrast, if Fred states, *"I offer to paint your house for $1,000,"* the offer contains certain terms. Alex knows what Fred is offering. The major matters are covered. We know the parties (Fred and Alex), we know the subject matter (painting Alex's house), and we know the price to be paid for painting the house ($1,000). Not every detail must be contained in the offer (for example, we don't know from the offer whether Fred will paint Alex's house with his right hand or his left hand), but Alex knows enough to ascertain what Fred is offering. So long as the major/material items are included in the offer, the element is met.

Third, the offeror must legally communicate his offer to the offeree. Notice the word *legally*. An offer need not be *actually* communicated to the offeree, in order to be valid. If the offeror makes a reasonable attempt to convey his offer to the offeree, a legal communication has occurred, even if an offer has been actually communicated. Perhaps the offer has arrived in the offeree's mailbox, but the offeree has yet to read the correspondence. Perhaps the offeror left an offer in the offeree's voicemail, but the offeree has yet to listen to the voicemail.

Perhaps the offeror gave the offer to the offeree's agent, but the offeree's agent has yet to communicate the offer to the offeree. In each case, an actual communication to the offeree has not occurred, but a legal communication has.

If each of these three elements is present, a valid offer has been made. Once a valid offer has been made, the offer is capable of being accepted by the offeree. But before we examine acceptance, there is more to say about an offer.

One of the common law's rules about offers is, once made, an offer can be revoked by the offeror before the offeree accepts the offer. In other words, if an offeree has not accepted an offer, the offeror can take back his offer. This is referred to as a *revocation* by the offeror. To be valid, a revocation must be legally communicated to the offeree. Once revoked, an offer is no longer capable of being accepted by the offeree. A revocation cancels an offer. The offer is no longer valid. However, the moment an offeree accepts an offer, the offeror may not revoke his offer.

There is, however, an exception to the common-law rule an offeror can revoke his offer before the offer is accepted. The exception is what is referred to as an *option contract*. If the offeror accepts payment (or something else of value) in return for keeping open the offer for a stated period of time, the offeror cannot revoke his offer during that time. For example, imagine Fred makes a valid offer to Alex. Alex wants time to think about it, but Fred has no obligation to leave open his offer. He can revoke his offer any time before Alex accepts it. But if Alex offers Fred, say, $10 to leave open his offer until noon the following day, and Fred accepts the money (he is under no obligation to accept the money), Fred cannot revoke his offer before noon the following day. Alex has literally bought herself time to consider Fred's offer, free from the possibility Fred will revoke his offer. Note, however, once noon tomorrow rolls around, the option expires, and we're back to the common-law rule: Fred can immediately revoke his offer, provided Alex has not already accepted it. Got it?

We've covered how an offeror can make a valid offer and how an offer can be revoked. Before examining how the offeree can accept an offer, we need to learn two other possible responses by the offeree to an offer: *rejection* and *counteroffer*.

A *rejection* is the opposite of an acceptance. The offeree does not agree to the offer. The offeree does not agree to enter into a contract with the offeror. In fact, he does the opposite: he expressly turns down the offer. A rejection terminates the offer. Once rejected, the offeror is no longer bound to the offer. So, if Fred offers to wash Alex's car for $100 and Alex replies, *"No,"* the offer is terminated. If Alex, moments later, says, *"Never mind, I accept your offer,"* there is no agreement. Why not? Because when she said, *No*, she terminated the offer. There was no longer a valid offer to accept. Now, in reality, Fred will take the deal, but he is actually accepting a new offer from Alex, since her previous rejection terminated his original offer. In other words, they swap places: Alex becomes the offeror and Fred the offeree.

A *counteroffer* changes the offer in a material way. It is as if the offeree says to the offeror, *"I don't accept your offer, but here is an offer for you."* For example, if Fred offers to wash Alex's car for $100 and Alex replies, *"I'll pay you $50 to wash my car,"* Alex counteroffers Fred's original offer. A counteroffer rejects the original offer and makes a new offer (in which case, the parties swap roles: Alex, the original offeree, becomes the offeror, when she counteroffers). If Alex's reply differs from Fred's offer on price, subject matter, the parties, or anything else a court would consider material, under the circumstances, her reply is a counteroffer. For example, price: *"You can wash my car but for $90, not $100,"* is a counteroffer. Subject matter: *"Yes, I'll pay you $100 but*

republic airways
Pilots Reject Contract Offer

By Associated Press

Pilots for Republic Airways overwhelmingly rejected a proposed four-year contract that the company said would have put them at or near the top of wages for pilots at regional airlines.

The voting that ended Friday affected more than 2,200 pilots represented by the Teamsters. The union said 85% of ballots cast were against ratification.

Republic Airways Holdings operates Republic Airlines, Chautauqua Airlines and Shuttle America, which operate flights for bigger airlines including Delta Connection, United Express and US Airways Express.

Republic CEO Bryan Bedford said he was disappointed in the vote and would work with the Teamsters to determine its next steps. Union local president Craig Moffatt called the offer inadequate and said the Teamsters would come up with a plan for an acceptable agreement.

Shares of Indianapolis-based Republic fell 38 cents, or 4.1%, to close at $8.88.

The vote came a week after pilots at another regional airline, American Eagle,rejected a proposed 10-year contract despite threats by parent American Airlines Group Inc. that doing so would cause the company to shrink Eagle.

Several regional airlines have said recently that they are struggling to recruit and keep pilots. On Thursday, Silver Airways announced it was doubling its signing bonus for new co-pilots to $12,000 payable over two years.

Pilot unions say pay is too low. The Air Line Pilots Association said average starting pay for a co-pilot at a regional airline is $22,400.

to clean my kitchen, not wash my car," is a counteroffer. The parties: *"I'll pay you $100 for your brother to wash my car,"* is a counteroffer. Again, a counteroffer rejects the offeror's offer and makes a new offer to the original offeror.

So, let's say Fred makes a valid offer to Alex. How does Alex accept the offer? As with an offer, an acceptance must contain certain elements, in order to be valid. Think back to the elements required to form a valid offer: (1) apparent, present intent to make an offer; (2) inclusion of material terms; and (3) legal communication to the offeree. These elements will help us understand the elements of a valid acceptance:

© Ditty_about_summer, 2014. Used under license from Shutterstock, Inc.

(1) apparent, present intent to accept the offer; (2) acceptance, without change, of the offer's material terms; and (3) legal communication to the offeror.

First, the offeree must exhibit an apparent, present intent to accept the offer. No magic language is required (unless the offer states so). Any word(s) and/or action(s) on the part of the offeree that can reasonably be received by the offeror as a genuine intention to accept the offer will suffice. So, what should count, in general? Words like *yes, you have yourself a deal*, and *all right, let's do this!* Actions like a nod of the head, a handshake, and so forth. What will not count? *I'll think about it. Maybe. I'll get back to you. It sounds good to me, but I have to check with my wife.* Any words not revealing a reasonable offeror a genuine intention to presently accept the offer will not suffice.

Second, the offeree must accept the offer, without materially changing the offer. The offeree must agree to the offeror's material terms. Nothing more, nothing less, nothing different. This is known as the *Mirror-Image Rule*. If you put the terms of the offer next to the terms of acceptance, it must be as if the two are looking in the mirror. The terms of the offer and acceptance must be the same. Recall an offer must include certain material terms: parties, subject matter, price, and anything else a court considers material under the circumstances. In other words, the major matters are covered in the offer. Well, the offeree must agree to the major matters. The offeree cannot change a material term, cannot add a material term, and cannot delete a material term. Any one of these would constitute a material change to the offer. In other words, any one of these would constitute a counteroffer and, thus, violate the Mirror-Image Rule. For example, Fred offers to paint the outside of Alex's house for $1,000. Alex replies, *"Yes, I agree to let you paint my house but for $900, not $1,000."* Alex's reply is not an acceptance. Why not? Because it changes a material term (price). Alex's reply is a counteroffer and, thus, violates the Mirror-Image Rule. What if Alex's reply were, *"Great! I will pay you $1,000 to paint the inside of my house."* Acceptance? No. Why not? Because the offer was to paint the *outside* of Alex's house, and Alex's reply was that Fred could paint the *inside* of her house. As such, Alex's reply changed a material term (subject matter). Thus, Alex's reply is a counteroffer and, thus, violates the Mirror-Image Rule.

Third, Alex must legally communicate her acceptance to Fred. As was the case with an offer, actual communication is not required (unless the offer states it is). So, Alex could tell Fred's authorized agent/representative she accepts. Alex could leave a voicemail on Fred's phone. Alex could put her written acceptance in Fred's hand. If Alex makes a reasonable attempt, under the circumstances, to convey her acceptance to Fred, she legally communicates her acceptance.

However, it is possible for Alex to accept Fred's offer *even before* she legally communicates her acceptance to him. Offers, revocations, rejections, and counteroffers are valid when legally communicated to the other party. The same is true for acceptances, but the common law contains a special rule allowing certain acceptances to be valid *prior* to legal communication. This rule, known as the *Mailbox Rule* or the *Reasonable-Medium Rule,* applies to *acceptances only*. It does not apply to offers, revocations, rejections, and counteroffers. So, acceptances are valid when legally communicated *but maybe sooner.*

The Mailbox Rule states an acceptance sent via reasonable medium is valid when dispatched. What is reasonable depends on the circum-

© Aina Jameela, 2014. Used under license from Shutterstock, Inc.

stances and/or the terms of the offer, but if a court feels the acceptance was sent by way of reasonable means, the acceptance was effective (valid) the moment it was sent.

Need an example? Probably so. Here's a simple one: On Monday, Fred mails Alex a valid offer, which stated any acceptance must be in writing. On Tuesday, Alex receives the letter. On Wednesday, Alex goes to the post office and mails an acceptance (accept for now mail is a reasonable medium). On Thursday, the letter is delivered to Fred. On Friday, Fred reads the letter. What do we have here? Actual communication occurs Friday: Fred read Alex's acceptance. Legal communication occurs Thursday: Alex's acceptance is delivered to Fred. So, we know the acceptance is valid Thursday, but since Alex sent her acceptance on Wednesday via reasonable medium, her acceptance is valid on Wednesday, thanks to the Mailbox Rule.

If a court is called upon to decide whether the Mailbox Rule kicked in when Alex mailed the acceptance, the court will likely find mail to be a reasonable medium. Why? First, Fred's offer didn't state mailing an acceptance is unreasonable or that Alex had to, for example, accept in person. Second, Fred's offer was sent via mail, so it is likely reasonable for her to communicate via the same medium. Third, the offer stated any acceptance must be in writing but didn't specify a particular type of writing, so mailing a letter (i.e., a writing) is likely reasonable. Obviously, what is reasonable varies from scenario to scenario, but these are some good rules of thumb.

The beauty of the rule for Alex (offeree) is she locks in the agreement sooner. This takes away Fred's ability to revoke sooner than if Alex's acceptance were not valid until legally communicated. Fred cannot, then, call Alex on Thursday morning, before her acceptance letter is delivered, and take back his offer. Why not? Because she accepted his offer when she mailed it at the post office.

Note, however, an offeror can avoid the Mailbox Rule by, for example, stating in his offer there is no Mailbox Rule (e.g., *To accept this offer, actual communication of acceptance is required.)* or that only certain mediums are reasonable.

Okay, then. Valid offer plus valid acceptance equals valid agreement. We have an agreement. To form a valid contract, what else do we need?

CONSIDERATION

Just having an agreement is not enough to form a contract. Both parties to the agreement must offer each other something of value, or *consideration.* Consideration is the element of contract requiring the parties to exchange things of value. Each side gives up something, in order to receive what the other side gives up. If Ella and Max have an agreement for Ella to play 10 songs on Max's guitar for $100, is there consideration present for both parties? Yes. The agreement calls for each side to give up something, in order to receive what the other gives up. Ella agrees to give up her time and effort. Max agrees to give up $100. This is a bargained-for exchange required to form a contract.

Another way to explain consideration is each side incurs a legal detriment. A person incurs a legal detriment by doing something she has no legal obligation to do or not doing something she has every legal right to do. There is no law requiring Ella to play songs on Max's guitar or requiring Max to pay money to Ella. So, Ella has no legal obligation to play Max's guitar, and Max has no legal obligation to pay money to

Ella. Thus, when the parties agree (for Max to pay Ella $100 to play 10 songs on his guitar), each incurs a legal detriment. And how about the type of legal detriment in which a party promises not to do something she has every legal right to do? Imagine Ella offers Max $100 if he doesn't play his guitar for the next 7 days. Is there consideration on the part of Ella and Max? Yes. Ella's consideration is offering $100, when she has no legal obligation to do so. Max's consideration is not playing his guitar for the next 7 days, when he has every legal right to do so.

Finally, an easy way to understand the concept of consideration: it's not a gift. Generally (with exceptions), a promise to make a gift to another is not enforceable, because only one party (the one promising the gift) gives up something of value. Stated differently, only one party (the one promising the gift) incurs a legal detriment, by promising to do something she has no legal obligation to do. Imagine Ella walks up to Max and promises him $100. Max holds out his hand and says, *"Show me the money!"* Ella then tells Max she has changed her mind and will not pay him the money. Does Max have an enforceable promise (a valid claim for breach of contract)? Certainly not. Why not? Because this was the promise of a gift. Max offered nothing of value. Max incurred no legal detriment. Ella offered consideration ($100), but Max did not. A contract requires consideration on the part of both parties to the transaction. This is referred to as *mutuality of obligation*: both sides have to obligate themselves to the passing of value.

So, each side has to offer something of value, but does the value one party offers have to equal the value the other side offers? The simple answer is *no*. So long as the respective considerations are adequate (referred to as *adequacy of consideration*), they do not have to be equal in value. What each side gives up must be reasonable/sufficient relative to what the other gives up. Consider this scenario: Ella and Max agree Ella will pay Max $20 to wash her car. The going rate for a carwash in their town is $25. In terms of market value, Max offers $25 of value, but Ella offers just $20. So, Ella receives a $25 value, but Max receives only a $20 value. The two sides do not offer equal consideration, but a court would surely find the agreement's considerations to be adequate. Only when an agreement is unconscionable (i.e., grossly unfair/inadequate, shockingly one-sided) with respect to the parties' respective considerations will a court disallow the agreement. Unconscionability is one of the grounds for a court's disallowance

of a contract on grounds of public policy. In essence, a court rules, though there is no law against the terms of the agreement, the court cannot, in good conscience, allow the agreement to stand, on the grounds the agreement is too unfair toward one of the two parties.

An example of when an agreement does not have consideration on both sides is when one side offers to do something she is already legally obligated to do or not do something she is already legally obligated not to do. So, if Ella and Max already have a contract for Max to wash Ella's car for $20, Max cannot start washing the car and then tell Ella he will finish washing the car for an additional $5 (for a total of $25). Max is already contractually obligated to wash Ella's car for $20, so he cannot offer his pre-existing obligation as consideration for more money. Also, Max offers Ella no consideration when he says to her, *"If you pay me $50, I won't punch you in the face."* Max is already legally obligated not to punch Ella (this is the tort of *battery*), so his pre-existing obligation is not sufficient consideration for a promise by Ella to pay him. Makes sense, yes?

As there are with so many common-law rules, there are exceptions to the requirement both parties offer consideration to an agreement. In other words, some gifts are enforceable. We won't cover all of the exceptions to the requirement of mutual consideration, but here is one for you to consider. Promising a gift can result in an obligation to pay when the promisee (i.e., the one to whom the promise is made) justifiably relies on the gift to her detriment. This is referred to as *promissory estoppel* (or *justifiable reliance* or *detrimental reliance*). If Max promises a gift to Ella, and Ella's reasonable/justifiable expectation of the gift causes her to incur expenses or suffer a monetary loss, Max will be on the hook for the reliance damages he causes if he reneges on his promise. Charities are common plaintiffs in legal actions seeking reliance damages, since charities often justifiably rely on gift pledges that are subsequently revoked. Ultimately, whether such plaintiffs receive damages depends on whether their detrimental reliance on the promise of the gift was reasonable, under the circumstances.

Two elements down. Two to go.

LEGAL CAPACITY

To enter into a contract with another, the law requires a person to have sufficient *legal capacity*. This means the person entering the contract understands the nature of a legally binding agreement. The person is of sound enough mind to comprehend she is legally obligating herself, per the terms of the agreement.

When will this element be lacking? Which people are ones who lack sufficient capacity to enter into a contract? Generally, capacity problems come in two forms: *lack of capacity* and *no reality of consent*. The former type involves issues with one's mental capacity. The latter type involves people who possess full capacity but whose consent to the terms of the agreement is otherwise problematic.

Full capacity will usually be lacking for one (or more) of three reasons: age, mental illness, and intoxication.

Some people are too young to possess full mental capacity to enter contracts, in the eyes of the law. These people are referred to as *minors*. In most states, the age of majority (adulthood) is 18; so, in those states, those who are 17 or younger are minors and, thus, lack full legal capacity.

Minors are further divided into those who understand the nature of a contract and those who do not. The former are minors, and the latter are minors of tender years. There is no set age dividing the two. Whether a person 17 or younger is a minor or a minor of tender years depends on the person. The law regards minors of tender years as lacking the capacity to enter into a contract. As such, contracts with such people are *void*. In other words, minors of tender years cannot be parties to contracts. By contrast, contracts with minors (not of tender years) are *voidable* at the option of the minor. This means, at least until the minor reaches the age of majority, she may *disaffirm* (repudiate) the contract, avoiding any future obligation, without having breached the contract. Obviously, a minor's ability to walk away from the contract before completion is a deterrent to an adult's willingness to enter into a contract with minors. As such, an adult/business would typically require a minor's parent(s), or other adult, to sign on to the contract, with the minor.

A person's mental health might also create capacity problems. If a person suffers from mental defect or impairment, such as dementia or a brain injury, the person lacks full legal capacity to enter a contract. If a person's mental illness causes the person to be unable to understand the nature of a legally binding agreement, any contract such person enters into is *voidable* at the person's option. So, for example, should a person with a mental illness enter into a contract to purchase a year's membership in a book-of-the-month club, the person's family could have the contract disaffirmed. Should a person be declared by a court to be legally incompetent (i.e., completely lacking mental capacity), any contract the person enters into without the supervision of his legal guardian is *void*.

Finally, a person can lack full capacity due to intoxication. However, intoxication provides fewer protections (than being a minor or being mentally ill) to parties who wish to be relieved of their contractual obligations. Whereas contracts with minors or the mentally ill are either void or voidable, contracts entered into by one who is intoxicated are either valid or voidable. In order for a contract to be *voidable* at the option of the intoxicated person (and, thus, allow disaffirmance by the intoxicated person), the person must prove to a court her intoxication prevented her from understanding she was entering a contract, that she was legally obligating herself. She must prove she was so affected by a substance (alcohol, drugs) that she was unaware of what she was doing when she entered the contract. Obviously, this can be difficult to prove.

In addition to lack of capacity, capacity problems can arise when one who possesses full capacity consents to an agreement, but the law finds such consent problematic. We can refer to these agreements as ones with *no reality of consent*, and they create contracts voidable at the option of the one whose consent is not real/genuine. Such agreements can result from mistakes (mutual or unilateral), fraud, innocent misrepresentation, duress, and undue influence.

A *mutual mistake* occurs when both parties are mistaken as to the subject matter of their agreement. If the mistake is material (substantially alters the nature of the agreement), either party can have a court refuse to enforce it. If both parties, for example, were independently mistaken in thinking they were transacting for (and, thus, mistaken in setting a price for) the sale/purchase of a painting by Monet when they were actually transacting for a Manet, the parties never had a meeting of the minds about the subject matter of the agreement. It is as if they thought they were dealing with apples when they were actually dealing with oranges. By contrast, a *unilateral mistake* occurs when one party is mistaken about the nature of the agreement, but the other is not. A unilateral mistake will not lead to non-enforcement by a court, unless the non-mistaken party is (or should be) aware the other party is mistaken and takes advantage of the mistaken party, as a result. For example, imagine Peter has a yard sale at his house. One of the items for sale is a painting Roger painted during elementary school. Judy stops by the yard sale, sees the painting, and exclaims, "*Why on earth are you selling this beautiful piece by Picasso?*" Clearly, Judy is mistaken about the painting. She thinks Picasso painted it, but Roger painted it. If Roger doesn't tell Judy he painted the painting and allows her to pay the going rate for a Picasso, Roger takes advantage of Judy's unilateral mistake, to her financial detriment. If Judy subsequently learns the truth, she can head to court to have the sale nullified.

Fraud is misleading another intentionally (on purpose). *Innocent misrepresentation* is misleading another unintentionally (not on purpose). Fraud is intentionally tricking another. Innocent misrepresentation is innocently tricking another. If Roger knows the painting he offers to sell Judy was not painted by Degas, yet he intentionally tricks her into buying what she believes (due to Roger's deceit) is a painting by Degas, Roger commits fraud. By contrast, if Roger truly believes it is by Degas (perhaps Roger was convinced of such by the previous owner, who sold him the painting with a forged certificate of authenticity) and leads Judy to believe the same, the sale was induced by innocent misrepresentation.[6] Both fraud and innocent misrepresentation result in contracts voidable for the misled parties.

Duress occurs when a party is forced to sign a contract. For example, if Johnny threatens Sarah with harm if she doesn't sign the contract he offers her, Sarah signs the contract under duress. The same would be true if Sarah signs the contract because Johnny blackmails her. In either case, Sarah is not a willing party to the contract. Obviously, in situations like these, there is no genuine mutual assent (meeting of the minds) between the parties, and courts will refuse enforcement.

Finally, *undue influence* occurs when a party with power/influence over another causes the latter (the weaker party) to enter into a contract she otherwise likely would not. For example, a caregiver might have influence over a patient. Likewise, a salesman might have sway over an elderly person. Also, a person who owes a fiduciary duty (e.g., financial advisor, lawyer) might be in a position to take advantage of one of his clients. Regardless of the type of parties, if a court feels a party exerts such control over another that the latter contractually binds herself when she normally would not, a court will refuse to enforce the contract on grounds of undue influence.

One more element to go!

6. Note: This hypothetical deals with the law of sales, which is covered in the following chapter. However, the elements required to form a contract under common law are the same required to form a sales contract.

estate planning

Dennis Fordham

On Jan. 1, 2014, California amended its statutory definition of "undue influence" in section 15610.70 of the Welfare and Institutions Code.

This new definition of "undue influence" applies both to "financial elder abuse" that affects the victim while alive and also to undue influence that affect the victim's "testamentary dispositions" after death.

Until 2014, proving undue influence often entailed proving the abuse of a "confidential relationship," i.e., a relationship in which the victim trusted and confided in the perpetrator, "for the purpose of obtaining an unfair advantage."

Now, "'undue influence' means excessive persuasion that causes another person to act or refrain from acting by overcoming that person's free will and results in inequity."

"Excessive persuasion" does not require the existence of any relationship whatsoever between the perpetrator and the victim, although that is one of the specific factors to be considered.

The old focus on a confidential relationship was sometimes preventing enforcement of elder abuse cases where the perpetrator had no real relationship, certainly not a confidential relationship, with the elderly victim.

It is not always the case that a confidential relationship exists between the victim and the perpetrator.

Now what is necessary is to show that an "inequitable result" was obtained through excessive persuasion.

That is a facts and circumstances analysis that requires consideration of each one the following factors: (1) victim's vulnerability; (2) the influencer's apparent authority; (3) the actions or tactics used; and (4) the fairness of the results. Each factor is elaborated upon in the statute.

The new definition's initial focus is on "excessive persuasion that overcomes a person's free will."

This derives from a long line of California decisions involving "will contests" where abnormal or excessive pressure either subverted or overcame the free will of the testator and resulted in a disposition contrary to what the testator would otherwise have done freely.

The definition's back end focus is on "inequity" as the end result. However, "evidence of an inequitable result, without more, is not sufficient to prove undue influence."

continued on next page...

Otherwise, without that language, whenever one beneficiary inherited more than someone else who arguablely should have inherited as much it might be argued that such an uneven result is unfair, even if it was freely intended by the testator.

For example, take a father who leaves most of his trust estate to a favored child and less to other not as favored children.

The new definition applies both to abusive transactions that take effect during a victim's lifetime and those that take effect at death.

These are very different spheres of abuse.

The former includes the scenario where the perpetrator, "[t]akes, secretes, appropriates, obtains, or retains real or personal property of an elder or dependent adult for a wrongful use or with intent to defraud, or both."

The second includes the scenario where the perpetrator coerces the elderly person into devising an estate plan that gift assets in a way that is not consistent with his free wishes.

Much remains to be seen as to how the statute will be applied by the courts. This is especially true in regards to what is considered to be an "inequitable result."

LEGALITY OF PURPOSE

Stated simply, people cannot create a contract to do something illegal. The subject matter of an agreement must be legal in nature. Illegal contracts are void. As such, and with only limited exceptions, courts will not enforce them. Obviously, agreements to violate criminal statutes (to commit crimes) are void. For example, a court would not enforce an agreement to rob a bank or a murder-for-hire contract. Likewise, agreements to violate civil statutes are void. For example, if a state has a civil statute outlawing wagering/betting, the states' courts will not enforce private bets.

In addition to being illegal on statutory (criminal or civil) grounds, some agreements are held by courts to be illegal on public-policy grounds. An example is unconscionability (discussed above, in the paragraph on adequacy of consideration), wherein a court might refuse to enforce an agreement it feels is grossly unfair to one party to the agreement. Also, courts often throw out certain agreements in which a party waives (gives up) a legal right (e.g., a right to sue the other party for negligently performing services).

court ruling confirms

Dartmouth's "Lifetime" Contracts Were Illegal

Auditi Guha

A Superior Court judge has ruled that the "lifetime" contracts former Select Board members granted some town employees in 2006 were illegal.

Among those who received the employment protection contracts were former Executive Administrator Michael Gagne and Finance Director Edward Iacaponi. The contracts were enacted March 1, 2006, before the composition of the Select Board changed.

Joseph Michaud, an attorney and former Select Board member, called the decision "outstanding," describing it as "an affirmation that we were correct that the 'lifetime' contracts were illegal and therefore unenforceable."

Michaud joined the Select Board just after the contracts were executed by the previous board. He said he was shocked they had been negotiated and charged they were "executed in complete secrecy" between the beneficiaries and the town, "clearly protecting certain employees" and "binding the hands of future boards."

The changes, he said, were not presented at Town Meeting and taxpayers didn't know about them until the new Select Board decided to investigate.

"I couldn't believe the town could enter into contracts like this," he said. "It's one of the most underhanded, dishonest things I have come across in government. I was very disappointed."

Gagne, now the town administrator in Mattapoisett, declined comment.

At the heart of the dispute was his contract, which included an employment protection clause stating it shall be renewed except for just cause. The cause "shall include but not be limited to the following: incapacity other than temporary illness, inefficiency, insubordination and conduct unbecoming the office."

On the board at the time were Robert Carney, Nathalie Dias, Robert Miller, Jreck Leduc and Kathleen Horan McLean.

Carney said Wednesday despite the clause, the town could fire employees who didn't do their jobs well. Asked why the board added the clause, he said, "The executive administrator recommended it."

The new board cited a desire to move in a new direction and members William Trimble, Diane Gilbert and Michaud voted not to renew Gagne's contract in November 2008. Gagne retaliated with a lawsuit alleging breach of contract.

Gagne's lawsuit was settled with a one-time payout of $56,831 in an effort to avoid trial and "best serve the town and leave the sordid business behind," Michaud said. "If I had to do it over, we would not have settled. We would've gone into trial."

continued on next page...

Gagne left in February 2009 and Iacaponi stepped in as interim director, then retired in 2010.

Contacted by phone Wednesday, Iacaponi declined to comment.

Another civil action suit was filed in April 2010 when plaintiff Doris Copley, a former paralegal employed by the town, also alleged she had been discharged in violation of her contract.

Copley was notified in June 2009 that the town was not renewing her contract, claiming that the wording violated the town charter and state law.

In his March 25 ruling, Judge Thomas F. McGuire confirmed what many town officials have long contended. He said "the automatic renewal provision of the contract was unenforceable."

Copley appealed the court's decision on April 5, according to court records. She did not return calls for comment and her lawyer was unavailable Wednesday.

The controversy goes back seven years when the former Select Board created the self-renewing contracts for eight town administrators. In addition to Gagne, Iacaponi and Copley, they included: Paul Bergman, director of assessing; David Hickox, director of the Department of Public Works; Steve Melo, harbormaster; Deborah Piva, town collector, and Joel Reed, former director of inspectional services.

Of those employees, Bergman, Hickox, Melo and Piva voluntarily waived the provision in their contracts.

Select Board member Michael Watson said he is happy about the recent court decision.

"The board's position has been that automatic contract renewals are not good public policy, and I am glad the courts are seeing it the same way, too," he said.

CONTRACT TERMINATION

We've learned how a contract is created, but how can a contract be terminated? In other words, we know how a contract starts, but how can it end? There are many ways a contract can be *discharged* (terminated). Let's learn a few of them.

DISCHARGE BY AGREEMENT

Parties to a contract are free to *rescind* the contract, by which I mean mutually agree to end their contract before it has been fully performed. Parties to a contract freely chose to come together, so they can freely choose to depart from each other. Provided all parties to the contract agree to end the contract, a discharge by *mutual agreement* (mutual rescission) is allowed.

© NLshop, 2014. Used under license from Shutterstock, Inc.

DISCHARGE BY PERFORMANCE

If parties to a contract have fully completed/performed what their contract requires of them, the contract is discharged by *performance*. The parties' obligations have ended, and they owe each other nothing more, under the (concluded) contract. For example, imagine Kory and Amy have a contract for Kory to rake the leaves in Amy's front yard for \$10. If Kory rakes the leaves, and Amy pays Kory \$10 for doing so, each has fulfilled the terms of the contract. The contract has been fully performed by each party. Thus, the contract is discharged. Each party owes the other nothing more.

© venimo, 2014. Used under license from Shutterstock, Inc.

DISCHARGE BY BREACH

The opposite of performing one's contractual obligations is what? Not performing them! Not fulfilling the duties required by a contract is referred to as a *breach of contract* (provided the non-performance has no legal justification/defense for her failure to perform). Using the scenario above, what if Kory refused to rake Amy's leaves? The contract requires him to rake her leaves, but he refuses. In such event, Kory willfully fails to perform his duties. He breaches the contract. Amy has a legal claim against Kory for breach of contract, and she, thus, has no obligation to pay him $10 (fulfill her contractual duties). Conversely, what if Kory rakes Amy's leaves, per the contract, but Amy refuses to pay him the $10 she owes him, per the contract? Here, Amy breaches the contract. Kory has a claim against Amy for breach of contract.

appeals court

Upholds Breach of Contract Ruling in Cerro Gordo Case

Mary Pieper

The Iowa Court of Appeals on Wednesday affirmed a Cerro Gordo County District Court ruling stating a Boone company must pay a Clear Lake couple $103,856 for breach of contract as part of a condominium project.

Constructive Consultants Inc. appealed Judge Colleen Weiland's April 2012 ruling that CCI must pay the damages to Jon and Mary Jo Banwart, who operate Cookies, Etc., a retail food store.

CCI entered into an arrangement with the Banwarts to provide project management services when the Banwarts opted to purchase a condominium unit. The upper floor would be a residential area, while the bottom level would be a retail store.

Delays in the 2007 projects and growing project costs created a rift between the Banwarts and specifically one of the company's owners, Jarrell Leigh Foster.

Eventually, the work was completed without the help of CCI. CCI filed a mechanics lien in Cerro Gordo County District Court in 2008. Charges and counter-charges were filed.

CCI argued that the parties entered into a "cost-plus-fee" contract, where Banwarts would pay CCI for labor and materials plus a fee for service.

The Banwarts said the parties entered into a guaranteed maximum price, or a "not-to-exceed" contract.

The district court agreed with the Banwarts, noting that its study showed that CCI was to finish the store and residential unit for a cost not to exceed $130,000. The Banwarts ended up paying additional costs to move the project along.

The appeals court stated it found no merit in CCI's argument that the Banwarts failed to mitigate their damages.

nike sued by Oakley for Breach of Contract

By Associated Press

Oakley is suing Rory McIlroy and Nike, accusing the world's top golfer and the sports gear giant he's recently been linked with of breaching McIlroy's contract with Oakley, according to an ESPN.com report.

The top money winner for both the PGA and European tours this year, McIlroy was signed through Dec. 31, 2012, to endorse Oakley eyewear and apparel.

McIlroy, who switched from Titleist to Nike clubs in late November, is expected to soon make official recent reports he will sign a 10-year equipment and apparel deal next year with Nike estimated to be worth between $200 million and $250 million.

Neither McIlroy nor officials from Nike have confirmed a deal between the two.

Oakley asserts in documents filed last week in federal court in Santa Ana, Calif., that it exercised its contractual "right of first refusal" to match Nike's ostensible offer, but both McIlroy and his agent ignored the company's overtures.

But on Friday the Irish golfer's management company, Horizon Sports Management, which he signed with in 2011 after bolting International Sports Management after four years, told ESPN.com: "McIlroy has fulfilled all of his obligations to Oakley, and the claims in the lawsuit are entirely baseless."

As part of its demands, Oakley wants an injunction to stop McIlroy and Nike from finalizing or implementing whatever contract is at the heart of the firm's lawsuit – which seems to confirm a deal has not yet been concluded.

Note, however, there are certain defenses to lawsuits for breach of contract. For example, imagine Kory, on the day before the contract requires him to rake Amy's leaves, is walking along a sidewalk. A drunk driver veers off the road, runs into Kory, and Kory is killed. Obviously, Kory will not be able to rake Amy's leaves the following day. So, he will fail to perform his contractual duties. But will Amy have a valid breach-of-contract claim against now-deceased Kory? Of course not. The amount of damages, if any, a plaintiff will receive in a breach-of-contract lawsuit depends on the particulars of the case. Is the breach major/material? Is the breach minor? Does the defendant have any valid defenses? Regardless of any potential damages owed the non-breaching party, non-performance (breach) of a contract brings the contract to an end.

DISCHARGE BY OPERATION OF LAW

Several situations can lead to a contract's discharge by *operation of law.* One example is when the subject matter of a contract becomes illegal. In other words, what the parties to the contract agreed to do was legal when they formed the contract, but a subsequent change in law makes the subject matter of their contract unlawful. In such cases, the contract ends by operation of *illegality*. Each party is freed of his contractual obligations. Another example of discharge by operation of law occurs when a performance required by the contract becomes *impossible.* Recall the example above of Kory's death via drunk driver. Because Kory was killed the day before the contract required him to rake Amy's leaves, it is impossible for Kory to perform the contract. As such, the contract is discharged by virtue of Kory's death. Amy has no valid breach-of-contract claim to bring against Kory's estate.

CONTRACTS IN WRITING

Contrary to popular belief, most agreements need not be in writing, to be enforceable. In fact, proof of an oral agreement is sufficient for most types of contracts. That said, all things being equal, it is much more difficult to prove the existence of an oral agreement than a written one. As such, it is always a good idea to get an agreement in writing.

Some types of agreements, however, are enforceable only if they are in writing (there are, as usual, exceptions to this rule). To be in writing, a writing must contain the major matters of the agreement (e.g., parties, subject matter, price) and be signed by the party against whom enforcement is sought. In other words, if Daniel wishes to have an enforceable written contract against Whittaker, Whittaker must sign the contract. A writing cannot be used against you if you do not sign it.

So, most agreements need not be in writing, to be enforceable, but which ones must be? The agreements in each state that must be written, to be enforceable, are determined via state statutes. These statutes are usually referred to as the state's *statute of frauds*. We won't learn each state's statute of frauds, not least because states are fairly consistent on which agreements must be in writing, to be enforced by the state's (state) courts. Typically, to be enforceable, the following

contracts are required to be in writing: (1) contracts for the sale of land, (2) contracts in consideration of marriage (e.g., prenuptial agreements), (3) contracts that cannot be performed within one year, (4) contracts in which the executor of a deceased person's estate promises to pay with his own money a debt of the estate, and (5) contracts to guaranty payment of another's debt (e.g., co-signing a loan).

South Carolina's statute of frauds[7] contains just these five types of agreements:

> *SECTION 32-3-10. Agreements required to be in writing and signed.*
>
> *No action shall be brought whereby:*
>
> *(1) To charge any executor or administrator upon any special promise to answer damages out of his own estate;*
> *(2) To charge the defendant upon any special promise to answer for the debt, default, or miscarriage of another person;*
> *(3) To charge any person upon any agreement made upon consideration of marriage;*

7. South Carolina Code of Laws, Title 32, Chapter 3, http://www.scstatehouse.gov/code/t32c003.php.

(4) To charge any person upon any contract or sale of lands, tenements, or hereditaments, or any interest in or concerning them; or

(5) To charge any person upon any agreement that is not to be performed within the space of one year from the making thereof;

Unless the agreement upon which such action shall be brought or some memorandum or note thereof shall be in writing and signed by the party to be charged therewith or some person thereunto by him lawfully authorized.

HISTORY: 1962 Code Section 11-101; 1952 Code Section 11-101; 1942 Code Section 7044; 1932 Code Section 7044; Civ. C. '22 Section 5516; Civ. C. '12 Section 3737; Civ. C. '02 Section 2652; G. S. 2019; R. S. 2151; 1712 (2) 545.

Some states' statute of frauds lists more than just these five types of agreements, however. Which agreements are enforceable only when in writing are the prerogative of each state, and many states' lists are longer. For example, Texas' statute of frauds[8] is as follows:

PROMISE OR AGREEMENT MUST BE IN WRITING.

(a) A promise or agreement described in Subsection (b) of this section is not enforceable unless the promise or agreement, or a memorandum of it, is
  - *(1) in writing; and*
  - *(2) signed by the person to be charged with the promise or agreement or by someone lawfully authorized to sign for him.*

(b) Subsection (a) of this section applies to:
  - *(1) a promise by an executor or administrator to answer out of his own estate for any debt or damage due from his testator or intestate;*
  - *(2) a promise by one person to answer for the debt, default, or miscarriage of another person;*
  - *(3) an agreement made on consideration of marriage or on consideration of nonmarital conjugal cohabitation;*
  - *(4) a contract for the sale of real estate;*
  - *(5) a lease of real estate for a term longer than one year;*

8. Texas Business and Commerce Code, Title 3, Chapter 26, Sec. 26.01, http://www.statutes.legis.state.tx.us/Docs/BC/htm/BC.26.htm.

(6) *an agreement which is not to be performed within one year from the date of making the agreement;*

(7) *a promise or agreement to pay a commission for the sale or purchase of:*

  (A) *an oil or gas mining lease;*

  (B) *an oil or gas royalty;*

  (C) *minerals; or*

  (D) *a mineral interest; and*

(8) *an agreement, promise, contract, or warranty of cure relating to medical care or results thereof made by a physician or health care provider as defined in Section 74.001, Civil Practice and Remedies Code. This section shall not apply to pharmacists.*

Acts 1967, 60th Leg., vol. 2, p. 2343, ch. 785, Sec. 1. Amended by Acts 1977, 65th Leg., p. 2053, ch. 817, Sec. 21.01, eff. Aug. 29, 1977; Acts 1987, 70th Leg., ch. 551, Sec. 1, eff. Aug. 31, 1987.

Amended by: Acts 2005, 79th Leg., Ch. 187 (H.B. 735), Sec. 1, eff. September 1, 2005.

Did you notice in Subsection (a) the *in writing* requirement can be met with either a signed agreement (contract) or a signed memorandum of the agreement? In other words, parties can put their agreement in writing when they form their agreement, or a memorandum (e.g., invoice, receipt, letter) confirming a previous oral agreement can suffice (provided the memorandum is signed by the party against whom enforcement is sought).

So, if Daniel and Whittaker sign a written contract when they form their agreement, the *in writing* requirement is met. But what if Daniel and Whittaker form an oral agreement, without putting their terms in writing and signing the contract? If, subsequent to the oral agreement, either party gives the other party a signed legal memorandum (which contains the major details of their oral agreement), the party who signed the memo can be held to the terms contained therein. If both sides send the other a signed legal memo, each side can hold the other to the terms of the contract. Got it? Let's look at an example, just to be sure we understand.

Daniel and Whittaker are both citizens of Texas living in Austin. They orally agree Daniel will clean Whittaker's swimming pool on Memorial Day for 3 consecutive years for the price of $200 each year. Does Texas require this agreement to be in writing? Yes! Why? Because this agreement cannot be performed within one year (remember, the contract calls for just three pool cleanings, but the cleanings are to take place on Memorial Day for three consecutive years), and one of the agreements listed in Texas' statute of frauds is *an agreement which is not to be performed within one year from the date of making the agreement.* A few hours after their oral agreement, Daniel sends Whittaker a signed copy of a work order listing the details of their oral agreement. Whittaker now has a signed legal memo with which he can enforce the agreement against Daniel. So, if Daniel doesn't show up to clean Whittaker's pool, per their oral agreement and per the signed legal memo Daniel sent Whittaker, Whittaker can use the signed memo in a lawsuit against Daniel for breach of contract.

Daniel, however, has nothing with which to hold Whittaker to the contract. Why not? Because the parties don't have a written contract and Whittaker has not sent Daniel a signed legal memo confirming their oral agreement. As such, Whittaker isn't required to allow Daniel to clean the pool. Of course, if he allows Daniel to clean the pool, Whittaker is required to pay for services rendered.

What if, in addition to the memo Daniel sends Whittaker, Whittaker sends Daniel a signed document listing the details of their oral agreement, for Daniel's records? Now, each has sent the other a signed legal memo confirming their oral agreement; and, as such, each can enforce the oral agreement against the other.

By now, you should have a better understanding of contracts (legally binding agreements). Can we *agree* to move on to the next chapter? Excellent. It's a deal!

chapter 10

SALES

In the previous chapter, we learned about common-law contracts, by which I mean contracts for such things as services (e.g., employment) and real estate (e.g., land). Over time, the state courts of the various states have developed the rules governing such transactions. State courts, however, are not the sources of (most of) the rules governing contracts for the sale of goods. In this chapter, we will learn about contracts for the sale of goods (as opposed to contracts for services and land), as well as other aspects of sales law. Sales of goods happen every day, all around us, and each of us is likely a regular party to such transactions. As such, a basic understanding of sales law will serve us well.

While general contracts law is rooted in common law, the law of sales is statutory in nature. Restated: Courts gave us general contracts law, but legislatures gave us sales law. To better understand the statutory nature of sales law, some background is necessary.

Do you recall from Chapter 1 the concepts of *primary law* and *secondary law*? Hopefully, you do. If not, I'll save you the time it takes to flip back to Chapter 1: primary law is binding in nature, while secondary law is not binding. In other words, if something is truly law, it is primary law. If something is not law but rather is a commentary, summary, analysis, etc., of law, it is secondary law. Though they are not bound to do so, sometimes legislatures and courts adopt secondary law, thus making it primary law. For example, a court could adopt a previous dissenting opinion (secondary law) and make it binding precedent (primary law). A court could also adopt certain parts of the various Restatements (secondary law) and make them common law (primary law). Keep this in mind, as we continue our history lesson.

In 1952, the Uniform Law Commission (ULC), in conjunction with the American Law Institute, published the Uniform Commercial Code (UCC). The UCC, like each of the more than 300 uniform acts that ULC has published since it first convened in 1892, is secondary law.[1] It is not binding. However, with the rapid rise of interstate commerce and

1. To learn more about the ULC and their various uniform acts, see http://www.uniformlaws.org/. See also http://www.law.cornell.edu/uniform/uniform.

the lack of state uniformity on sales law, the UCC was appealing to the various states. In an effort to promote efficient interstate commerce, the various states started enacting the UCC, thus turning a piece of secondary law into primary law. Legislatively, widespread adoption of the UCC began to grease the wheels of commerce, so to speak.

This makes sense, right? If each state had separate/different rules governing the sale of goods in that state, imagine how frustrating and inefficient conducting multi-state sales would be to sellers. Having to comply with certain sales law in, say, California, while having to comply with different rules in another state would take more time and more money than conducting transactions in states with similar (or even identical) rules.

To date, each state has adopted, in full or in part, the UCC. Article 2 of the UCC (Article 2), the part of the UCC dealing specifically with the law of sales, has been adopted fully or partially by each state but Louisiana. Although minor changes to Article 2 have been made by some states' legislatures and/or courts, the various states' laws of sales are largely the same. The rules we learn in this chapter come from the original version of Article 2 that was published by ULC in 1952. With minor exceptions, these are the rules of most states.[2] Article 2 is meant to aid commerce, not hinder it. I'm painting with broad strokes here, but think of the common law as law that is strict and inflexible; think of Article 2 (sales law) as lenient and flexible.

So, what does Article 2 say? What is the law of sales in most of the country? Let's examine some key portions of Article 2. But before we learn some of the rules of Article 2, we need a firm grasp on when Article 2 applies to a transaction and when it does not.

Article 2 governs the sale of goods. §2-102 makes this clear: *Unless the context otherwise requires, this Article applies to transactions in goods.* What do *sale* and *goods* mean? No need to guess, as Article 2 defines these terms. §2-106 defines *sale* as *the passing of title from the seller to the buyer for a price.* §2-105 defines *goods*, in part, as follows: *all things (including specially manufactured goods) which are movable at the time of identification to the contract for sale.*

---

2. To learn more about the UCC and its adoption by various states, see http://www.law.cornell.edu/uniform/ucc. From American Law Institute – Uniform Commercial Code, Article 2. Copyright © 2011 by ALI and NCCUSL. Reproduced with the permission of the Permanent Editorial Board for the UCC. All rights reserved.

© TaniaLerro, 2014. Used under license from Shutterstock, Inc.

Most movable goods are tangible (e.g., truck, table), but some movable goods are intangible (e.g., natural gas [a commodity]). Goods are personal property; thus, Article 2 governs transactions involving personal property (including bartering goods for other goods). While personal property is governed by Article 2, the sale of real property (e.g., land) and the sale of intellectual property (i.e., trademark) are not. Moreover, Article 2 applies to new goods, as well as used goods.

We've learned contracts for services are governed by common law and contracts for goods are governed by Article 2. What if a transaction involves goods *and* services, such as a transaction involving parts and labor or the purchase of a product with an extra charge for delivery? What then?

Since the rules of the common law and Article 2 are not the same, the two cannot govern the hybrid/mixed (goods and services) transaction simultaneously. Either the common law governs or Article 2 governs. Not both. But which will govern? Most jurisdictions use the test laid down in *Bonebrake v. Cox*, 499 F.2d 951 (8th Cir. 1974): *whether their predominant factor, their thrust, their purpose, reasonably stated, is the rendition of service, with goods incidentally involved (e.g., contract with artist for painting) or is a transaction of sale, with labor incidentally involved (e.g., installation of a water heater in a bathroom).* In other words, is the transaction really about a good or a service? A court will answer this question, based on the relevant factors/circumstances surrounding the transaction. If the predominant gist (to state the rule simply) of the transaction is to buy and sell a good, Article 2 governs. If the gist of the transaction is to pay for a service, the common law governs.

While Article 2 applies to all sales of goods, certain parts of Article 2 apply to *merchants* only. And who is a merchant under Article 2? §2-104(1) tells us:

> *"Merchant" means a person who deals in goods of the kind or otherwise by his occupation holds himself out as having knowledge or skill peculiar to the practices or goods involved in the transaction or to whom such knowledge or skill may be attributed by his employment of an agent or broker or other intermediary who by his occupation holds himself out as having such knowledge or skill.*

What does this mean? First, *goods of the kind* means the goods involved in a particular transaction. So, if Ollie has a contract to sell oranges to Maggie, oranges are the *goods of the kind*. Second (and continuing the scenario), a merchant is one who regularly buys/sells oranges, portrays to the public he has special knowledge or skill with regard to oranges, or employs an agent with special knowledge or skill with regard to oranges. Which people are likely merchants of oranges? For starters, orange farmers, distributors, and retailers. Also, commercial buyers of oranges. Next, orange experts/consultants. Finally, anyone who employs (as an agent for a transaction involving oranges) an orange expert/consultant. In the eyes of Article 2, all of these people presumably know more about oranges than the lay public. Given merchants are better positioned to take advantage of non-merchants (than vice versa), merchants will likely be held by courts to higher duties of good faith in transacting than non-merchants. §2-103(1)(b) states, *"Good faith" in the case of a merchant means honesty in fact and the observance of reasonable commercial standards of fair dealing in the trade.* Lastly, just because someone is an orange merchant does not mean he is, say, an apple merchant. Merchant status is determined on a transaction-by-transaction basis. To be an apple merchant, a party to the transaction must be one of the three types of people listed above *with respect to apples*.

Now that we know what Article 2 is, when it applies, who merchants are, and what *sale* and *goods* mean, let's turn to some rules of Article 2. Let's begin with the rules for forming contracts for the sale of goods. What does it take to form a valid contract under Article 2?

The elements required to form a contract under Article 2 are the same elements required to form a contract under common law: agreement, consideration, capacity, and legality. However, there is a big difference between forming a valid agreement under common law and forming a valid agreement under sales law. Recall Article 2 is meant to make it easier to conduct transactions. As such, and all things being equal, it is much easier to form a sales contract than to form a non-sales (i.e., common-law) contract. Why? Because forming an *agreement* (one of the four elements of a contract) under sales law is easier than forming an agreement under common law. Let's look at the difference.

Recall from Chapter 9 a common-law agreement requires a detailed offer and a detailed acceptance materially consistent with each other. In other words, the acceptance cannot be fundamentally different than the offer in terms of the material parts of the offer: parties, subject matter, consideration, and anything else material to the transaction. Relative to the offer, the acceptance cannot add a material term, delete a material term, or change a material term. Remember what this is called? The Mirror-Image Rule. By contrast, a sales agreement does not require an offer and an acceptance to be identical to one another. Article 2 rejects the common law's Mirror-Image Rule in favor of rules that make it easier than the common law to form an agreement.

What does it take to form an agreement under Article 2? §2-204 tells us:

> (1) *A contract for sale of goods may be made in any manner sufficient to show agreement, including conduct by both parties which recognizes the existence of such a contract.*

> (2) *An agreement sufficient to constitute a contract for sale may be found even though the moment of its making is undetermined.*
>
> (3) *Even though one or more terms are left open, a contract for sale does not fail for indefiniteness if the parties have intended to make a contract and there is a reasonably certain basis for giving an appropriate remedy.*

Catch that? Article 2 allows contract formation *in any manner sufficient to show agreement* (including conduct by the parties) even if the moment of formation is not known. And does a sales contract require all of the material elements required to form a common-law contract? No. So long as a court feels (based on the evidence presented to the court) the parties intended to form a contract, and so long as the court has enough before it to craft a remedy for the parties' dispute, a contract can exist. To be simple, when it comes to forming a sales contract, the parties' intentions matter far more than the agreement's particulars.

This notion of a court's crafting a remedy to a sales dispute gets to the heart of one of the most important functions of the UCC: gap filling. When the parties to a sales contract cannot work out disputes over terms (whether missing, additional, deleted, and/or altered), a court will be there to settle their dispute. When parties cannot agree on an important matter, default provisions of Article 2 fill in the gaps. Obviously, courts do not fill gaps when the minimum requirements of contract formation have not been met. But if a sales contract has been formed, and the parties subsequently cannot reconcile differences on material matters, a court can settle their disputes by using Article 2's default gap fillers. Are you confused? Probably so. Let's stay on this for a bit.

Recall from above Article 2, unlike the common law, does not require an agreement to contain all material information in order to be valid. So, whereas an agreement to paint a house would not be valid without, say, a price, an agreement to buy a bucket of paint can be valid, even if it doesn't state a price. In the event the parties cannot agree on a price for the paint, a court can craft a remedy by filling in the gap with a market price. Courts use Article 2 to fill in gaps with reasonable terms for such matters as price, delivery date, and place of delivery.

§2-207 is the gap-filling section of Article 2. The rules laid down in the section are referred to as *Battle of the Forms*. In its entirety, §2-207 states:

> *(1) A definite and seasonable expression of acceptance or a written confirmation which is sent within a reasonable time operates as an acceptance even though it states terms additional to or different from those offered or agreed upon, unless acceptance is expressly made conditional on assent to the additional or different terms.*
>
> *(2) The additional terms are to be construed as proposals for addition to the contract. Between merchants such terms become part of the contract unless:*
>
> *(a) the offer expressly limits acceptance to the terms of the offer;*
>
> *(b) they materially alter it; or*
>
> *(c) notification of objection to them has already been given or is given within a reasonable time after notice of them is received.*
>
> *(3) Conduct by both parties which recognizes the existence of a contract is sufficient to establish a contract for sale although the writings of the parties do not otherwise establish a contract. In such case the terms of the particular contract consist of those terms on which the writings of the parties agree, together with any supplementary terms incorporated under any other provisions of this Act.*

§2-207 guides us through a situation where the parties to a potential transaction intend to transact and swap writings, but the writings are not identical (typically, parties swap boiler-plate forms that contain different terms). In other words, the offer and the acceptance are inconsistent in one or more material ways. Remember: If an acceptance materially differs from an offer, the acceptance would not be valid under common law. §2-207 rejects this common-law Mirror-Image Rule, finding the acceptance to be valid, even though it is materially different than the offer. Subsection (1) states so long as the offeree (the party to whom the offer was made) definitely meant to accept and did not make his acceptance contingent upon the offeror's acceptance of the additional (new) and/or different (contradictory) terms, the acceptance (and thus the agreement) is valid. Okay, so, we have a valid agreement, but does the agreement consist of the offeror's original terms or the offeree's terms? §2-207 tells us what to do with additional and/or different terms.

The short answer is the additional and/or different terms contained in the offeree's acceptance *might* become part of the contract. How the terms are dealt with first depends on whether *both* parties to the transaction are merchants. If both buyer and seller are merchants, §2-207 tells us such terms automatically become part of the contract *unless* the offer was limited to its terms only, the additional and/or different terms alter the offer in a material way, or the offeror objects to such terms in advance or within a reasonable time after receiving them. And what if both parties are non-merchants or if just one of the two parties is a merchant? §2-207 tells us the offeree's additional and/or different terms are merely proposals to the contract. They don't become part of the contract unless the offeror agrees to them.

Finally, what if a contract is not formed pursuant to the first two subsections of §2-207 but the parties begin to perform the transaction anyway? Restated, what if the writings don't form a valid contract but the parties' conduct evidences a valid contract between them? In such a case, Subsection (3) governs, stating the terms binding upon the parties are those on which their forms/writings agree. Article 2 will dictate any other material terms not agreed upon. In other words, Article 2 will fill the material gaps.

Now that we have an understanding of how valid sales contracts are formed, let's learn some more key parts of Article 2.

Think back to Chapter 9. We learned various states' common law requires certain agreements to be in writing, in order to be enforceable. Such law in each state is referred to as the state's *statute of frauds*. Likewise, Article 2 contains a statute of frauds (§2-201), specifying which sales agreements must be in writing, in order to be enforceable. Subsection (1) of §2-201 states the general rule:

> *Except as otherwise provided in this section a contract for the sale of goods for the price of $500 or more is not enforceable by way of action or defense unless there is some writing sufficient to indicate that a contract for sale has been made between the parties and signed by the party against whom enforcement is*

sought or by his authorized agent or broker. A writing is not insufficient because it omits or incorrectly states a term agreed upon but the contract is not enforceable under this paragraph beyond the quantity of goods shown in such writing.

So, a sale of goods valued at $500 or more must be in writing, in order to be enforceable.[3] There are, however, exceptions to the general rule (hence the beginning of the §2-201(1): *Except as otherwise provided in this section).* In other words, certain oral contracts for sales of goods valued at $500 or more *are* enforceable. §2-201(2) contains an exception that applies only when both parties (buyer and seller) are merchants. We will save for another day an examination of this merchant exception, but let's learn the exceptions applying to all transactions, regardless of whether the parties are merchants. §2-201(3) lists these exceptions:

A contract which does not satisfy the requirements of subsection (1) but which is valid in other respects is enforceable

(a) if the goods are to be specially manufactured for the buyer and are not suitable for sale to others in the ordinary course of the seller's business and the seller, before notice of repudiation is received and under circumstances which reasonably indicate that the goods are for the buyer, has made either a substantial beginning of their manufacture or commitments for their procurement; or

(b) if the party against whom enforcement is sought admits in his pleading, testimony, or otherwise in court that a contract for sale was made, but the contract is not enforceable under this provision beyond the quantity of goods admitted; or

(c) with respect to goods for which payment has been made and accepted or which have been received and accepted (Sec. 2-606).

These sections apply when the contract to buy/sell goods valued at $500 or more is based on an oral agreement, not a written agreement, as required by the statute of frauds.

§2-201(3)(a) would apply when, for example, Molly orders dinner plates customized with an image of her face on each plate from Dinah's Din-

3. The UCL has since increased the dollar amount from $500 to $5,000, but the change has not been adopted by a state.

nerware, a local retail store. The plates Molly orders are not ordinary plates that, if Molly backs out, can easily be resold. Rather, the plates are specialty plates. They are plates not demanded by other customers. In such case, if Molly backs out of her agreement to buy them after Dinah's Dinnerware has already made the plates or has substantially begun to make them or has ordered custom parts for the plates, the exception applies. Molly is on the hook for any monetary loss Dinah's Dinnerware incurs, as a result of Molly's backing out of her agreement to buy.

What about §2-201(3)(b)? Imagine James (seller) and Lucas (buyer) have an oral agreement for the sale of $1,500 of ordinary (i.e., non-custom) tennis balls. When James attempts to deliver the tennis balls to Lucas, Lucas refuses to accept them, telling James the relevant statute of frauds requires their agreement to be in writing. If James sues Lucas for breach of contract and, in his answer to Lucas' complaint, James admits to orally agreeing to the sale but not agreeing in writing, §2-201(3)(b) applies. James' admission puts him on the hook for the monetary losses Lucas suffers, as a result of James' refusal to accept and pay for the goods.

Finally, §2-201(3)(c) covers situations where transactions barred by the statute of frauds have been either partially or fully completed. For example, Butch orally agrees to buy two ordinary motorcycles from Hog Wild, each costing $2,000. The transaction is greater than $500, so the statute of frauds requires it to be in writing. Thus, neither party is obligated to perform. However, if Hog Wild delivers the motorcycles to Butch and Butch accepts them, Butch is then obligated to pay. Why? Because he accepted the goods. What if Hog Wild only has one of the two motorcycles in stock and, thus, delivers just one? Again, Butch has no obligation to accept the motorcycle, but if he does, he must pay for it. The second motorcycle remains barred by the statute of limitations, so Butch can refuse delivery of it. This exception would operate the same way if Hog Wild were to accept payment from Butch. If they accept payment for one motorcycle, they are bound to deliver one motorcycle. If they accept payment for both motorcycles, they are bound to deliver both motorcycles.

Before leaving the statute of frauds, note not every state that has adopted Article 2 uses the $500 figure. For example, the statute of frauds in Michigan's Uniform Commercial Code is, in part, as follows:[4]

4. Michigan Uniform Commercial Code, 440.2201, https://legislature.mi.gov/(S(2edh5v45p52teq45ua3ucg55))/mileg.aspx?page=GetMCLDocument&objectname=mcl-440-2201

(1) *Except as otherwise provided in this section, a contract for the sale of goods for the price of $1,000.00 or more is not enforceable by way of action or defense unless there is a writing sufficient to indicate that a contract for sale has been made between the parties and signed by the party against whom enforcement is sought or by his or her authorized agent or broker. A writing is not insufficient because it omits or incorrectly states a term agreed upon but the contract is not enforceable under this subsection beyond the quantity of goods shown in the writing.*

Subsection (1) of §2-305 authorizes a court to set a reasonable price (at the time of delivery) for a transaction if, *(a) nothing is said as to price; or (b) the price is left to be agreed by the parties and they fail to agree; or (c) the price is to be fixed in terms of some agreed market or other standard as set or recorded by a third person or agency and it is not so set or recorded.* Imagine Baxter's Blenders agrees to sell blenders to Hadley, a large buyer of blenders. The two sides exchange forms (offer and acceptance), but the forms do not include a price for the blenders. If the parties cannot subsequently agree on a price, a court can set a reasonable price. Finding a reasonable price will not be difficult for a court, as the market price range for blenders is not one of life's great mysteries!

Though a court will not arbitrarily set a specific quantity to be purchased and will not enforce a contract beyond an agreed-upon quantity, a court might enforce a contract in which the parties agree the quantity to be purchased is the output of the seller or the requirements of the buyer. For example, a contract doesn't set a specific quantity (such as, say, 50 units) but rather states the buyer agrees to buy as many as the seller produces (i.e., output) or the seller agrees to sell as many as the buyer requires (i.e., requirements). Authority to enforce such output or requirements contracts is found in Subsection (1) of §2-306: *A term which measures the quantity by the output of the seller or the requirements of the buyer means such actual output or requirements as may occur in good faith, except that no quantity unreasonably disproportionate to any stated estimate or in the absence of a stated estimate to any normal or otherwise comparable prior output or requirements may be tendered or demanded.*

What if the parties' forms are sufficient to form a contract but are silent about, or in conflict about, place of delivery of the goods? No problem. §2-308 fills the gap: *Unless otherwise agreed (a) the place for delivery of goods is the seller's place of business or if he has none, his residence; but (b) in a contract for sale of identified goods which to the knowledge of the parties at the time of contracting are in some other place, that place is the place for their delivery; and (c) documents of title may be delivered through customary banking channels.* And if the contract is silent about, or in conflict about, time of delivery? Subsection (1) of §2-309 comes to the rescue: *The time for shipment or delivery or any other action under a contract if not provided in this Article or agreed upon shall be a reasonable time.*

What if the goods a seller delivers to the buyer are not acceptable, given the terms of the contract? What if the goods are the wrong goods or are broken or otherwise fail to conform to the parties' agreement? §2-601 reveals that, with certain exceptions, *if the goods or the tender of delivery fail in any respect to conform to the contract, the buyer may (a) reject the whole; or (b) accept the whole; or (c) accept any commercial unit or units and reject the rest.* Per Subsection (1) of §2-602, *Rejection of goods must be within a reasonable time after their delivery or tender. It is ineffective unless the buyer seasonably notifies the seller.* As for what constitutes acceptance, §2-606 states,

> *(1) Acceptance of goods occurs when the buyer (a) after a reasonable opportunity to inspect the goods signifies to the seller that the goods are conforming or that he will take or retain them in spite of their non-conformity; or (b) fails to make an effective rejection (subsection (1) of*

Section 2-602), but such acceptance does not occur until the buyer has had a reasonable opportunity to inspect them; or (c) does any act inconsistent with the seller's ownership; but if such act is wrongful as against the seller, it is an acceptance only if ratified by him.

(2) *Acceptance of a part of any commercial unit*[5] *is acceptance of that entire unit.*

Among the consequences of acceptance of goods is the buyer's obligation to pay for the goods.[6] Also, with limited exceptions, once a buyer accepts goods, he may not subsequently reject them, for non-conformity,[7] or revoke his acceptance.[8]

Article 2 offers myriad remedies to buyers who deserve recourse from sellers. §2-711, for example, offers such remedies as the right to cancel a contract, the right to money damages, and the right to a security interest in goods from the seller already in the buyer's possession. Subsections (1) and (2) of §2-715 authorize incidental damages and/or consequential damages, respectively, when warranted. What if a seller refuses to deliver unique goods? §2-716(1) states the buyer is entitled to the equitable remedy of specific performance: *Specific performance may be decreed where the goods are unique or in other proper circumstances.*

Just as Article 2 provides for a range of remedies to aggrieved buyers, Article 2 has a long list of remedies available to aggrieved sellers. §2-702, for example, lists a seller's remedies in the case of an insolvent buyer. §2-703 provides a range of remedies in the event the *buyer wrongfully rejects or revokes acceptance of goods or fails to make a payment due on or before delivery or repudiates with respect to a part or the whole.* §2-709 states

5. §2-105(6) defines commercial unit as such a unit of goods as by commercial usage is a single whole for purposes of sale and division of which materially impairs its character or value on the market or in use. A commercial unit may be a single article (as a machine) or a set of articles (as a suite of furniture or an assortment of sizes) or a quantity (as a bale, gross, or carload) or any other unit treated in use or in the relevant market as a single whole.

6. See §2-607(1): The buyer must pay at the contract rate for any goods accepted.

7. See §2-607(2): Acceptance of goods by the buyer precludes rejection of the goods accepted and if made with knowledge of a non-conformity cannot be revoked because of it unless the acceptance was on the reasonable assumption that the non-conformity would be seasonably cured but acceptance does not of itself impair any other remedy provided by this Article for non-conformity.

8. See §2-608: (1) The buyer may revoke his acceptance of a lot or commercial unit whose non-conformity substantially impairs its value to him if he has accepted it (a) on the reasonable assumption that its non-conformity would be cured and it has not been seasonably cured; or (b) without discovery of such non-conformity if his acceptance was reasonably induced either by the difficulty of discovery before acceptance or by the seller's assurances. (2) Revocation of acceptance must occur within a reasonable time after the buyer discovers or should have discovered the ground for it and before any substantial change in condition of the goods which is not caused by their own defects. It is not effective until the buyer notifies the seller of it. (3) A buyer who so revokes has the same rights and duties with regard to the goods involved as if he had rejected them.

what remedies are available to a seller if a buyer does not pay the purchase price when the payment is due. These and other sections offer myriad forms of redress for sellers, when such redress is warranted.

Before ending our look at sales law, I should note Article 2 offers buyers various warranties for purchased goods. A *warranty* is a promise/guarantee goods purchased will conform to certain standards. If goods purchased do not live up to the standards promised/guaranteed, the buyer will have the ability to sue the seller for a breach of warranty (a form of breach of contract, since a warranty is a contract, a binding promise). The warranties potentially available to buyers are title warranties, express warranties, and implied warranties.

§2-312(1) states a sale of goods comes with two *title warranties*: *(a) the title conveyed shall be good, and its transfer rightful; and (b) the goods shall be delivered free from any security interest or other lien or encumbrance of which the buyer at the time of contracting has no knowledge.* In other words, when a buyer purchases goods, she does so with an implied promise she buys the goods from the goods' rightful owner and the goods are not subject to a third party's mortgage, lien, or any other security interest on the goods.

Express warranties are detailed in §2-313. Express warranties are created by words or actions of the seller. In other words, a seller brings express warranties upon himself. And what are the words or actions imposing on the seller obligations that would not otherwise exist? Subsection (1) lists them:

> *(a) Any affirmation of fact or promise made by the seller to the buyer which relates to the goods and becomes part of the basis of the bargain creates an express warranty that the goods shall conform to the affirmation or promise.*
> *(b) Any description of the goods which is made part of the basis of the bargain creates an express warranty that the goods shall conform to the description.*
> *(c) Any sample or model which is made part of the basis of the bargain creates an express warranty that the whole of the goods shall conform to the sample or model.*

All of the items on the above list are typical in sellers' attempts to sell products to buyers. But if the seller's sales tactics include any of the means listed (affirmation of fact, promise, description of goods, showing of a sample or model), the seller creates express warranties.

For example, imagine Callie Camper wants to buy a new tent for her next camping trip. She goes to Tina's Tents, a retail store specializing in, you guessed it, tents. A sales agent greets Callie, as Callie makes her way to a group of tents. The agent directs Callie's attention to a model tent, which is fully erected on the showroom floor. The agent describes certain characteristics of the exterior and interior of the model. She tells Callie the tent weighs 25 pounds and, if properly secured, can withstand wind gusts up to 50 miles per hour. Callie decides the tent will meet her specific needs and decides to purchase. Does Callie's purchase include any express warranties? Certainly. Thanks to Subsection (1)(a), Callie has an express guarantee the tent weighs 25 pounds and, if properly secured, can withstand 50-mph wind gusts. Per Subsection (1)(b), Callie has express guarantees the tent will conform to the tent descriptions the agent provided. Finally, since the agent showed Callie a model, Subsection (1)(c) creates for Callie an express guarantee the tent she purchased will conform to the standards/characteristics of the model shown her. Make sense?

Two other matters to address, before leaving express warranties. First, notice all three subsections of §2-313 include the phrase *which is made part of the basis of the bargain* (BOTB). This means whatever creates an express warranty for a certain good must be a reason the buyer purchased the good. In other words, the promise, affirmation of fact, description of the good, or sample or model of the good must have played a part in the buyer's decision to buy. It must have mattered to the buyer. In the example above, the seller's guarantees matter to Callie, who had specific needs met by the tent shown her. But what if a promise a seller makes is unimportant to a buyer. If Holly Homebody wants to purchase a tent to use only inside her house, she does not care whether a tent can withstand 50-mph wind gusts. So, a guarantee a tent will withstand 50-mph wind gusts does not matter to Holly and is, thus, not part of Holly's BOTB. And if something is not part of the buyer's BOTB, she does not have a valid claim for breach of warranty if the good does not conform to the express guarantee. However, the law presumes an express warranty is part of the buyer's

© Africa Studio, 2014. Used under license from Shutterstock, Inc.

BOTB, so the buyer does not have to prove it was. The seller, though, can offer evidence rebutting the presumption.

Second, it is one thing for a seller to state a tent weighs 25 pounds and can withstand 50-mph wind gusts. It is entirely another thing to puff up a good by, for example, assuring the buyer all her friends will love the good or she will look hip and stylish when using the good. What's the difference between the former and the latter? A tent either weighs 25 pounds, or it doesn't. A properly-secured tent can either withstand 50-mph wind gusts, or it cannot. These guarantees are objectively verifiable. They are fact-based. They are objectively true or false. By contrast, whether others will love the product is not objectively verifiable. Neither is whether a buyer will look hip and stylish. Such matters are subjective. §2-313(2) states,

> *It is not necessary to the creation of an express warranty that the seller use formal words such as "warrant" or "guarantee" or that he have a specific intention to make a warranty, but an affirmation merely of the value of the goods or a statement purporting to be merely the seller's opinion or commendation of the goods, does not create a warranty.*

Unlike express warranties, *implied warranties* are not created by words or actions of a seller. Instead, they are implicit promises coming with

the sale of a good. So, a buyer could have no direct interaction with the seller and still leave the store with implied warranties for the good she buys. Imagine Lory Loner finds a product at a retail store, takes the good to the self-checkout station, swipes her credit card, takes her receipt, and exits the store. She had no direct interaction with the seller. She spoke to no one in the store. No agent made any promise about the good, described the good, or showed her a sample or model. She, thus, leaves the store with no express warranty. But does she leave the store with an implied warranty? Yes. The purchase creates one.

There are two types of implied warranties: implied warranty of merchantability and implied warranty of fitness for a particular purpose. In the example above, Lory's purchase created an *implied warranty of merchantability*, which, per §2-314, is an implied promise a good purchased from a merchant (of said good) is merchantable (i.e. safe for its normal use).[9] The only requirement is the good is purchased from a merchant of that good. If a buyer purchases a good from a merchant, the buyer purchases with implied assurance the good is merchantable. And what does *merchantable* mean? §2-314(2) tells us:

> *Goods to be merchantable must be at least such as (a) pass without objection in the trade under the contract description;*

9. See §2-314(1): Unless excluded or modified (Section 2-316), a warranty that the goods shall be merchantable is implied in a contract for their sale if the seller is a merchant with respect to goods of that kind. Under this section the serving for value of food or drink to be consumed either on the premises or elsewhere is a sale.

> *and (b) in the case of fungible goods, are of fair average quality within the description; and (c) are fit for the ordinary purposes for which such goods are used; and (d) run, within the variations permitted by the agreement, of even kind, quality and quantity within each unit and among all units involved; and (e) are adequately contained, packaged, and labeled as the agreement may require; and (f) conform to the promise or affirmations of fact made on the container or label if any.*

By contrast, an *implied warranty of fitness for a particular purpose* is created via a different scenario, one involving a buyer's interacting with the seller. If a buyer purchases a good for a specific use/purpose, a fitness warranty is possible. §2-314 states,

> *Where the seller at the time of contracting has reason to know any particular purpose for which the goods are required and that the buyer is relying on the seller's skill or judgment to select or furnish suitable goods, there is, unless excluded or modified under the next section, an implied warranty that the goods shall be fit for such purpose.*

So, for a sale to create an implied warranty of fitness, two circumstances surrounding the sale must exist: the seller must know of the buyer's particular purpose for the good and must know the buyer is relying on him (the seller) to furnish goods suitable for such purpose. For example, if Cliff Climber asks a sales agent at Gary's Gloves for help choosing gloves suitable for rock climbing, both conditions are present. Purchase of the gloves comes with an implied warranty the gloves are suitable for rock climbing. If the agent recommends gloves not suitable for rock climbing (Cliff's stated purpose), Cliff has a valid claim for breach of warranty. By contrast, if Cliff selects gloves himself, without the seller's knowledge and assistance, his purchase comes with an implied warranty of merchantability (an implied promise the gloves are suitable for their ordinary use) only.

Before leaving the topic of warranties, note sellers have various ways to disclaim warranties, meaning there are avenues for sellers to avoid the creation of warranties. Moreover, even when warranties are created, multiple defenses to breach of warranty lawsuits are potentially available to sellers. In other words, just because a buyer receives one or more warranties does not mean she will have a winning claim if a warranty is breached.

wal-mart case

Highlights UCC Notice Requirements

By Rieck and Crotty, P.C.

In April, 2009, John Whitwell purchased a DVD player at a Wal-Mart store in Collinsville, Illinois for $214.04, including $16.04 in sales tax. He returned the DVD player shortly thereafter, but returned it to a different Wal-Mart store in Glen Carbon, Illinois. He received a refund of $211.56. The $2.48 difference between what he paid and what was refunded resulted from different sales tax rates in Glen Carbon and Collinsville.

Whitwell sued Wal-Mart in a proposed class action. He claimed that Wal-Mart's failure to pay him the additional $2.48 was a breach of contract. He claimed that Wal-Mart "promises each of its customers, through its use of store plaquards [sic], its web site, sales associates and other means, that they may return goods to [Wal-Mart] within a certain number of days from the original date of sale and receive a refund of all amounts paid for the good(s)," and that Wal-Mart's failure to refund the full price he paid was a breach of contract.

Wal-Mart moved to dismiss Whitwell's complaint. It argued that the complaint failed to state a claim upon which relief could be granted. According to Wal-Mart, the contract, as alleged, was indefinite. In addition, Whitwell failed to give notice to Wal-Mart of the alleged breach of contract before filing suit, as required under the Illinois Uniform Commercial Code (the "UCC").

The court noted that a complaint generally should not be dismissed on a motion unless it fails to provide adequate notice of a claim or does not contain sufficient facts to state a "claim to relief that is plausible on its face." A complaint need not contain detailed factual allegations, but must contain more than mere labels and conclusions, or a simple recitation of the elements of a cause of action. Although Whitwell's complaint did not specify the terms of the alleged contract with particularity, the court found it reasonable to assume that when Wal-Mart sells goods it contracts with the buyer to refund all amounts paid in exchange inefor the buyer's promise to comply with Wal-Mart's return and refund policies. The Court concluded that Whitwell's alleged contract did not fail for indefiniteness, although it was ambiguous as to refund specifics, which would require factual proof. The complaint, however, failed for other reasons.

Whitwell did not provide notice of claim to Wal-Mart before filing his suit. The policy of the UCC is to favor the resolution of contract disputes without litigation. To advance this policy, the UCC requires a buyer of goods, within a reasonable time after he discovers or should have discovered any breach, to notify the seller of breach or be barred from any remedy. This policy and notice requirement has been consistently recognized by Illinois courts. Whitwell argued that the notice requirement did not apply because he never accepted goods from Wal-Mart; the

continued on next page...

notice requirement applies only to a claim for breach of warranty, which he did not assert; and that notice was not required because Wal-Mart had actual knowledge of Whitwell's claim when he filed suit. The court rejected each argument.

First, Whitwell accepted the DVD player because he had opportunity to inspect it, paid for it, took it home and used it. Second, the UCC notice requirement applies to any breach without differentiating between warranty and contract claims. Finally, although there may be a general exception under Illinois law to pre-suit notices where a seller has actual knowledge of a breach, "it is essential that the seller be notified that this particular transaction is troublesome and must be watched.." Whitwell did not allege that he gave pre-suit notice of the claimed breach, and alleged no facts to suggest that Wal-Mart had actual knowledge of the claimed breach of contract. Wal-Mart may have had "generalized information" that variations in local rates of sales tax could affect or were affecting its refunds to customers, but that did not establish actual notice of the breach in this case; what is required is that Wal-Mart have "actual knowledge of the alleged breach of the particular product[ ] purchased by [Whitwell] in this lawsuit," namely, the DVD player Whitwell purchased in Collinsville and returned in Glen Carbon. In view of Whitwell's failure to comply with the pre-suit notice requirement of the UCC, the case was dismissed.

This case illustrates the ramifications of failing to take all required steps in asserting a claim for recovery in any situation involving a sale of goods under the UCC. Please contact us if you require guidance in pursuing such a claim.

I could devote this entire book to the rules (and exceptions) of Article 2, but hopefully you now have a good overview of the source of states' sales law. As with torts, contracts, and all other state-based areas of law, check the specific sales laws of a given state to learn the similarities and differences, relative to the general rules we've learned in this chapter.

chapter 11

AGENCY

An agency is a consensual relationship in which one party (the agent) serves on behalf of the other party (the principal). The agent represents the principal; the principal is represented by the agent. Agencies are usually created in order for an agent to represent the principal in business dealings or transactions. In a valid agency, the agent's actions are deemed to be your actions. In other words, when an agent acts on your behalf, it is as if you are acting yourself. A common example of an agency is an employer-employee relationship, in which an employee acts on behalf of his/her employer. Imagine a salesman for a large medical-supplies company. The company gives the salesman the authority to meet with clients and make sales. When a client conducts business with the salesman (the agent), the client is, in effect, conducting business with the company (the principal).

REQUIREMENTS

To create an agency, several requirements must be met. First, both parties must consent to the agency. As mentioned above, an agency is a consensual relationship. Such consent must be given freely, not as the result of duress or fraud or any other improper means. Secondly, an agency requires that the principal has sufficient mental capacity. Unlike a contract, which requires both parties to have legal capacity, an agency requires the principal only to possess legal capacity. In other words, you don't need to be sane to be an agent, but you do need to be sane to be a principal. Thirdly, the agency must have a legal purpose. In other words, you cannot create a valid agency in order to carry out an illegal venture or transaction. If these three requirements are met, you generally have what you need to create a valid agency. That said, sometimes an agency requires the consent between the parties to be in writing. If the purpose of the agency is one in which the principal would be required to sign a writing, then the agency itself must be evidenced by a writing signed by the principal. This is known as the equal-dignities rule. Take buying real estate, for example. If your state's Statute of Frauds requires a signed writing for the purchase of real estate, then in order for an agent to purchase real estate on the principal's behalf, the agency must be created via a writing signed by the principal. Another time when an agency requires a writing signed by the principal, in order to be valid, is when that agency is created by way of a power of attorney.

Before moving on, you might have noticed that the requirements for forming an agency are similar, but not identical, to the requirements to forming a contract. Generally, a contract requires the following: (1) mutual agreement, (2) mutual consideration, (3) sufficient mental capacity of both/all parties, and (4) a legal purpose. By contrast, and as stated above, an agency requires: (1) mutual agreement (i.e. consent), (2) sufficient capacity of the principal, and (3) a legal purpose. So, unlike a contract, an agency does not require both/all parties to have sufficient mental capacity and does not require mutual consideration. In essence, not requiring mutual consideration means a principal is not required to compensate his/her agent, in order for the agency to be valid. In other words, agencies can be gratuitous in nature.

FORMATION

With an understanding of the general requirements of a valid agency, I'd like to dive into the different manners of forming an agency. In other words, how might two parties end up in an agency? There are several possibilities, explored in no particular order.

First, and as already covered, an agency can be created by agreement between/among the parties. An agency is a consensual relationship; thus, parties can consent (i.e. agree) to the creation of an agency, provided the consent is voluntary. In essence, a principal can authorize an agent to act on her behalf; if that agent agrees to serve as the principal's agent, then that agent has the authority to represent the principal. Such authority can exist in actual form or apparent form.

Actual authority exists when a principal grants power to an agent. Such actual authority can be created expressly or impliedly. Express actual authority is created when a principal grants power to an agent in writing or orally. By contrast, implied actual authority arises whenever an agent performs an act that is reasonably necessary to carry out the express wishes of the principal. In such situations, even if a certain act was not expressly authorized by the principal, if the act is necessary to complete the task the principal expressly authorized, the agent has implied authority to perform the act. For example, if a principal instructs an agent to purchase a certain good or service for the principal, the agent has implied authority to make any additional purchase required for that good of service (e.g. handling fee, delivery fee, or government-mandated fee). Regardless of whether actual authority exists in express or implied form, principals are bound to the acts performed by agents acting with actual authority to perform said acts.

Apparent authority exists when a third party reasonably believes a person is an agent, even though that person is not actually an agent. In other words, it appears the person has the authority to represent the principal, even though she does not. Obviously, whether such apparent authority exists depends on the circumstances of the particular situation. For example, if a company regularly does business with the general manager of a retail store, and that general manager enters into a contract with the company without the authority to do so, the retail store will likely be bound to the contract. The reason is that, given these circumstances, the company is likely reasonable in its belief that the general manager has his employer's consent to enter into the contract, given that the company has regularly done business with the general manager, on behalf of the retail store. On the other hand, if a party unreasonably believes a person is an agent, the principal will not be bound to the acts of the illegitimate agent.

Secondly, an agency can be created by estoppel. This occurs when a principal causes a third party to believe a person is the principal's agent, when, in fact, that person is not the principal's agent. Perhaps a person, while in the presence of a business owner, tells a third party she is one of the business's agents. If the business owner does not disavow the false statement, then the third party will justifiably believe the person is, in fact, an agent for the business. If the person subsequently transacts with the third party, the principal is held to the transaction.

Thirdly, an agency can be created by ratification. Ratification occurs when a principal agrees to an action of someone who is not an agent or to an action of a legitimate agent who acted outside of his/her authority. Consider the following scenario: James wants to purchase a birthday cake for his daughter but doesn't have the time to shop for a cake. So, he asks Frankie if she will find a suitable cake. Frankie agrees. Frankie orders a cake from Party Plus and also orders flowers and balloons from Party Plus. James did not authorize Frankie to order flowers and balloons, so Frankie has acted outside her authority. However, if Party Plus calls James to verify the order (or sends James the final contact), and he approves it, he ratifies the contract. In effect, if a principal "signs off on" an unauthorized act, the act is authorized, and the agency is valid.

Finally, an agency can be created by operation of law. Stated differently, even if two parties did not agree to create an agency, the law might create one anyway. Perhaps an emergency causes someone who is not an agent to act on the principal's behalf, in order to prevent a loss (or further loss) to the principal. For example, imagine that Tim, a custodian employed by Eddie's Electronics, is cleaning the store after it has closed for the day. While cleaning, a pipe bursts, causing the store to flood. Eddie, the owner and manager of the store, has turned off his phone, so Tim cannot reach him. Faced with the emergency of a flooding showroom floor, Tim calls an after-hours plumbing service. The plumbing service fixes the pipe, drains the water from the showroom floor, and bills Eddie's Electronics for the work. Though Eddie did not agree to the work, he is liable for the bill. Tim acted outside of his authority but did so for the benefit of his employer. Thus, the law will recognize a valid agency.

DUTIES

The law of agency imposes upon the parties certain legal duties. One duty that is imposed on both principals and agents is the duty of good faith. Principals and agents are required to act with good faith throughout the duration of the agency. In essence, each is required to act honestly and fairly. Lying to the other party is an obvious violation of the duty of good faith, for example.

Some duties are unique to principals; others unique to agents. For example, principals have a duty to compensate agents for services rendered. To be sure, the parties can agree that the agency will be a gratuitous one; but in the absence of an understanding that the agent will not be compensated, the agent is entitled to reasonable compensation for performing her agency tasks. Principals also have a duty to reimburse agents for any reasonable expenses agents incur, in carrying out their agency duties. If Scarlet tasks Houston with selling her house, then Scarlet is legally obligated to reimburse Houston for any money he spends reasonably, in his efforts to sell her house. For example, basic marketing materials typically would be reimbursable, as would paying to have the house cleaned, before holding an open house for prospective buyers. On the other hand, any unreasonable expenses Houston incurs while trying to sell Scarlet's house are not reimbursable. For example, paying for vacations for each interested buyer would not be reimbursable. Another duty the law of agency imposes on principals is a duty to indemnify agents for any losses they suffer, while lawfully carrying out the principal's wishes. For example, if an agent enters his principal into a contract, in accordance with his principal's instructions, and the other contracting party later sues the agent, the principal must pay the agent for any losses the agent suffers, as a result. Principals also have a duty to cooperate with their agents. The duty of cooperation means principals must assist (reasonably) in agents' efforts to carry out their principals' instructions and must not obstruct/hinder agents in such efforts. In other words, principals must offer reasonable help to their agents and must not get in their way.

The law of agency also imposes several duties on agents. For example, agents have a duty of obedience to their principals' reasonable instructions. Obviously, however, agents have no duty to obey instructions to break the law and will likely violate the duty of obedience if they act reasonably, when instructions are unclear or when exigent/emergency circumstances exist; but if an agent's failure to abide by clear, lawful instructions causes harm to his principal, the agent is liable for the harm. Agents also have a duty to carry out their principals' instructions with exercise reasonable care. Failing to do so will put the agent on the hook for any damage the principal suffers, as a result. Additionally, agents have a duty to be loyal to their principals. In effect, an agent cannot work against a principal, while he is working for her. Undermining the principal (by going behind the principal's back and working for the benefit of one of the principal's competitors, for example) is an obvious violation of the duty. Finally, agents have a duty to render an accounting to their principals, whenever the agency agreement calls for one and/or whenever the principal makes a reasonable request for one. Thus, agents must keep accurate, up-to-date records of monies coming into and going out of the agency; and agents must not mix (i.e. commingle) their personal funds with the agency's funds.

LIABILITY TO THIRD PARTIES

As you can see, principals and agents owe duties to each other, but what about liability to third parties? Obviously, each party (principal and agent) can be liable to third parties for his/her own wrongful actions. In other words, each party is directly liable for its own actions. For example, if an agent commits a tort against a third party, at the request of the principal, the principal is certainly liable. Likewise, if an agent commits a tort against a third party, the agent is liable. But agents' actions can also create indirect liability for their principals. For example, principals are typically liable for any negligence committed by their agents acting within the scope of their employment, such as when a company's delivery driver negligently drives a delivery truck and strikes a pedestrian. Such vicarious (i.e. indirect) liability is rooted in the doctrine of respondeat superior (Latin for let the master answer). On the other hand, principals are generally not liable for intentional torts or crimes committed by their agents, though there are exceptions.

In addition to liability for torts/crimes, contracts can also create liability to third parties. For starters, if an agent enters a principal into a contract with a third party and fully discloses the identity of the principal to the agent, the principal becomes contractually obligated to that third party. Meanwhile, the agent is not bound (i.e. is not a party to the contract), for she was simply acting in the place of the principal. This is the very essence of an agency. The agent represents the principal, and the third party is aware of the parties (principal and agent) and of their agency relationship. By contrast, if an agent partially discloses the agency relationship—meaning she informs the third party that she is acting on another's behalf but does not identify the principal—then she and the principal are bound to any contract she enters into on behalf of the principal. Likewise, if an agent acts on behalf of a principal, but the third party is not aware the agent is acting on behalf of another (i.e. the principal is undisclosed), the agent and principal are contractually bound. On the other hand, if an agent enters into an unauthorized contract, meaning one for which she has none of the authority described above, the agent is contractually bound, but the principal is not.

TERMINATION

We now have a pretty good idea how agencies are created and what agencies entail, but how do agencies come to an end? As is true for contracts, agencies can be terminated by the parties or by operation of law.

Termination by the parties can arise via several means. For starters, the parties can mutually agree to terminate their agency relationship. This makes sense, right? If parties can freely agree to begin an agency, surely they can freely agree to end one. Likewise, either party can unilaterally terminate the agency, via word or conduct (If the principal terminates unilaterally, we refer to the termination as a revocation; if the agent terminates, it's a renunciation.). You cannot be held to an agency against your will. So, if you want out, you can get out. That said, if your agency relationship involves a contract, getting out of your agency early can result in a breach of contract. Regardless, you can end the agency. It should be noted that interested third parties should be notified, whenever an agency is terminated, since a person who no longer has actual authority might still have apparent authority. Parties can also terminate a contract by the terms they set for their agency. Lapse of time, for example. If Lindsey and Bill agree that Bill will be Lindsey's agent for a period of 15 days, then the agency terminates at the end of the 15 days (assuming it has not already been terminated). Lindsey and Bill could also make the agency conditional. For example, they agree Bill will be her agent until the next time it snows in Chicago. In such a case, Bill is Lindsey's agent until the next time it snows in Chicago. Whenever it snows, the agency terminates by condition. Finally, an agency terminates whenever its purpose is achieved. If the purpose of the agency is for Bill to find a buyer for Lindsey's house, then should Bill find a buyer for Lindsey's house, the agency terminates, as its purpose has been achieved.

Agencies can also terminate by operation of law, which means the occurrence of an event that automatically ends the agency. A few examples are instructive. First, the death or insanity of either party. Generally speaking, if either the principal or the agent dies or becomes insane, the agency terminates. Second, in certain situations, the bankruptcy of one of the parties would end the agency. Third, destruction of the subject matter of the agency would end the agency. Using the example above, where Bill is Lindsey's agent for the purpose of funding a buyer for her house, if Lindsey's house is destroyed by a tornado, the agency ends, because the subject matter of the agency (Lindsey's house) has been destroyed. Fourth, if a party to an agency is a company, the agency is terminated if the company is dissolved. The company is no more, so the agent (and, thus, the agency) is no more. There are other examples, but hopefully you have a good idea of the some of the ways an agency might come to an end. And, with that, this chapter comes to an end!

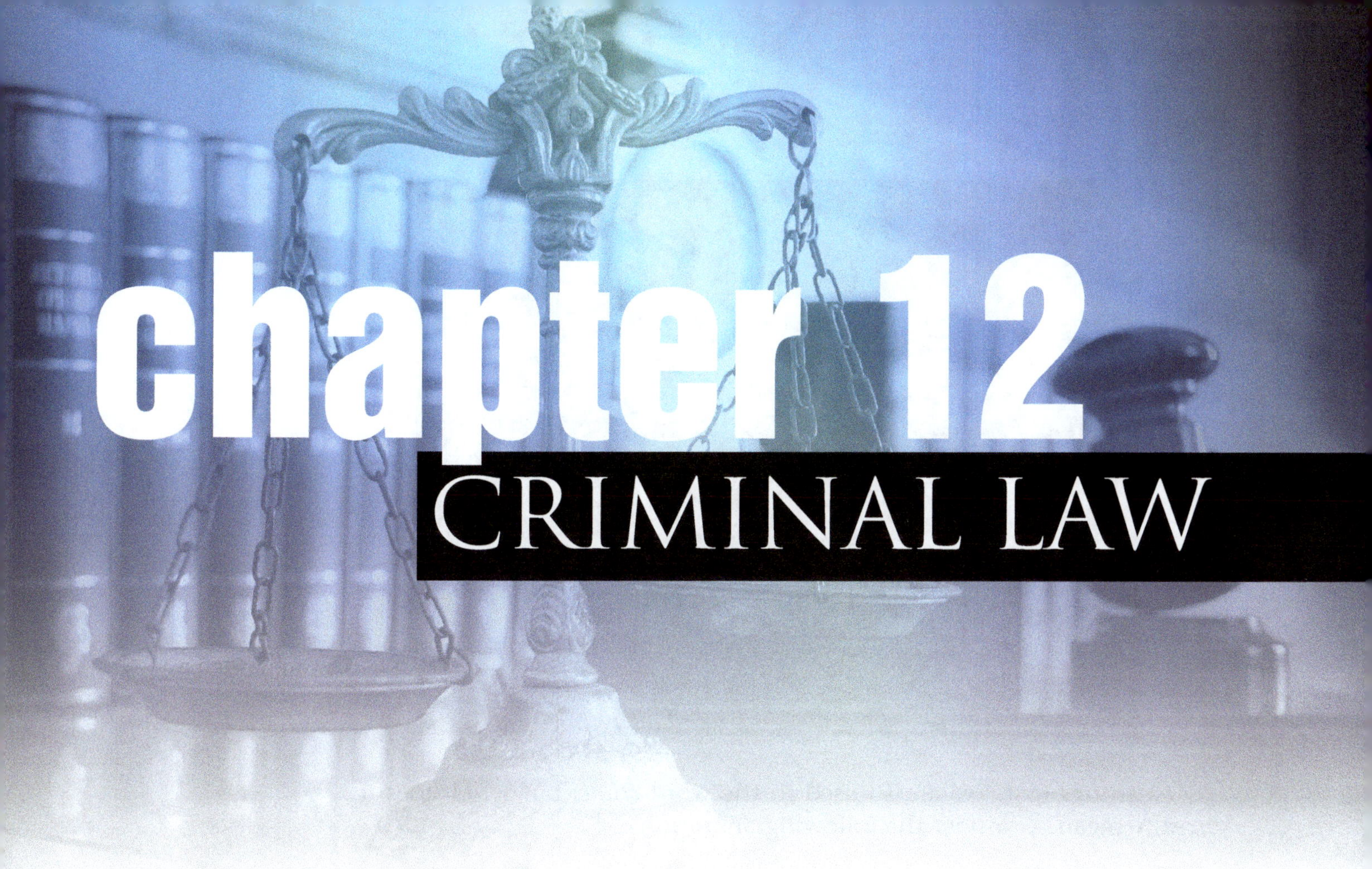

chapter 12 CRIMINAL LAW

Until now, the book's only mentions of criminal law are in the first chapter, which outlined different areas of law; and in the chapter on torts, when we learned a tort is a type of civil (not criminal) wrong. Otherwise, the book's focus has been on areas of civil law, such as torts and contracts.

Obviously, my hope is any reader will never encounter criminal law (either as a victim or a perpetrator). However, I feel the book should at least give a brief look at the vast area of law focused on criminal wrongs, not least because news outlets and entertainment mediums are so full of crimes. Movies and televisions are replete with crime dramas, but when was the last time you turned on the television and watched a tort drama? That's right: never! So, I can't end our time together without examining the area of law to which we are so often exposed.

© Everett Collection, 2014. Used under license from Shutterstock, Inc.

First things first. We are so used to the word *crime*, but what does it really mean? Consider the following definitions:

> *An illegal act for which someone can be punished by the government* – Merriam-Webster.com[1]

> *An action or an instance of negligence that is deemed injurious to the public welfare or morals or to the interests of the state and that is legally prohibited* – Dictionary.com[2]

> *Any act or omission (of an act) in violation of a public law forbidding or commanding it* – Legal Information Institute[3]

Did you notice any pattern? The use of the words *government* and *public* reveal a crucial element to our understanding of crime. Broadly, a crime is an offense against the government. This stands in contrast to civil wrongs, such as torts and breaches of contract, which are offenses against private parties. The reason a crime is an offense against the government is the government decides what constitutes a crime. That said,

1. http://www.merriam-webster.com/dictionary/crime
2. http://dictionary.reference.com/browse/crime
3. http://www.law.cornell.edu/wex/criminal_law

the various states classify crime according to whom or what they harm, such as crimes against the state (e.g., treason), a person (murder), and property (theft). As an example, Title 18.2 of the Code of Virginia classifies crimes as follows:[4]

Chapter 3	Inchoate Offenses (18.2-22 thru 18.2-29)
Chapter 4	Crimes Against the Person (18.2-30 thru 18.2-76.2)
Chapter 5	Crimes Against Property (18.2-77 thru 18.2-167.1)
Chapter 6	Crimes Involving Fraud (18.2-168 thru 18.2-246.15)
Chapter 7	Crimes Involving Health and Safety (18.2-247 thru 18.2-324.1)
Chapter 8	Crimes Involving Morals and Decency (18.2-325 thru 18.2-403.4)
Chapter 9	Crimes Against Peace and Order (18.2-404 thru 18.2-433.3)
Chapter 10	Crimes Against the Administration of Justice (18.2-434 thru 18.2-480.1)
Chapter 11	Offenses Against the Sovereignty of the Commonwealth (18.2-481 thru 18.2-492)
Chapter 12	Miscellaneous (18.2-493 thru 18.2-511.1)
Chapter 13	Virginia Racketeer Influenced and Corrupt Organization Act (18.2-512 thru 18.2-517)

Criminal law is an area of law governed mostly by the various states and their localities. Each state's legislature determines what is considered a crime in that state; and the crimes in each state are listed in the state's criminal code, referred to as the *penal code*.[5] As with torts, we won't look at how every state categorizes crimes or what is considered

4. https://leg1.state.va.us/cgi-bin/legp504.exe?000+cod+TOC1802000

5. Note: Almost all crimes are created statutorily (e.g., by legislatures and local governments), but some crimes are created via common law. Many states, such as Arizona, have abolished common-law crimes: *All common law offenses and affirmative defenses are abolished. No conduct or omission constitutes an offense or an affirmative defense unless it is an offense or an affirmative defense under this title or under another statute or ordinance.* Arizona Revised Statutes, Title 13, Chapter 1, Section 13-103(1), http://www.azleg.gov/FormatDocument.asp?inDoc=/ars/13/00103.htm&Title=13&DocType=ARS

a crime, but we will cover what is generally true among the states. Also, notice I wrote criminal law is governed *mostly* by the various states. The U.S. Congress also classifies certain actions as crimes.[6] So, while most crimes are state-based, some crimes are federally-based.

While civil offenses are pursued in court via lawsuits (i.e., litigation), criminal offenses are pursued in court via prosecution. Plaintiffs initiate lawsuits, while government prosecutors initiate prosecutions. State prosecutors, often known as district attorneys, prosecute state crimes and are organized at the local (usually county) level. Federal prosecutors, known as U.S. attorneys, prosecute federal crimes and are organized by U.S. federal districts (which we covered at the beginning of the book).

As for the burden of proof required to find a defendant guilty of a crime, we learned this earlier in the book. Do you recall our look at the case of O.J. Simpson? Do you remember why O.J. Simpson was found not guilty at his criminal trial but found liable at his civil trial? The reason is the criminal burden of proof (*beyond a reasonable doubt*) is higher than the civil burden of proof (*by a preponderance of the evidence*). Why does this make sense? Why must the evidence required to find a defendant guilty of a crime be stronger than the evidence required to find someone liable in a lawsuit?

TYPES OF CRIME

Crimes are separated into two categories: *misdemeanors* and *felonies*. Compared to one another, misdemeanors are less serious, and felonies are more serious. Generally, misdemeanors are punishable by fines, the forfeiture of certain privileges (e.g., driver's license, occupational license), and/or up to one year of incarceration (usually in a jail). By contrast, felonies are punishable by fines, the forfeiture of certain constitutional rights (e.g., right to carry a gun, right to vote), and/or more than one year of incarceration (usually in a prison). Let's see how some states classify felonies and misdemeanors.

> Alabama: *FELONY. An offense for which a sentence to a term of imprisonment in excess of one year is authorized by this*

6. See Title 18, Chapter 1, of the United States Code: http://www.gpo.gov/fdsys/pkg/USCODE-2009-title18/html/USCODE-2009-title18.htm

title. MISDEMEANOR. An offense for which a sentence to a term of imprisonment not in excess of one year may be imposed.[7]

Arizona: *"Misdemeanor" means an offense for which a sentence to a term of imprisonment other than to the custody of the state department of corrections is authorized by any law of this state. 18. "Felony" means an offense for which a sentence to a term of imprisonment in the custody of the state department of corrections is authorized by any law of this state.*[8]

Massachusetts: *A crime punishable by death or imprisonment in the state prison is a felony. All other crimes are misdemeanors.*[9]

county commissioner
Jernigan Arrested for Misdemeanor Theft

By Murfreesboro Post

Sixth District Rutherford County Commissioner Joe Frank Jernigan, 69, of Readyvile was charged with misdemeanor theft Wednesday.

Jernigan was allegedly caught on camera stealing his opponent's political advertising sign.

To further complicate the issue, the family on whose property the sign was located claims that Jernigan was driving a vehicle with Rutherford County government license tags. The commissioner works for the Rutherford County Highway Department and has use of a county car.

He was booked into Rutherford County Adult Detention Center on a criminal summons that was taken out by the Anderson family who reportedly confronted Commissioner Jernigan on their property.

It is important to note that a summons is not a warrant, but a document that orders the suspect to appear in General Sessions Court.

From "County Commissioner Jernigan arrested for misdemeanor theft," *The Murfreesboro Post*, April 10, 2014.

7. The Code of Alabama 1975, Chapter 5, Section 13A-1-2, Subsections 8 and 9, respectively, http://alisondb.legislature.state.al.us/acas/codeofalabama/1975/coatoc.htm
8. Arizona Revised Statutes, Title 13, Chapter 1, Section 13-105, Subsections 18 and 25, respectively, http://www.azleg.gov/FormatDocument.asp?inDoc=/ars/13/00105.htm&Title=13&DocType=ARS
9. Massachusetts General Laws, Part IV, Title I, Chapter 274, Section 1, https://malegislature.gov/Laws/GeneralLaws/PartIV/TitleI/Chapter274/Section1

Felonies and misdemeanors are further divided into classes/degrees. For example, the Nebraska Criminal Code[10] categorizes felonies[11] and misdemeanors[12] as follows:

> *28-105. Felonies; classification of penalties; sentences; where served; eligibility for probation.*
>
> *(1) For purposes of the Nebraska Criminal Code and any statute passed by the Legislature after the date of passage of the code, felonies are divided into nine classes which are distinguished from one another by the following penalties which are authorized upon conviction:*

Class I felony	*Death*
Class IA felony	*Life imprisonment*
Class IB felony	*Maximum — life imprisonment*
	Minimum — twenty years imprisonment
Class IC felony	*Maximum — fifty years imprisonment*
	Mandatory minimum — five years imprisonment
Class ID felony	*Maximum — fifty years imprisonment*
	Mandatory minimum — three years imprisonment
Class II felony	*Maximum — fifty years imprisonment*
	Minimum — one year imprisonment
Class III felony	*Maximum — twenty years imprisonment, or twenty-five thousand dollars fine, or both*
	Minimum — one year imprisonment

10. Nebraska Revised Statutes Chapter 28, http://nebraskalegislature.gov/laws/browse-chapters.php?chapter=28
11. Nebraska Revised Statute 28-105, http://nebraskalegislature.gov/laws/statutes.php?statute=28-105
12. Nebraska Revised Statute 28-106, http://nebraskalegislature.gov/laws/statutes.php?statute=28-106

Class IIIA felony	*Maximum — five years imprisonment, or ten thousand dollars fine, or both* *Minimum — none*
Class IV felony	*Maximum — five years imprisonment, or ten thousand dollars fine, or both* *Minimum — none*

(2) *All sentences of imprisonment for Class IA, IB, IC, ID, II, and III felonies and sentences of one year or more for Class IIIA and IV felonies shall be served in institutions under the jurisdiction of the Department of Correctional Services. Sentences of less than one year shall be served in the county jail except as provided in this subsection. If the department certifies that it has programs and facilities available for persons sentenced to terms of less than one year, the court may order that any sentence of six months or more be served in any institution under the jurisdiction of the department. Any such certification shall be given by the department to the State Court Administrator, who shall forward copies thereof to each judge having jurisdiction to sentence in felony cases.*

(3) *Nothing in this section shall limit the authority granted in sections 29-2221 and 29-2222 to increase sentences for habitual criminals.*

(4) *A person convicted of a felony for which a mandatory minimum sentence is prescribed shall not be eligible for probation.*

28-106. Misdemeanors; classification of penalties; sentences; where served.

(1) *For purposes of the Nebraska Criminal Code and any statute passed by the Legislature after the date of passage of the code, misdemeanors are divided into seven classes which are distinguished from one another by the following penalties which are authorized upon conviction:*

Class I misdemeanor...	*Maximum — not more than one year imprisonment, or one thousand dollars fine, or both* *Minimum — none*

Class II misdemeanor...	*Maximum — six months imprisonment, or one thousand dollars fine, or both* *Minimum — none*
Class III misdemeanor...	*Maximum — three months imprisonment, or five hundred dollars fine, or both* *Minimum — none*
Class IIIA misdemeanor...	*Maximum — seven days imprisonment, five hundred dollars fine, or both* *Minimum — none*
Class IV misdemeanor...	*Maximum — no imprisonment, five hundred dollars fine* *Minimum — one hundred dollars fine*
Class V misdemeanor...	*Maximum — no imprisonment, one hundred dollars fine* *Minimum — none*
Class W misdemeanor...	*Driving under the influence or implied consent* *First conviction* *Maximum — sixty days imprisonment and five hundred dollars fine* *Mandatory minimum — seven days* *imprisonment and five hundred dollars fine* *Second conviction* *Maximum — six months imprisonment and five hundred dollars fine* *Mandatory minimum — thirty days imprisonment and five hundred dollars fine* *Third conviction* *Maximum — one year imprisonment and one thousand dollars fine* *Mandatory minimum — ninety days imprisonment and one thousand dollars fine*

(2) *Sentences of imprisonment in misdemeanor cases shall be served in the county jail, except that in the following circumstances the court may, in its discretion, order that such sentences be served in institutions under the jurisdiction of the Department of Correctional Services:*
   (a) *If the sentence is for a term of one year upon conviction of a Class I misdemeanor;*
   (b) *If the sentence is to be served concurrently or consecutively with a term for conviction of a felony; or*
   (c) *If the Department of Correctional Services has certified as provided in section 28-105 as to the availability of facilities and programs for short-term prisoners and the sentence is for a term of six months or more.*

So, we know states consider some criminal acts (felonies) as more serious than others (misdemeanors), and we know states further divide felonies and misdemeanors into classes, based on seriousness. But what, specifically, are some examples of crimes? Let's look at a random sampling of crimes in various states.

A common type of crime is *homicide*. As with all crimes, each state decides what constitutes homicide in that state. The Texas Penal Code lists several types of criminal homicide:

Sec. 19.01. TYPES OF CRIMINAL HOMICIDE.

(a) A person commits criminal homicide if he intentionally, knowingly, recklessly, or with criminal negligence causes the death of an individual.

(b) Criminal homicide is murder, capital murder, manslaughter, or criminally negligent homicide.

Sec. 19.02. MURDER.

(a) In this section:

(1) "Adequate cause" means cause that would commonly produce a degree of anger, rage, resentment, or terror in a person of ordinary temper, sufficient to render the mind incapable of cool reflection.

(2) "Sudden passion" means passion directly caused by and arising out of provocation by the individual killed or another acting with the person killed which passion arises at the time of the offense and is not solely the result of former provocation.

(b) A person commits an offense if he:

(1) intentionally or knowingly causes the death of an individual;

(2) intends to cause serious bodily injury and commits an act clearly dangerous to human life that causes the death of an individual; or

(3) commits or attempts to commit a felony, other than manslaughter, and in the course of and in furtherance of the commission or attempt, or in immediate flight from the commission or attempt, he commits or attempts to commit an act clearly dangerous to human life that causes the death of an individual.

(c) Except as provided by Subsection (d), an offense under this section is a felony of the first degree.

(d) At the punishment stage of a trial, the defendant may raise the issue as to whether he caused the death under the immediate influence of sudden passion arising from an adequate cause. If the defendant proves the issue in the affirmative by a preponderance of the evidence, the offense is a felony of the second degree.

Sec. 19.03. CAPITAL MURDER.

(a) A person commits an offense if the person commits murder as defined under Section 19.02(b)(1) and:

(1) the person murders a peace officer or fireman who is acting in the lawful discharge of an official duty and who the person knows is a peace officer or fireman;

(2) the person intentionally commits the murder in the course of committing or attempting to commit kidnapping, burglary, robbery, aggravated sexual assault, arson, obstruction or retaliation, or terroristic threat under Section 22.07(a)(1), (3), (4), (5), or (6);

(3) the person commits the murder for remuneration or the promise of remuneration or employs another to commit the murder for remuneration or the promise of remuneration;

(4) the person commits the murder while escaping or attempting to escape from a penal institution;

(5) the person, while incarcerated in a penal institution, murders another:

(A) who is employed in the operation of the penal institution; or

(B) with the intent to establish, maintain, or participate in a combination or in the profits of a combination;

(6) the person:

(A) while incarcerated for an offense under this section or Section 19.02, murders another; or

(B) while serving a sentence of life imprisonment or a term of 99 years for an offense under Section 20.04, 22.021, or 29.03, murders another;

(7) the person murders more than one person:

(A) during the same criminal transaction; or

(B) during different criminal transactions but the murders are committed pursuant to the same scheme or course of conduct;

(8) the person murders an individual under 10 years of age; or

(9) the person murders another person in retaliation for or on account of the service or status of the other person as a judge or justice of the supreme court, the court of criminal appeals, a court of appeals, a district court, a criminal district court, a constitutional county court, a statutory county court, a justice court, or a municipal court.

(b) An offense under this section is a capital felony.

(c) If the jury or, when authorized by law, the judge does not find beyond a reasonable doubt that the defendant is guilty of an offense under this section, he may be convicted of murder or of any other lesser included offense.

16-year-old Sentenced for Intox Manslaughter

CASEY KNAUPP

A 16-year-old boy was sentenced Monday to 20 years in prison for driving intoxicated and causing a collision in Tyler that killed a pregnant woman and seriously injured a young girl.

Jaime Arrellano, of Carthage, pleaded guilty to two counts of intoxicated manslaughter and one charge of intoxicated assault. He was sentenced to 20 years in prison for causing the death of Martha Fidela Mondragon, 31, of Tyler, in the June 23 wreck. Arrellano was also sentenced to 16 years in prison for causing the death of Ms. Mondragon's unborn child and 10 years for injuring 6-year-old Bianca Mondragon.

Judge Cynthia Stevens Kent, of the 114th District Court, also assessed a $5,000 fine and ordered that the sentences run at the same time. Arrellano, who was certified to stand trial as an adult, will be eligible for parole after serving 10 years in prison because Judge Kent found that Arrellano used a deadly weapon - his vehicle - during the offense.

Arrellano, who used a Spanish-speaking interpreter, cried as Ms. Mondragon's niece spoke to the defendant on behalf of the family during victim allocution.

She said Arrellano made a decision that affected both of their families, but he was still able to see his when they can no longer see Martha. She told him to think about the decisions he makes when he gets out of jail and that he didn't know the damage he caused her family.

Tyler police said the crash happened at around 11 p.m. on June 23. Ms. Mondragon was driving her Ford Mustang westbound on Front Street with 6-year-old Bianca in the car, when a black Ford Explorer, driven by Arrellano and traveling northbound on Broadway Avenue, ran a red light and slammed into her car in the intersection.

Bianca was seriously injured in the crash and was flown by helicopter to Children's Hospital in Dallas. Ms. Mondragon, who was pregnant, was transported to the emergency room at East Texas Medical Center, where doctors performed an emergency Caesarean section to deliver a baby boy. Both Ms. Mondragon and the baby died several hours later.

Arrellano was taken to the Mother Frances Hospital emergency room, where he was treated for minor injuries and then taken into police custody.

He faced two to 20 years in prison for the intoxicated manslaughter charges and two to 10 years for the intoxicated assault.

> *Sec. 19.04. MANSLAUGHTER.*
> *(a) A person commits an offense if he recklessly causes the death of an individual.*
> *(b) An offense under this section is a felony of the second degree.*
>
> *Sec. 19.05. CRIMINALLY NEGLIGENT HOMICIDE.*
> *(a) A person commits an offense if he causes the death of an individual by criminal negligence.*
> *(b) An offense under this section is a state jail felony.*

Burglary and *larceny* (theft) are common crimes. Let's see how North Carolina defines each. Article 14, §14-51, of the North Carolina General Statutes, defines burglary as follows:

> *There shall be two degrees in the crime of burglary as defined at the common law. If the crime be committed in a dwelling house, or in a room used as a sleeping apartment in any building, and any person is in the actual occupation of any part of said dwelling house or sleeping apartment at the time of the commission of such crime, it shall be burglary in the first degree. If such crime be committed in a dwelling house or sleeping apartment not actually occupied by anyone at the time of the commission of the crime, or if it be committed in any house within the curtilage of a dwelling house or in any*

building not a dwelling house, but in which is a room used as a sleeping apartment and not actually occupied as such at the time of the commission of the crime, it shall be burglary in the second degree. For the purposes of defining the crime of burglary, larceny shall be deemed a felony without regard to the value of the property in question.

Per Article 16, §14-72, of the North Carolina General Statutes,[13] larceny can be a misdemeanor or a felony:

(a) Larceny of goods of the value of more than one thousand dollars ($1,000) is a Class H felony. The receiving or possessing of stolen goods of the value of more than one thousand dollars ($1,000) while knowing or having reasonable grounds to believe that the goods are stolen is a Class H felony. Larceny as provided in subsection (b) of this section is a Class H felony. Receiving or possession of stolen goods as provided in subsection (c) of this section is a Class H felony. Except as provided in subsections (b) and (c) of this section, larceny of property, or the receiving or possession of stolen goods knowing or having reasonable grounds to believe them to be stolen, where the value of the property or goods is not more than one thousand dollars ($1,000), is a Class 1 misdemeanor. In all cases of doubt, the jury shall, in the verdict, fix the value of the property stolen.

(b) The crime of larceny is a felony, without regard to the value of the property in question, if the larceny is any of the following:

(1) From the person.

(2) Committed pursuant to a violation of G.S. 14-51, 14-53, 14-54, 14-54.1, or 14-57.

(3) Of any explosive or incendiary device or substance. As used in this section, the phrase "explosive or incendiary device or substance" shall include any explosive or incendiary grenade or bomb; any dynamite, blasting powder, nitroglycerin, TNT, or other high explosive; or any device, ingredient for such device, or type or quantity of substance primarily useful for large-scale destruction of property by explosive or incendiary action or lethal injury to persons by explosive or incendiary action. This defini-

13. http://www.ncga.state.nc.us/EnactedLegislation/Statutes/HTML/BySection/Chapter_14/GS_14-72.html

tion shall not include fireworks; or any form, type, or quantity of gasoline, butane gas, natural gas, or any other substance having explosive or incendiary properties but serving a legitimate nondestructive or nonlethal use in the form, type, or quantity stolen.

(4) *Of any firearm. As used in this section, the term "firearm" shall include any instrument used in the propulsion of a shot, shell or bullet by the action of gunpowder or any other explosive substance within it. A "firearm," which at the time of theft is not capable of being fired, shall be included within this definition if it can be made to work. This definition shall not include air rifles or air pistols.*

(5) *Of any record or paper in the custody of the North Carolina State Archives as defined by G.S. 121-2(7) and G.S. 121-2(8).*

(6) *Committed after the defendant has been convicted in this State or in another jurisdiction for any offense of larceny under this section, or any offense deemed or punishable as larceny under this section, or of any substantially similar offense in any other jurisdiction, regardless of whether the prior convictions were misdemeanors, felonies, or a combination thereof, at least four times. A conviction shall not be included in the four prior convictions required under this subdivision unless the defendant was represented by counsel or waived counsel at first appearance or otherwise prior to trial or plea. If a person is convicted of more than one offense of misdemeanor larceny in a single session of district court, or in a single week of superior court or of a court in another jurisdiction, only one of the convictions may be used as a prior conviction under this subdivision; except that convictions based upon offenses which occurred in separate counties shall each count as a separate prior conviction under this subdivision.*

teen shoots at Intruders During Home Invasion

Diana Rugg

A Kannapolis teen is recovering after his second home invasion in two weeks – but this time he managed to shoot one of his attackers during the assault.

"I pulled out a gun and shot one of them," said Chris Ludwick, 19.

Ludwick said he shot at the men four times with a .22-caliber pistol that his father gave him after the first home invasion on February 7. He was prepared when the men broke down the back door just before 4:30 a.m. Sunday.

"I was sleeping and was woken up to a disturbing outrage," said Ludwick, "and they came inside my house and started trying to beat me up."

Ludwick has cuts on his face and four staples in the back of his head from where one of the men grabbed the gun and pistol whipped him after the shooting.

He doesn't know why he was targeted twice in as many weeks.

"The first time they took a lot of hats and my phone and some of my money, and the second time all they got was my watches," he said.

Kannapolis police arrested two men shortly after the attack, after Ludwick gave police a description of their car.

Kristopher Garret Welch, 20, and Andrew Christopher Calamari, 21, are both in the Cabarrus County jail under $200,000 bond each. Each faces charges for two counts of first degree burglary and felony larceny. Police say one of the suspects was found at CMC Northeast with a gunshot wound to the leg, while the other was picked up by Concord Police.

Welch also faces a charge of assault and battery, while Calamari faces additional charges of assault with a deadly weapon and larceny of a firearm.

Police have not yet found the gun.

Ludwick's father Terry doesn't regret giving his son the gun after the first home invasion.

"I hate to do it. I didn't want to do it – but when it comes to my son's life, I want him to be protected," said Terry Ludwick.

"He's my son and I love him, I love him dearly," he said, choking up.

"I really do... and I don't want nothing to happen to him."

Arson is another common crime. South Carolina defines arson as follows:[14]

> (A) *A person who wilfully and maliciously causes an explosion, sets fire to, burns, or causes to be burned or aids, counsels, or procures a burning that results in damage to a dwelling house, building, structure, or any property whether the property of himself or another, which results, either directly or indirectly, in the death of a person is guilty of the felony of arson in the first degree and, upon conviction, must be imprisoned not less than thirty years.*
>
> (B) *A person who wilfully and maliciously causes an explosion, sets fire to, burns, or causes to be burned or aids, counsels, or procures a burning that results in damage to a dwelling house, building, structure, or any property whether the property of himself or another, which results, either directly or indirectly, in serious bodily injury to a person is guilty of the felony of arson in the second degree and, upon conviction, must be imprisoned not less than three nor more than twenty-five years.*
>
> (C) *A person who wilfully and maliciously causes an explosion, sets fire to, burns, or causes to be burned or aids, counsels, or procures a burning that results in damage to a dwelling house, building, structure, or any property, whether the property of himself or another, which results, either directly or indirectly, in bodily injury to a person or damage to the property is guilty of the felony of arson in the third degree and, upon conviction, must be imprisoned not more than fifteen years.*
>
> (D) *For purposes of this section, "damage" means an application of fire or explosive that results in burning, charring, blistering, scorching, smoking, singeing, discoloring, or changing the fiber or composition of a building, structure, or any property specified in this section.*

14. South Carolina Code of Laws, Title 16, Article 3, Section 16-11-110, http://www.scstatehouse.gov/code/t16c011.php

south carolina man
Facing Murder

By Associated Press

A South Carolina man faces attempted murder charges after law officers say he set fire to his rental house while officers were inside trying to arrest him.

The Spartanburg County Sheriff's Office said Monday that 44-year-old Larry Morris needed medical treatment after the early-morning incident.

Deputies were sent to help police in Cowpens arrest Morris on criminal sexual conduct warrants.

A deputy involved in serving the warrants said he and his partner went inside the home to find Morris. The deputy says he noticed a fire coming from a back bedroom and Morris leaving the room.

Sheriff's Lt. Tony Ivey said investigators decided Morris intentionally set the fire. He's charged with second-degree arson and five counts of attempted murder. It wasn't known if he had a lawyer.

In addition to arson, *vandalism* is a type of crime involving damage to property. South Dakota defines vandalism as follows:[15]

> *Intentional damage to property—Degree of offense according to value—Application. Any person who, with specific intent to do so, injures, damages, or destroys:*
>
> *(1) Public property without the lawful consent of the appropriate governing body having jurisdiction thereof; or*
> *(2) Private property in which any other person has an interest, without the consent of the other person;*
>
> *is guilty of intentional damage to property. If the damage to property is four hundred dollars or less, the person is guilty of intentional damage to property in the third degree, which is a Class 2 misdemeanor. If the damage to property is one thousand dollars or less but more than four hundred dollars, the person is guilty of intentional damage to property in the second degree, which is a Class 1 misdemeanor. If the damage*

15. South Dakota Codified Laws, Title 22, Chapter 34, http://legis.sd.gov/Statutes/Codified_Laws/DisplayStatute.aspx?Type=Statute&Statute=22-34-1

to property is one hundred thousand dollars or less but more than one thousand dollars, the person is guilty of intentional damage to property in the first degree, which is a Class 4 felony. If the damage to property is more than one hundred thousand dollars, the person is guilty of aggravated intentional damage to property, which is a Class 3 felony.

The provisions of this section do not apply if the intentional damage to property was accomplished by arson or reckless burning or exploding pursuant to chapters 22-33.

These common crimes and many others are found in states' criminal codes. Space does not allow for a more detailed look at various crimes; but, to give you an idea of additional crimes common among the states, on the next page is the table of contents for North Dakota's criminal code:[16]

sheriff says missing
South Dakota Woman's Home Vandalized

By Associated Press

Authorities in east-central South Dakota say the home of a missing woman has been vandalized.

News outlets report that the Sanborn County sheriff's office says vandals shattered a window, entered the home of 30-year-old Rachel Cyriacks, and broke a table and a light fixture.

Sheriff Tom Fridley says nothing was taken. He says the vandals spray-painted "riverside for life" and an expletive on the front of the home.

Fridley says he doesn't know whether the phrase is connected to the disappearance.

Cyriacks was last seen on the morning of Nov. 13 in Woonsocket. She is 5 feet 5 inches tall and weighs about 140 pounds.

The Woonsocket woman was last seen in a silver Chevrolet c1500 pickup that authorities say has a lot of damage underneath.

16. North Dakota Century Code, Title 12.1, http://www.legis.nd.gov/cencode/t12-1.html

Chapter	Chapter Name
12.1-01	Application - Purposes - Proof - Definitions
12.1-02	Liability and Culpability
12.1-03	Accomplices - Corporations - Agents
12.1-04	Juveniles - Intoxication - Defenses
12.1-04.1	Criminal Responsibility and Post-Trial Responsibility Act
12.1-05	Justification - Excuse - Affirmative Defenses
12.1-06	Criminal Attempt - Facilitation - Solicitation - Conspiracy
12.1-06.1	Racketeer Influenced and Corrupt Organizations
12.1-06.2	Criminal Street Gangs
12.1-07	Treason - Flag Desecration
12.1-08	Obstruction of Law Enforcement - Escape
12.1-09	Tampering and Unlawful Influence
12.1-10	Contempt - Obstruction of Judicial Proceedings
12.1-11	Perjury - Falsification - Breach of Duty
12.1-12	Bribery - Unlawful Influence of Public Servants

12.1-13	Confidential Information - Conflict of Interest - Impersonation
12.1-14	Official Oppression - Elections - Civil Rights
12.1-15	Defamation - Interception of Communications
12.1-16	Homicide
12.1-17	Assaults - Threats - Coercion - Harassment
12.1-17.1	Offenses Against Unborn Children
12.1-18	Kidnapping
12.1-19	Abortion [Repealed]
12.1-20	Sex Offenses
12.1-21	Damaging Property or Public Services
12.1-21.1	Animal Research Facility Damage
12.1-22	Robbery - Breaking and Entering Offenses
12.1-23	Theft and Related Offenses
12.1-23.1	Theft of Cable Television
12.1-24	Forgery and Counterfeiting
12.1-25	Riot
12.1-26	Firearms and Destructive Devices [Repealed]
12.1-27	Obscenity [Repealed]
12.1-27.1	Obscenity Control
12.1-27.2	Sexual Performances by Children
12.1-28	Gambling and Related Offenses
12.1-29	Prostitution
12.1-30	Sunday Closing Law
12.1-31	Miscellaneous Offenses
12.1-31.1	Drug Paraphernalia [Repealed]
12.1-31.2	Disorderly Conduct Restraining Order
12.1-32	Penalties and Sentencing
12.1-33	Rights of Convicts
12.1-34	Fair Treatment of Victims and Witnesses
12.1-35	Child Victim and Witness Fair Treatment Standards
12.1-36	Female Genital Mutilation
12.1-37	Child Support Nonpayment

12.1-38	Assumption of Risk in Crimes
12.1-39	Human Cloning
12.1-40	Human Trafficking

ELEMENTS OF A CRIME

As you can see, states are very specific about what constitutes a given crime. To find a person guilty of most crimes, the government prosecutor must prove beyond a reasonable doubt *actus reus* and *mens rea*. *Actus reus*, or guilty act, refers to the specific acts (of commission or omission) constituting crimes. As noted above, these acts are listed in states' criminal codes. In addition to the specific acts that must be proved, a prosecutor must prove *mens rea*, or a guilty mind, meaning the prosecutor must prove the defendant intentionally committed an act he knows is criminal. In other words, a person willingly acts with a criminal purpose. Note, however, some crimes require only *actus reus* and not *mens rea*. In other words, to be found guilty of these crimes, a prosecutor must prove only the criminal act was committed, not that the act was committed with criminal intent. These crimes, such as statutory rape, are referred to as crimes of *strict liability*.

DEFENSES TO A CRIME

As with all civil claims, there are certain defenses to all crimes. In other words, a defendant might be able to avoid or lessen his criminal liability via proving a valid defense/excuse. Examples of such defenses are self defense, defense of another, duress, intoxication, and insanity. Intoxication and insanity, for example, are valid defenses to some crimes by virtue of negating the crimes' required element of criminal intent. However, intoxication might be insufficient to negate the intent of related, lesser crimes. For example, one who voluntarily becomes intoxicated might not be guilty of murder but might be guilty of manslaughter.

By now, you should have a basic understanding of criminal law. We will save for another day the topic of *criminal procedure* — the process of enforcing criminal law in accordance with federal and state laws. Stay tuned!

www.ingramcontent.com/pod-product-compliance
Lightning Source LLC
LaVergne TN
LVHW080650011026
849160LV00014B/1379